"A wise father and son have written a wise commentary on the greatest book on wisdom ever written. Read it, and you will be much the wiser for it!"

**James Merritt**, senior pastor of Cross Pointe Church, Duluth, Georgia

"Danny and Jon have written great fresh insight from the very old wisdom of God through Solomon. They have mined the text to explain the practical insights of Proverbs, yet their illustrations are wonderfully relevant to the age in which we live. What a blessing to the church to combine 'timeless' wisdom with such 'timely' illustrations!"

**Bryant Wright**, senior pastor, Johnson Ferry Baptist Church of Marietta, Georgia

# CHRIST-CENTERED Exposition

OT / COMMENTARY

AUTHORS Daniel L. Akin and Jonathan Akin
SERIES EDITORS David Platt, Daniel L. Akin, and Tony Merida

CHRIST-CENTERED

# Exposition

EXALTING JESUS IN

## PROVERBS

HOLMAN®
REFERENCE
NASHVILLE, TENNESSEE

Christ-Centered Exposition Commentary: Exalting Jesus in Proverbs


B&H Publishing Group
Brentwood, Tennessee


ISBN: 978-0-8054-9766-3

Dewey Decimal Classification: 220.7
Subject Heading: BIBLE. O.T. PROVERBS—
COMMENTARIES \ JESUS CHRIST



Printed in the United States of America
5 6 7 8 9 10 • 27 26 25 24 23
BTH

## SERIES DEDICATION

Dedicated to Adrian Rogers and John Piper. They have taught us to love the gospel of Jesus Christ, to preach the Bible as the inerrant Word of God, to pastor the church for which our Savior died, and to have a passion to see all nations gladly worship the Lamb.

—David Platt, Tony Merida, and Danny Akin
March 2013

## AUTHORS' DEDICATION

To our families, where we enjoy the fear of the Lord, feasting, and love.

"Better a little with the fear of the LORD than great treasure with turmoil. Better a meal of vegetables where there is love than a fattened ox with hatred." (Prov 15:16-17)

# TABLE OF CONTENTS



## Proverbs

### Section 1—Selected Passages



### Section 2—Riddle Me This: Unlocking the Difficult Proverbs

## Section 3—Family Relationships



## Section 4—Sticks and Stones: The Power of Words



## Section 5—Seven: The Deadly Follies

# ACKNOWLEDGMENTS

Plans fail when there is no counsel, but with many advisers they succeed" (Prov 15:22). Many advisers and helpers have aided us in successfully completing this project. We owe them a debt of gratitude.

I (Danny) want to thank Shane Shaddix, Mary Jo Haselton, and Kim Humphrey for their work on this project.

I (Jon) want to thank Ken Mathews, who supervised my doctoral work on the book of Proverbs; Russell Moore, who taught me a Christ-centered approach to Proverbs; Jim Hamilton, who helped me develop a biblical theological approach to Proverbs; and my Fairview Church family, for faithfully enduring hours and hours of sermons in Proverbs.

Furthermore, we are grateful to God for families. Our wives, children, and grandchildren are a constant source of joy and blessing in our lives. Solomon wisely said, "Grandchildren are the crown of the elderly, and the pride of children is their fathers" (Prov 17:6). His twelve grandchildren crown Danny; and Nathan, Jonathan, Paul and Timothy are extremely proud of their dad.

Finally, to the Greater Solomon, our Savior and King, the Lord Jesus, be all glory now and forevermore. Amen.

# SERIES INTRODUCTION

Augustine said, "Where Scripture speaks, God speaks." The editors of the Christ-Centered Exposition Commentary series believe that where God speaks, the pastor must speak. God speaks through His written Word. We must speak from that Word. We believe the Bible is God breathed, authoritative, inerrant, sufficient, understandable, necessary, and timeless. We also affirm that the Bible is a Christ-centered book; that is, it contains a unified story of redemptive history of which Jesus is the hero. Because of this Christ-centered trajectory that runs from Genesis 1 through Revelation 22, we believe the Bible has a corresponding global-missions thrust. From beginning to end, we see God's mission as one of making worshipers of Christ from every tribe and tongue worked out through this redemptive drama in Scripture. To that end we must preach the Word.

In addition to these distinct convictions, the Christ-Centered Exposition Commentary series has some distinguishing characteristics. First, this series seeks to display exegetical accuracy. What the Bible says is what we want to say. While not every volume in the series will be a verse-by-verse commentary, we nevertheless desire to handle the text carefully and explain it rightly. Those who teach and preach bear the heavy responsibility of saying what God has said in His Word and declaring what God has done in Christ. We desire to handle God's Word faithfully, knowing that we must give an account for how we have fulfilled this holy calling (Jas 3:1).

Second, the Christ-Centered Exposition Commentary series has pastors in view. While we hope others will read this series, such as parents, teachers, small-group leaders, and student ministers, we desire to provide a commentary busy pastors will use for weekly preparation of biblically faithful and gospel-saturated sermons. This series is not academic in nature. Our aim is to present a readable and pastoral style of commentaries. We believe this aim will serve the church of the Lord Jesus Christ.

Third, we want the Christ-Centered Exposition Commentary series to be known for the inclusion of helpful illustrations and theologically driven applications. Many commentaries offer no help in illustrations, and few offer any kind of help in application. Often those that do offer illustrative material and application unfortunately give little serious attention to the text. While giving ourselves primarily to explanation, we also hope to serve readers by providing inspiring and illuminating illustrations coupled with timely and timeless application.

Finally, as the name suggests, the editors seek to exalt Jesus from every book of the Bible. In saying this, we are not commending wild allegory or fanciful typology. We certainly believe we must be constrained to the meaning intended by the divine Author Himself, the Holy Spirit of God. However, we also believe the Bible has a messianic focus, and our hope is that the individual authors will exalt Christ from particular texts. Luke 24:25-27,44-47 and John 5:39,46 inform both our hermeneutics and our homiletics. Not every author will do this the same way or have the same degree of Christ-centered emphasis. That is fine with us. We believe faithful exposition that is Christ centered is not monolithic. We do believe, however, that we must read the whole Bible as Christian Scripture. Therefore, our aim is both to honor the historical particularity of each biblical passage and to highlight its intrinsic connection to the Redeemer.

The editors are indebted to the contributors of each volume. The reader will detect a unique style from each writer, and we celebrate these unique gifts and traits. While distinctive in their approaches, the authors share a common characteristic in that they are pastoral theologians. They love the church, and they regularly preach and teach God's Word to God's people. Further, many of these contributors are younger voices. We think these new, fresh voices can serve the church well, especially among a rising generation that has the task of proclaiming the Word of Christ and the Christ of the Word to the lost world.

We hope and pray this series will serve the body of Christ well in these ways until our Savior returns in glory. If it does, we will have succeeded in our assignment.

David Platt
Daniel L. Akin
Tony Merida
*Series Editors*
February 2013

# Proverbs

# Section 1—Selected Passages

# Wisdom: A Person, Not Tips

## PROVERBS 1:1-7

**Main Idea:** A relationship with the Lord will make you wise for everyday life.

---

**I. What Is Wisdom (1:1-6)?**
   A. Wisdom is royal (1:1).
   B. Wisdom is correction and understanding (1:2).
   C. Wisdom is the knowledge of good and evil (1:3).
   D. Wisdom is discernment (1:4).
   E. Wisdom is obtaining guidance (1:5-6).

**II. How Do You Get Wisdom (1:7)?**
   A. You get wisdom by reverent trust in the Lord (1:7).

---

People desperately want to "win" at life. They want to succeed in everyday life, and Christians are no different. They search frantically for tips from books, from "experts" on TV talk shows, or in magazines. The problem is that many Christians look everywhere but the Bible to learn how to "win" at parenting, finances, marriage, the workplace, and other areas of life. They look to Dr. Phil or Oprah or Dear Abby or *Delilah After Dark* or *Intelligence for Life* by John Tesh. If you have to look to John Tesh for intelligence on life, you're in trouble!

Even Christians who want a "Christian" perspective on these topics are more likely to look to a Christian book than to *the* Book—the Bible! So often we don't want the Word. Instead, we want practical tips and strategies that have been plucked from the world. Sure, we believe the Bible is God's Word and it's authoritative, but we somehow buy into the misconception that it doesn't do a great job of addressing the nitty-gritty details of daily life. So Christians will do no more than skim the Word devotionally to get some helpful tips for their day. The philosophies of the world primarily shape and fashion their worldview.

However, the problem doesn't stop there. The problem is that even if we do look to the Book, and even if we do somehow pull out some tips for how to live a better life, more often than not we don't follow what we already know. Oftentimes we know what to do, but we can't bring ourselves to do it. Think of how often we mess up. Think of the hurtful words you've said to a friend or your spouse or your parents. Think of the times you've said more than you should say. Think of the times you spoke too quickly and couldn't get your words back. Think about the time someone confronted you with something you needed to hear, and in anger you blew them off with, "Who do you think you are?!" Think about the times you should've lovingly confronted someone and didn't. Think about that person whose feelings you hurt. Think about that lie you desperately hope your parents won't find out or your boyfriend won't find out or your wife won't find out. Think about those things you keep hidden from your parents. Think about that time you screamed, "I hate you!" to your mom. Think about that secret that you just couldn't keep to yourself, and in a moment of supposed confidential privacy you whispered in someone's ear, "Well, did you hear what happened to . . . ?" Think about the times you've bragged about yourself so others would think you're something. Think about the mistakes you've made with your children. Think about the times you didn't discipline a behavior that has now gotten out of hand. Think about the times your children saw you do something you had told them not to do or heard you say something you told them not to say. Think about that grudge you've held and refused to let go because someone really hurt you. Think about the times you've been stingy with your money instead of generous to a person with a real need. Think about the frivolous spending that got you in trouble. Think about the get-rich-quick scheme that ruined you. Think about the times you didn't finish your job assignment on time because you got sidetracked by Facebook. Think about the people you're jealous of because they got the promotion that passed you by. Think about the times you've nagged or ignored helping your spouse. Think about how you repeat the same stupid mistake over and over and don't learn from it. On and on and on we could go.

What does all of this tell us? It tells us that we have a major problem that no amount of tips will solve. It tells us that we are not wise and are often foolish. It tells us that we are broken and don't work right. It tells us that we are in desperate need of wisdom to make decisions and navigate our way through life. But we can't just say that we need wisdom and then go after it. Since we are broken, we don't even follow the wisdom we already know. We do things we know are hurtful and foolish. We just can't help ourselves.

The Bible says at creation there was perfect harmony between people and God, between people themselves, and between people and the world around them (Gen 1–2). There was an order to things. Human sin—the fall—broke all of that because people sought knowledge and wisdom apart from God (Gen 3). That messed everything up. Once a man's vertical relationship with God was out of whack, so were his horizontal relationships with other people and the world around him. Are we really surprised that the first murder in history (Gen 4) followed soon after the fall of humanity?

Because of sin, there are barriers now between us and God, between us and others, and between us and the world around us. We no longer rightly perceive the way the world works—we no longer recognize the order—so we can't navigate through daily life. God created the world with an order to work in a certain way, and we must live according to that to be truly wise; but in our brokenness we don't see it.

Proverbs is all about restoring that harmony through Jesus Christ. Proverbs is all about becoming wise in everyday life through a relationship with Jesus—through the gospel. It's about the life of the kingdom that God always meant for humankind to live. When our vertical relationship with God is right through Jesus, we can be right with others and the world around us.

## What Is Wisdom?

### PROVERBS 1:1-6

Proverbs chapters 1–9 are the introduction to the book. It's a long introduction—like most preachers' sermons. Proverbs 1:1-7 is the preamble, the introduction to the introduction. This section tells us what the book is about and the book's purpose. These are the "proverbs" (v. 1). The proverbs proper are the sentences of wisdom found in the book. Primarily what we think of when we think of "proverbs" are the short, pithy sayings contained in chapters 10–31. Proverbs 1–9 sets those up and shows us how to interpret them. This word for "proverbs" in verse 1 of the LXX (the Septuagint, the Greek translation of the Old Testament) is a word sometimes used for the parables of Jesus (e.g., John 10:6). Indeed, Jesus is the one "Greater than Solomon" who instructs us in the wisdom of the kingdom.

These are the proverbs "of Solomon" (v. 1). Solomon is the main author of Proverbs, which means that he is responsible for the majority of it. There are other authors like Agur and King Lemuel, but it should be no shock that Solomon is the main author. Solomon was the wisest man in Israel's history because the Lord granted him a wish for wisdom (1 Kgs 3). First Kings 4:30-34 states,

> *Solomon's wisdom was greater than the wisdom of all the people of the East, greater than all the wisdom of Egypt. He was wiser than anyone. . . . His reputation extended to all the surrounding nations.*
>
> *Solomon spoke 3,000 proverbs, and his songs numbered 1,005. He spoke about trees, from the cedar in Lebanon to the hyssop growing out of the wall. He also spoke about animals, birds, reptiles, and fish. Emissaries of all peoples, sent by every king on earth who had heard of his wisdom, came to listen to Solomon's wisdom.*

There are basically seven divisions in the book of Proverbs: (1) The Introduction (1:1–9:18); (2) Solomon's Proverbs (10:1–22:16); (3) The Sayings of the Wise (22:17–24:22); (4) Further Sayings of the Wise (24:23-34); (5) Solomon's Proverbs Collected by Hezekiah's Men (25:1–29:27); (6) The Sayings of Agur (30:1-33); and (7) The Sayings of King Lemuel (31:1-31) (Waltke, *Proverbs, Chapters 15–31*, 4).

Here, in the "introduction to the introduction," Solomon tells us what wisdom is.

### *Wisdom Is Royal (1:1)*

These are the proverbs of Solomon, "son of David, king of Israel." Wisdom is royal because it's how kings rule their people. In 1 Kings 3:9 Solomon asks God for wisdom, which was for him the ability to rule well as king of Israel. He says, "So give your servant a receptive heart to judge your people and to discern between good and evil. For who is able to judge this great people of yours?" And in Proverbs 8:15-16 Wisdom states, "It is by me that kings reign and rulers enact just law; by me, princes lead, as do nobles and all righteous judges." Immediately Proverbs connects wisdom with the kingship and with the Messiah. "Son of David" is a messianic title. The Son of David will establish God's eternal kingdom on earth, but he can only do it through wisdom—through justice (see 2 Sam 7; Isa 11). In Proverbs, Solomon is training his "son" in wisdom so that he can establish the messianic kingdom. As we will see, he is also instructing the youth of the nation in wisdom in hopes of producing it in them as well. But the king embodies the nation and represents the nation. If the king is wise, the people will be wise; but if the king is unwise, the people will be foolish. There is a need for a wise king who can produce a wise nation—a wise kingdom. Throughout Israel's history the foolishness of the kings led to the difficulties and ultimately the destruction of the kingdom. The kings were fools, so the people were fools. As a result, there was death and chaos.

What does this mean for us? We need to see that the Son of David—Jesus of Nazareth—has established the messianic kingdom by fulfilling the wisdom of Proverbs. He is the wise Messiah promised in Isaiah 11 who will reestablish the harmony forfeited at the fall. We need to submit to his loving and wise rule so that he can produce wisdom in us. That's our only path to wisdom. Proverbs is laying out how kingdom citizens should live and what the wise King will produce in them. Also, in the consummated kingdom the saints of Christ will rule the cosmos with him by the wisdom of God. Therefore, we need to learn this wisdom so we can rule rightly. In the "already" of the kingdom seen in the church—the outposts of the kingdom—we are in an internship for eternity, ordered now by the wisdom of God.

So Solomon's purpose is to give wisdom in order to bring harmony to the kingdom. Proverbs 1:2 clearly states the purpose of the book—to impart wisdom to the reader. But what is wisdom besides the necessary means to rule? Solomon uses several words to help us grasp all that wisdom entails.

### *Wisdom Is Correction and Understanding (1:2)*

Proverbs 1:2 says the purpose of the book is to know "wisdom and discipline," or "understanding and correction." *Wisdom* is the kind of knowledge that helps you know what is going on around you. Are you able to read situations and people correctly? If not, you need discipline.[1] This requires the humility to recognize that you don't know everything and to receive counsel from another. How do you respond to correction, to teaching, to counsel? That has a lot to do with whether or not you are wise. The know-it-all is not as wise as he thinks; the Bible says he's a fool.

This word *correction* or *discipline* entails a discipleship-type relationship where you can be warned about going in the wrong direction, rebuked when needed, corrected to go in a different way or to think

[1] Most English translations have the word "instruction" here in verse 2, but the Hebrew word is better translated "correction or discipline" (*Brown-Driver-Briggs Hebrew and English Lexicon*, 416).

differently, and punished if you do not listen. Do you have any relationship in your life right now where someone can correct you? Do you have any relationship in your life where someone can call you to account and say, "What do you think you're doing?" We all need pastors or parents or brothers and sisters in Christ who can correct us. That's wisdom.

### *Wisdom Is the Knowledge of Good and Evil (1:3)*

Solomon says that wisdom is ethical. He says the purpose of the book is for you as the reader to receive correction in order to be wise "in righteousness, justice, and integrity." Therefore, biblical wisdom is not intelligence or a high IQ; it's the knowledge of good and evil. A wise person can tell the difference between right and wrong in the situations in which they find themselves.

The problem for us is that even in the church we so often think of foolishness and wisdom as morally neutral. Pastors will even say things like being wise or foolish is not about right and wrong so much as best and not best. So foolishness is when I break my hand by slamming it on the floor because Tony Romo threw another interception to cost the Cowboys a playoff spot. That's not necessarily a sin; it's just stupid, a pastor will say. No! That's not what the Bible means by wisdom and foolishness according to Proverbs 1:3. Foolishness lacks the ability to discern good and evil. It is a sin to be a fool. If I were to ask most people who on the sitcom *The Simpsons* is a fool, almost everyone who has ever watched it would say Bart because he does dumb things that get him in trouble. If I were to ask who is wise on *The Simpsons*, many would say Lisa because she has her head on straight. According to Proverbs, Lisa is just as foolish as Bart because she treats her parents like idiots. Folly is sinfulness and wisdom is righteousness according to Proverbs.

Adam and Eve are prohibited access to the tree of the knowledge of good and evil in the garden of Eden. Why? God forbids them to eat that fruit not because he's giving them an arbitrary rule to break so that one day he can send his Son to die for sinners and save us from hell. He wants to teach humanity to depend on God for that knowledge instead of determining it for ourselves. God determines what is good and what is evil; that's not for us to decide. So we fear him by submitting to his Word. However, humans decided to trust the voice of the serpent and what their "own eyes" said was best. Adam and Eve sought wisdom apart from God and his Word. That's foolishness. The fruit appeared desirable "to make one wise"—it seemed right to them, but it was foolish, and foolishness according to Genesis and Proverbs always ends in death. Wisdom comes from the mouth of God (Prov 2:6), so submit to the Word of God and not what you think is right.

The chaos and confusion in our society is due to humankind doing what is right in our own eyes rather than what God has revealed in his Word. That's not just true for those "outsiders" who reject a sanctity of life ethic and those who redefine marriage. Many of us in the church also have failed to submit to God's way. We agree that wisdom is to be found in God's Word. And we agree that we should submit to what it says in all things, except for our own situations, which for some reason we always think are the exceptions. "I know God's Word says I have no grounds for a divorce, but I also know God doesn't want me to be miserable." "I know God's Word says I should submit to my husband, but you don't know my husband." "I know God's Word says I should be generous, but I also know that God realizes I just don't have a lot right now." We find all kinds of ways to evade God's Word for what is better in our own eyes. That's foolishness.

Instead, we need to submit to the wisdom—the knowledge of good and evil—that God gives us clearly in the Word. The Lord reveals to us wisdom in his Word through the law. The law tells us right from wrong. Deuteronomy 4:6 says that Israel's wisdom is to be found in keeping the law. Parents are instructed to teach the law to their kids so that the nation can remain in the land and not die in exile (Deut 6). The king was to be a man of the law so that his kingdom would be secure (Deut 17). In the book of Proverbs, Solomon is obeying both Deuteronomy 6 and 17 by instructing his son in the wisdom of right and wrong (Hamilton, *God's Glory in Salvation*, 290). This is exactly what Solomon asked the Lord for in 1 Kings 3:9—the ability to "discern between good and evil." What was denied to humanity in the garden is now given to humanity through the wisdom of Proverbs—the fear of the Lord!

### *Wisdom Is Discernment (1:4)*

Proverbs 1:4 says that wisdom is shrewdness and discretion. Wisdom is the ability to read a situation and make the right decision. That's the point of the book. Solomon wants to give this discernment to the inexperienced and the youth. As we will see, Proverbs gives categories of people (inexperienced, mocking, foolish, wise, etc.). Inexperienced people are not wise or foolish yet; instead, they are open to instruction in wisdom or folly. They are gullible and usually believe the most recent thing they have heard. They are easily enticed or persuaded (see the discussion in Longman, *Proverbs*, 96–97). This is the audience that Solomon is going after because there is still hope. Inexperience and youthfulness often go hand in hand, and that is why Solomon is so concerned (as is Moses in Deut 6) with parents teaching their children right and wrong. Proverbs tells those of us who are parents (and grandparents) that it is our task to instruct our children in wisdom. Those who are young and those who are inexperienced need to acquire the ability to perceive what's going on, make the right decisions, and avoid the bad ones.

### *Wisdom Is Obtaining Guidance (1:5-6)*

Solomon says that a wise man will listen and increase in learning; a wise man will acquire direction and guidance. This is interesting. The audience that Solomon refers to in this verse is "a wise person." He says that the wise need to grow in learning and get direction. Huh? Doesn't being wise mean that you've arrived at the place where you don't need to learn anymore? Solomon says that's a foolish outlook on life. The truly wise will have the humility to know that they still need to listen to counsel instead of having the arrogance to think they have arrived. The wise recognize that no one graduates. We all need to hear the wisdom of Proverbs again and again throughout our lives. Wisdom is not a goal to attain; it's a pursuit that you spend your whole life on.

Solomon says the point of the book is to help you understand these wise sayings so you can be wise and make wise decisions in your daily life. He's laid out in this preamble the multifaceted nature of wisdom. Wisdom is being corrected and disciplined. Wisdom understands and reads situations. Wisdom is godly morality. Wisdom is justice. Wisdom is discretion and discernment of right and wrong, stupid and smart, what path to take and which one to avoid. Wisdom is listening to instruction and receiving guidance. But now that we know what wisdom is, the question remains, "How can we get it?"

## How Do You Get Wisdom?

**(WHAT IS THE KEY TO BEING WISE LIKE THIS?)**

### *You Get Wisdom by Reverent Trust in the Lord (1:7)*

How can we be wise like this? How can we learn to read situations and make wise decisions? How do you get this multifaceted wisdom? As we will see throughout the book, Solomon says that all wisdom is "religious" or spiritual in nature because it's only through a relationship with the Lord that one can be wise. The fear of—the reverence for—Yahweh is the beginning of wisdom. Fools despise wisdom and discipline, but the wise person is the one who fears, trusts, and reverences Yahweh. This is the first step and the essential component in gaining wisdom—the fear of the Lord. Proverbs is quite clear that the way to get wisdom is to depend on God rather than on yourself (cf. 3:5-6). The everyday, nitty-gritty details of your life are to be lived in fear of God. There is no sacred and secular divide in your life. We so often think that "going to church" and mission efforts and quiet times are the godly things we do in life. Other things like our work, our kids' soccer teams, or how we spend our money are the secular or neutral parts of our lives. Solomon crushes that. The everyday decisions that we make are to be done in fear of the Lord, and the everyday decisions we make reveal whether or not we fear the Lord. God is concerned with your whole life. The everyday decisions we make are indicators of whether we fear him or not. How you eat dinner, how you finish tasks assigned to you, how you spend money, how you parent your kids, and how you respond to your parents are all before the Lord. Every nook and cranny of your life is to be governed by God.

We all view the world in a certain way—through a certain lens. However, the fall of humankind into sin has assured that we do not see the world rightly. As an analogy, I (Jon) am colorblind. I can't tell the difference between red and green and a whole host of other colors. I don't see the world the way it actually is. As a result, I make poor decisions with regard to fashion. In a very real way, that's what is true of all of us in our sin. We don't view the world the way it really is, so we make wrong decisions that go against the grain of how the world really is. However, if we will observe the world through the lens that God has given in fear of him, we can start perceiving how things really are. And once we start living according to that pattern, we will walk in wisdom.

The only way to be wise is to trust in the Lord and be in a relationship with him. Wisdom comes from Yahweh (2:6), so we are taught in the Bible to ask him for it (e.g., Jas 1). According to Proverbs, this wisdom is filtered through receiving instruction from a human mediator like a sage or a parent. In our context that might mean a parent, a godly and wise friend, a Bible teacher, or a pastor.

Fools are arrogant and refuse correction (Prov 1:7). They are worse than the inexperienced because they aren't open to changing their minds. This means that really, really smart people can actually be fools. The question we all need to ask ourselves is, what category am I in? Am I one who is open to the instruction of the Lord? Am I one who is humble enough to seek counsel? Or am I a know-it-all? Am I a person who always thinks I'm right? Foolishness is doing what is right in your own eyes instead of what God has revealed. Disney says to "follow your heart," but the Bible says those who are left to themselves and to their hearts will choose the wrong path. Following our heart is foolishness because we are broken people. Doing what is right in our own eyes is a recipe for disaster. Just read the book of Judges. There was no king in Israel, everyone did what was right in his own eyes, and the result was chaos (see esp. Judg 17–21). We need a loving and wise King who can rule over us. Proverbs reveals that Solomon is training a Son of David to do just that, and in the fullness of time we see that his name is Jesus of Nazareth. You see, Solomon fails to live out the wisdom of Proverbs, and so does his son King Rehoboam, who shows his foolishness by listening to his peers rather than the elders of Israel (see 1 Kgs 12). But Isaiah 11 promises that the Messiah will be the embodiment of the book of Proverbs. In fact, he is described with the words of Proverbs. Isaiah 11:2-3 states,

*The Spirit of the Lord will rest on him—*
*a Spirit of wisdom and understanding,*
*a Spirit of counsel and strength,*
*a Spirit of knowledge and of the fear of the Lord.*
*His delight will be in the fear of the Lord.*

And when Jesus of Nazareth bursts onto the scene, he grows in wisdom and in stature and in favor with God and people (Luke 2:52). He's called greater than Solomon (Matt 12) and the "wisdom of God" for us (1 Cor 1:24,30). "In him are hidden all the treasures of wisdom and knowledge" (Col 2:3).

Getting wisdom is important because it will help you make decisions in everyday life. It will help you "win" at life. But failing to get wisdom will wreck your life. The problem for all of us is that we have failed repeatedly because even when we know what to do, we often don't do it. This reveals our brokenness. Where do we turn? What's the answer for us? How can we become wise when we are so broken we can't even do what we know is right?

What if wisdom wasn't a concept or an idea or a set of ideas you had to learn at all? What if Wisdom was a person you could know and have a relationship with? What if Wisdom was a person you could love and walk with, and just by knowing, loving, and walking with this person it would actually make you wise?[2] What if Wisdom was a person who spoke to you, and by listening to Wisdom's voice you could actually grow in wisdom? Proverbs will teach us that Wisdom isn't an Israelite *Dear Abby*[3]; it's not a bunch of tips you learn to live out. Wisdom is a person—Jesus of Nazareth. Through a relationship with him you can be reconciled to God, to others, and to the world around you. Through a relationship with him, he will begin to produce in you the wisdom he lives out—the wisdom of Proverbs!

## Reflect and Discuss

1. Why are we drawn to resources with "quick and easy steps to success"? Why do we approach Proverbs like this?
2. Why does the Bible say that tips to a better life are not sufficient?
3. How did the fall mess up our wisdom? How did it affect our relationship to the world, to God, and to other people?
4. Solomon, the king of Israel, uses proverbs to teach his son to rule an earthly kingdom in righteousness. What then do they have to do with Jesus? In the big picture how are we to see Jesus from Proverbs?
5. With whom can you pursue a discipleship relationship where you can be warned about going in the wrong direction, be rebuked, be corrected, and be punished if you do not repent?
6. How is wisdom more than "good vs. best" or "smart vs. stupid"?
7. Why did God tell Adam and Eve not to eat from the tree of the knowledge of good and evil? How can the moral confusion in our world today be traced back to the first sin?
8. What is the first step and the essential component in gaining wisdom?
9. How does Proverbs push back against the "follow your heart," Disney-fied culture? How can you apply the wisdom of Proverbs in your decision-making?
10. Instead of a concept or set of ideas, what does Proverbs ultimately teach is wisdom?

---

[2] Paraphrased from Tim Keller, "True Wisdom."

[3] I (Jon) learned the phrase "Israelite *Dear Abby*" from Russell Moore's messages on Proverbs.

## Falling Among Thieves

### PROVERBS 1:8-19

**Main Idea:** Unchecked greed for money and stuff is foolish because it will destroy you.

---

I. **Getting Money the Wrong Way Will Destroy You (1:8-19).**
II. **The Problem: It Doesn't Always Work Out Immediately, but It Will Work Out Ultimately (1:19).**
III. **Our Biggest Problem Is That We Have All Failed at This (1:8-19).**
IV. **Jesus Can Save You from Your Foolishness (1:8-19).**

---

In his book *Counterfeit Gods,* Tim Keller tells the story of a French money manager who invested the wealth of many of Europe's royal and leading families. This money manager lost $1.4 billion of his clients' money in Bernard Madoff's Ponzi scheme. As a result, he slit his wrists in his Madison Avenue office (Keller, *Counterfeit Gods,* ix–x). His greed to gain easy money through a get-rich-quick scheme destroyed his life. The truth that "naked greed" destroys is testified to again and again in our day. The "culture of greed" has been destructive to our national economy (the collapse of 2008), to our companies (like Enron), and to individual lives as well. Many families have been ruined by pursuing the Joneses. We've wanted money and stuff at any cost, and we've paid dearly for it.

The problem for so many of us is that we think this is only a problem for people on Madison Avenue. This is a problem that really rich people have to worry about. We can't see our own greed. We think our pursuit of nice things is normal and healthy. And yet, many families have been destroyed by the desire to accumulate nice things. Pastors never have someone schedule a counseling visit to confess, "My greedy lust for money and things is destroying me and my family." These families eventually feel the weight of the decisions they've made, but most of the time it is too late. We are too foolish to see our own greed, and we're too foolish to see the trap we are setting for ourselves right now. Solomon writes Proverbs 1:8-19 to warn his son that greed will destroy him, and the Spirit calls us to hear the warning as well.

## Getting Money the Wrong Way Will Destroy You

### PROVERBS 1:8-19

King Solomon—the father—instructs the crown prince—his son—to avoid greedy gain. He pleads with his son, "Listen to me!" Not only should the son listen to his father's instruction, he should also listen to the "teaching" (Hebrew word *torah*, often translated "law") of his mother. So both parents are responsible to teach their children the law (the knowledge of good and evil). Parents are tasked with instructing their children in the way the world works (i.e., wisdom). Parents, do not abdicate this responsibility or farm it out to teachers, coaches, day care workers, or Bible study teachers. This is your job! Teach your children the Word of God. Teach them how life works best because you know from God's Word what is best for them.

Not only does Solomon plead with his son to listen to his parents (v. 8); he also tells him why to do so. He says, "for they will be a garland of favor on your head and pendants around your neck" (v. 9). Since jewelry is a sign of health, prosperity, and honor, Solomon is saying that heeding his instructions will give the son a good life (Garrett, *Proverbs*, 69).

After making this exhortation, the father turns to the specific life lesson he wants his son to learn. He gives him a parable—a story. The story is about resisting the temptation to join a gang (a peer group), kill someone, and take their money. This calls to mind the story of the Good Samaritan where robbers beat the man and take his stuff (Luke 10:25-37). The father pleads with his son not to be enticed by this gang. Don't be pressured by your sinful peers. The reason he is so concerned is that he knows where that leads. He makes a common-sense observation about the outcome of such a decision: the outcome is death. So he appeals to his son not to walk in this way (Prov 1:15).

Proverbs repeatedly presents the idea of two paths. There is a wise, righteous path that leads to life; and there is a foolish, wicked path that leads to death. So there is a double meaning in Proverbs 1:15. Solomon says, "Don't go their way" (i.e., don't follow them); and he is implicitly saying, "Don't follow this course of life" (i.e., the foolish path that leads to destruction).

Solomon explains the outcome because he is a good teacher. A good teacher doesn't just tell his students what to do; he tells them why they should do it. Don't follow this gang because "they hurry to shed blood" (v. 16); and it's not just the blood of the innocent that they shed, they also shed their own blood! Their devices turn back on them (v. 18). Solomon uses the illustration of a trap set in plain view so that a bird can see it. Even a dumb bird recognizes a trap if it's not camouflaged; so the youth should have the sense to avoid an obvious trap, especially if a stupid animal has that much sense. The father is calling the robbers dumber than birds. They don't have enough sense to see the trap and avoid it. No, they step into it. So, son, don't be foolish. Recognize that this will end badly. Solomon concludes, "Such are the paths of all who make profit dishonestly; it takes the lives of those who receive it" (v. 19). Being greedy to get stuff at any cost will wreck your life. Don't do it!

The wisdom principle is clear: Getting money or stuff the wrong way (i.e., at others' expense) will destroy you. Using people, abusing people, or cheating people to get money will end badly. Unchecked greed, lustful desire, or ravenous craving for money and stuff at any cost will destroy you. It does not deliver what it promises.

## The Problem: It Doesn't Always Work Out Immediately, but It Will Work Out Ultimately!

**PROVERBS 1:19**

This story and lesson raises a problem for many of us, and the problem is a question: Is this true?[4] Maybe someone robbed you and never got caught. We all know the stories of people who cheated and got away with it. We all suspect there are business people who have enriched themselves through unethical practices. We know stories of those who used and abused others to get money, and they never got what was coming to them. Perhaps you've gotten away with something. Maybe you've cheated on your income taxes or taken money from your parents' dresser. And, on the flip side, we know the stories of those who said no to bribes, refused to cheat, did things the right way, kept their integrity, and suffered loss for it. They didn't get rich. They missed out on the big bucks they could have had.

I knew a missionary couple in Central Asia who ran a business selling school items as their platform to share the gospel. When I met the missionary, he told me, "We are the only business in this marketplace that

[4] The structure and flow of this sermon was helped tremendously by Dennis Johnson's discussion of how to preach the wisdom literature of the OT in *Him We Proclaim*, 303–13.

goes through the right channels to get our business permits. Everyone else here bribes to operate their business, but we follow the law. We want to be honest citizens." I went back to that city a year later, and those missionaries had been kicked out of the country for not having a business permit. The government refused to renew theirs. This couple did things the right way, and they lost big time in return.

Some cheat and never face the consequences in this life, and others are honest and lose everything. So how are we to understand this passage now? Is this proverb true? Is its warning a promise? Some scholars solve this tension—their observation of cases to the contrary—by saying that the proverbs are just rules that are generally true but not always true. So they say these are not promises, just how things work out most times. That's not the whole story. The proverbs are promises. The proverbs will always come true. You can bank on them. We need to understand this about the proverbs. Proverbs are promises that generally come true now but always come true later. They are generally true in this life, but they are absolutely true in the life to come. Eventually these will come true even if they don't come true immediately.[5] Again, wisdom is an order by which God made the world and behind which he stands to make sure that it happens. We see this in God's Word. Achan's greed was found out pretty quickly, and it cost him and his family their lives (Josh 7). Ahab and Jezebel's greedy murder of Naboth to take possession of his vineyard didn't cost them their lives for years after their sin, but it did cost them their lives eventually (1 Kgs 22; 2 Kgs 9).

So naked greed will destroy you—sometimes now and sometimes later. Your unethical business practice may be exposed shortly and send you to jail. You may steal petty cash and get fired or cheat on your taxes and get audited. Your greed may run your family into the ground, and you not see the toll it takes on your wife and kids for years to come; but eventually you will see it. But even if none of those things is uncovered in this life, they will be at the judgment. Any discomfort you feel right now for your greed is only a tiny foretaste of the ultimate judgment to come in hell (see Rev 20:11-15, the Great White Throne Judgment).

---

[5] See the great discussion by Waltke on the proverbs as promises in *The Book of Proverbs, Chapters 1–15*, 107–9.

## Our Biggest Problem Is That We Have All Failed at This (1:8-19)

Our biggest problem with this proverb is not whether or not it's true immediately. Our biggest problem is that we've all failed to live out the warning given by Solomon. We have all walked in this foolish course of life and earned wrecking our lives now and receiving death later. The problem is that we can easily bypass this text and ease our consciences with, "I've never been tempted to join a gang to kill and rob someone, so I guess I'm in pretty good shape." That's probably true for most of us. We've never been tempted in that specific way, though perhaps some have. The problem is that you think that absolves you of any guilt, and you are wrong!

You may have never joined a gang to kill and rob someone, but what about the force of the text? Have you ever given into peer pressure to do something you shouldn't? Have you ever done something wrong to be accepted by the crowd? Have you ever been so lonely and desired relationships so badly you found them in the wrong place and in the wrong way? Have you ever used people or manipulated them to get what you want? Have you ever swindled someone? Have you ever lied or cheated to make a sale? Have you ever taken money from your parents or the government? Have you ever taken a friend to lunch and said, "Ask me about my job, and I can pay for this with the company credit card"?

James, the brother of Jesus, tells us what leads to violence and murder. James says unmet cravings are the source for violence. James 4:1-2 says,

> *What is the source of wars and fights among you? Don't they come from your passions that wage war within you? You desire and do not have. You murder and covet and cannot obtain. You fight and wage war.*

The reason you lash out at people is because you don't have something you want, including money and things. That's exactly what Solomon is talking about. Who among us has never craved this way? We can't ease our consciences with, "I haven't acted on it." James says you are a murderer in training if you are driven by unmet desires. You already have the motive—perhaps someday the opportunity will arise. This is in all of us, and we should be very afraid.

We see this in our children. Not one of us has to teach our children to punch their brother, push their sister, or scream at the top of their lungs to get a toy they want. That's just part of our sinful nature.

When we see something we want, we will do what we have to do to get it, including violence. The means of lashing out may change as we age, but the rage is still there. Some will be pressured into the violence of abortion simply to ensure economic stability or a life free of stress. Some will throw trash or scream hateful things at refs who don't give their team the call. Some will fight at a funeral over the exact division of the inheritance. Who among us has not been green with envy of what someone else has and at least thought, "I wish I had that life"? Have you ever bad-mouthed someone behind his back because he got the promotion instead of you? Who among us has never used people to get something we want out of them?

The problem is not money or things in and of themselves. "*Profit*" is a neutral term here (v. 19). It can be good or bad; it depends on how you get it (and how you use it). Proverbs is positive about wealth if a good work ethic is the means to getting it and generosity is the way you use it. However, sinful means of accumulating wealth are wrong (Longman, *Proverbs*, 109). Everywhere in Proverbs it condemns and warns about easy money, get-rich-quick schemes (i.e., pyramid schemes), or using others to get what we want. Proverbs 15:27 says, "The one who profits dishonestly troubles his household, but the one who hates bribes will live." This is true, yet we foolishly do it. Most of us justify our greed with "Well, it's my money not the government's," or "My company doesn't need this as much as I do," or "I know I'm a workaholic, but I am just trying to provide the best for my family."

Solomon warns his son not to follow this path, but our problem is that we all fall into it. The "American Dream" is a nightmare according to the sage. It will destroy you. In high school I often used to sleep over at a friend's house, and we would sneak up to the pantry after midnight to get a snack. We loved to stay at his house because his dad was a very rich businessman, which meant they had a big house and awesome snacks. Many nights, while sneaking into the pantry, we would find his mom passed out on the rug in front of their TV. She would drink herself to sleep because her husband was so busy making money he rarely came home. He was never at his son's ball games. His drive to succeed absolutely tore his family apart. The sad part is he didn't see it coming because he thought all that money and success was enough to make them happy, and instead it made them miserable.

Solomon says that we will reap what we have sown. Our greed may cause us to lose a job, our reputation, or our family in this life; and it will certainly lead to judgment when we stand before God. Eventually it will be exposed. Eventually you will fall into the trap if you don't walk in the way of wisdom. First Timothy 6:9 says, "Those who want to be rich fall into temptation, a trap, and many foolish and harmful desires, which plunge people into ruin and destruction." We've got a big problem: we are headed for a trap, and we can't see it in ourselves as easily as we see it in others. Of course this isn't a good path. Of course it destroys families. We can look at the miserable lives of the rich and famous and see that. And yet we never see it in ourselves until it's too late! But there is good news . . .

## Jesus Can Save You from Your Foolishness

### PROVERBS 1:8-19

All of the Bible is about Jesus, including the Proverbs. Jesus is the "son" who grows in wisdom and stature and favor with God and man. Paul says that Jesus is the "wisdom of God" for us (1 Cor 1:24,30). Jesus is the one who can rescue us from our foolishness and make us wise.

Amazingly, this proverb—this parable—plays out in the life of Jesus. Judas is enticed to join a gang who in turn sets a trap for an innocent man (cf. Prov 1:11). Judas does this to get money. The gang sets the trap, and they take the innocent man's life. Jesus is executed among thieves. Again, it looks like the proverb is not true. The innocent man dies the death that thieves deserve to die, and the guilty man lines his pockets. Judas threw in his lot with the gang to ambush an innocent man for profit, and it looked like he won; but by Sunday morning Judas is in the grave, and Jesus stands up and walks out of his!

Jesus can rescue us from our foolish greed. Even though he was innocent, he was hung on the cross between robbers. He took the punishment that thieves deserve so that thieves like us could be forgiven. He took the punishment for our greed, for our cravings, for our violent hearts, so that we could be set free. He gives his Spirit to his followers to empower them to walk in his wisdom. He empowers us to avoid easy money, to be content, and to use our money to help others instead of using others to help us get more money. He gives us a new community—the church—a community that does not entice us to sin but spurs us on to love and good deeds.

## Conclusion

The eschatological reward of wisdom is far greater than ill-gotten riches that shimmer and fade and ultimately destroy you. They're not worth it. Yes, some do cheat to get money and never face the consequences in this life. And yes, some are honest and lose everything. What now? Wait on the Lord; he will turn the tables. Sometimes he does it in three days; sometimes he waits longer, but he will do it. In his song "Death In His Grave," John Mark McMillan sings of Jesus, "On Friday a thief, on Sunday a king." That's the story of Christ. And that's our story if we are in Christ!

## Reflect and Discuss

1. Why is it easy for us to think that greed is only a problem for the rich?
2. How can you live out Solomon's example and exhortation for parents to instruct their children in God's law and in the way the world works?
3. While you may never be tempted to join a gang and commit murder, what are some ways you are tempted to get money or stuff the wrong way?
4. What are some ways you have been influenced and possibly enslaved by the "American Dream"?
5. We don't always see the Proverbs prove true. How in your life have you seen greedy people succeed or faithful people fail or be punished?
6. How have you seen the temporal consequences of greed in your own life or in the life of someone close to you?
7. How does Solomon's parable play out in the life of Jesus?
8. How does Jesus's life reaffirm the eternal consequences in the teaching of Proverbs?
9. How did Jesus rescue us from our greed? How does he change our lives moving forward?
10. What's the "eschatological reward" for wisdom? How should that impact our daily lives and decisions?

# Wisdom Is a Street Preacher

## PROVERBS 1:20-33

**Main Idea:** Wisdom is a person who pleads with us to repent and not perish.

---

**I. You Need to Accept Jesus, the Wisdom of God (1:20-23).**
**II. Refusing to Accept Jesus Will Wreck Your Life (1:24-32).**
**III. Accepting Jesus Leads to True Life (1:33).**

---

Several years ago I (Jon) went on a mission trip to a country in Southeast Asia. We would travel from place to place preaching the gospel, and then at lunchtime we would stop in an open air market to eat. Our trip leader was a passionate evangelist, so after we had time to eat he would appoint someone to stand up on our jeep and use a megaphone to preach the gospel to the hundreds of people in the marketplace. One day I was chosen to preach, so I got on the jeep and as passionately as I could I gave the gospel. At the end of my sermon I invited anyone who wanted to respond to the gospel to come forward to talk with me. No one came, so I prepared to get down off the jeep. Our trip leader looked at me and motioned with his hand for me to continue to preach. So I preached for a few more minutes, gave the invitation and no one came. Our leader motioned for me to keep going. This went on for several minutes. Finally, some teenage boys who were watching me began to laugh at me. This enraged our group leader. He snatched the megaphone from me and walked toward the boys and shouted with a red face, "You think this is funny! God is gonna laugh at you in hell one day!" I was shocked, and so were the teenagers. It was quite the scene.

Hellfire and brimstone preaching can be harsh, and there are definitely wrong ways to do it. Many people can use the threat of hell as a way to manipulate people into making decisions. But many people preach with this kind of passion—like our group leader—because they really do love people and do not want them to perish. We can debate the most effective methods of evangelism and the best ways to go about it, but what we can't debate is that there is an urgent need to plead with those headed toward destruction to repent and believe the gospel.

Shockingly, in Proverbs 1:20-33 Wisdom is presented as a "turn or burn" street preacher who appeals to "the inexperienced" to turn and not perish. Wisdom warns that we are heading for disaster because of our foolishness and brokenness. Wisdom pleads with us to repent. This passage is essential to rightly understanding the book of Proverbs and the biblical concept of wisdom. Ultimately, wisdom is not a set of ideas; wisdom is a person—Jesus Christ. You need to begin a personal relationship with him by faith. If you do, he will forgive your sin and give you his Spirit. This will lead you to wisdom for abundant life here and eternal life hereafter. But rejecting Wisdom—Jesus—will wreck your life here and condemn you eternally hereafter. Whether or not you have a relationship with Jesus determines if you walk in wisdom or in a way that seems right to you.

There are three inescapable realities that we see in Proverbs 1:20-33.

## You Need to Accept Jesus, the Wisdom of God

### PROVERBS 1:20-23

Too often we think of Proverbs as an Israelite version of *Dear Abby*. We think Solomon is simply giving us wise tips on how to live a successful life. The problem is that we are broken; so even if we know the right things to do, we often choose to do the wrong things. We say things before we think; we don't listen to advice; we tell lies; we disrespect our parents; we brag arrogantly on Twitter, Facebook, and Instagram; we waste time at work with Angry Birds; and we are stingy with our money. Proverbs has very good news for us. Wisdom is not primarily tips on how to live life; Wisdom is a person with whom you can be in a relationship—Jesus of Nazareth. When your vertical relationship with God is right through Jesus Christ, your horizontal relationships with others and the world around you will be right as well. Proverbs teaches very clearly here that Wisdom is personal. You have to know Wisdom to walk the wise path in daily relationships, in the work place, or in how you use your words.

Wisdom cries out in the most public places where there will be a maximum number of people. She cries out in the streets, the open squares, the noisy places, and the city gates (Fox, *Proverbs 1–9*, 96). Solomon personifies his wise teaching as a woman—Woman or Lady Wisdom. He presents her as a preaching prophetess. This is a poetic device. *Personification* is representing an abstract idea as a person or creature. This mechanism grabs our attention. We use it to talk about the flag ("these colors don't run") and when we say "opportunity knocked" or "Lady Justice is blind."

This may raise an objection in your mind: "Pastor, you said that Jesus is Wisdom, but Solomon says Wisdom is a woman." Why does Solomon present a woman here? First, Solomon is symbolically talking about his wise teaching. He uses the poetic device of personification to get the reader's attention. Second, the Hebrew noun for wisdom is a feminine noun, so the personification will take on feminine characteristics (again this is poetry; it's not saying that Jesus is a woman). Hebrew, like Spanish and French, has gender identities for its nouns; so when there is a metaphor, it takes on that identity (Waltke, *Proverbs, Chapters 1–15*, 83). Third, Solomon knows that his son—a young man—will be drawn to an attractive woman. In order to get his son to listen to his teaching, he personifies it as a beautiful woman whom he wants his son to marry. This might have helped me (Jon) in high school. I hate biology. I almost failed the subject. It was boring to me, and I didn't understand it. But if my teacher had presented biology to me as Ashley—the beautiful, smart, funny, complex woman that I married and seek to learn about on a daily basis—then I would have been all ears! That's exactly what Solomon is doing here. He is telling his son that learning the wisdom of Proverbs is as scintillating, exhilarating, enjoyable, and satisfying as pursuing and marrying a knockout woman!

Later, in Proverbs 8–9, Solomon will reveal that Woman Wisdom doesn't just stand for Solomon's wisdom; she also stands for God's Wisdom that is being revealed through Solomon in Proverbs. In the fullness of time, God reveals to us what Solomon couldn't have fully known: that Jesus is God's Wisdom in the flesh. First Corinthians 1:24 and 30 state,

> *Yet to those who are called, both Jews and Greeks, Christ is the power of God and the wisdom of God. . . . It is from him that you are in Christ Jesus, who became wisdom from God for us—our righteousness, sanctification, and redemption.*

Christ is the embodiment and fulfillment of the wisdom of Proverbs in the same way that he is the embodiment of the Word itself (John 1). So ultimately, the only way to become wise is to accept Jesus's invitation into a personal relationship by faith.

That invitation is presented here with Woman Wisdom being a "turn or burn" street preacher who gives an urgent invitation to the inexperienced: If they listen to her voice and begin a relationship with her, they will be wise and live; but if they refuse, they will be foolish and die. Like a good street evangelist, she goes to where the people are—the crowded places. She urgently warns them to respond instead of heading on a destructive path. She pleads with three classes of people who have not yet made a decision one way or the other about wisdom (about Jesus!): (1) the inexperienced (i.e., gullible), (2) the mocker (i.e., the hard-hearted), and (3) the fool (the middle of the three classes) (Longman, *Proverbs*, 112).

She calls them to repent upon hearing her sermon. In the fullness of time Jesus calls us to repent when we hear the gospel—to receive him and his word. Repentance is the key response to Jesus's message. You must recognize that you're on the wrong path because of the foolish choices you've made and continue to make, then you must choose to follow Jesus.

Jesus does very much the same as Woman Wisdom. In the Gospels he goes to people and calls them to follow him. You have a choice between two paths (wisdom or foolishness), which is ultimately a choice between two persons (Jesus or Satan). Turn around and run toward Jesus—that's conversion. That's salvation. That's wisdom!

If you do repent, Wisdom promises two things to you. First, you will receive Jesus's Spirit. Turning to Wisdom will lead to receiving the spirit of wisdom (v. 23). There is much going on here. The Spirit of God hovered over the waters at creation to make the world. The Spirit and wisdom were given to temple builders in the Old Testament like Solomon (see Exod 31:1-2 and the building of the tabernacle). The tabernacle and the temple were patterned after the garden of Eden, so they were in a real sense a rebuilding of creation or a "new creation." The Spirit of wisdom is also given to Messiah since he will ultimately make all things new (Isa 11). Since the Spirit built creation according to the pattern of wisdom and harmony, having the Spirit is essential to walking according to that pattern. The Spirit is given to you to transform you and to empower you to walk in wisdom, but you must repent to receive the Spirit. When you do, the Lord promises in Ezekiel 36:27, "I will place my Spirit within you and cause you to follow my statutes."

The New Testament reveals that not only is Jesus the Wisdom of God who gives the Spirit, but he is also the Son of David who receives the Spirit; so the only way we can experience the Spirit of Wisdom is if we are found in Christ.

Second, if you repent you will understand Jesus's Word. Wisdom will illuminate his teaching so you can understand it and walk in obedience to it. The Word of God and the Spirit of God go together. The Spirit is the one who inspires the Word to be written (see John 14–16; Eph 6:17 "the sword of the Spirit"). We see the connection of the Spirit and the Word clearly in Colossians 3 and Ephesians 5. Colossians 3:16 states, "Let the word of Christ dwell richly among you, . . . through psalms, hymns, and spiritual songs." Ephesians 5:18-19 says, "Be filled by the Spirit: speaking to one another in psalms, hymns, and spiritual songs." These are parallel texts that link the "Word of Christ" with being "filled with the Spirit." The Spirit who inspired the Word to be written will illuminate you to understand it through Jesus. So respond to the invitation of Jesus—the Wisdom of God—by repenting!

## Refusing to Accept Jesus Will Wreck Your Life

### PROVERBS 1:24-32

Wisdom recounts a past record of refusing the invitation (i.e., the teachings of Wisdom). All of us have failed to live up to the standard of Wisdom. So Wisdom will laugh at your calamity and terror and distress when it comes like a storm (this language is reminiscent of the wisdom conclusion to Jesus's Sermon on the Mount). Wisdom here is clearly linked to the Lord and the judgment he pours out. The Lord is the one who ridicules and laughs at the wicked (Ps 2). The judgment of the Lord is a storm (Ps 83:15). This passage reminds us of a modern parable: hell hath no fury like a woman scorned. Those who scorn Woman Wisdom will encounter fury.

She moves from accusation to sentencing. She says that trouble will come. Rejecting Wisdom will lead to calamity and terror. There will be ruinous consequences in this life. *Calamity* refers to things that will wreck your life or things that go bad. *Terror* refers to the things you fear most. Wisdom says that refusing her means your nightmares will come true. The things about which you lie awake at night, strategizing how you will avoid them, are the very things that will happen to you if you refuse Wisdom. Perhaps that hidden sin of pornography will be exposed, and your wife will be devastated. Perhaps that affair with your coworker will be exposed, and your children will never forgive you.

Perhaps your refusal to discipline your children while they are young will lead to them wrecking their lives. Your refusal of Wisdom will catch up with you.

And even if it doesn't catch up with you in the short run, it will catch up with you in the end. There may be some of you who think everything is OK because you're able to hide the porn, you're able to hide the flirtatious relationship on Facebook, and you think you will always be able to manage it. You think it won't ever catch up to you. It will! There will be a final judgment where all things are exposed and brought into the light. You will ultimately reap what you have sown, even if you don't in this life. You may walk in foolishness and even prosper in the short term, but eventually it will ruin you. Payday someday (as R. G. Lee famously preached) comes to all of us.

Wisdom says that there is a final judgment, and it is certain. She says that at some point people will call for her and search for her, but it will be too late. She will have eye-for-an-eye retribution. They didn't listen to her, so she won't listen to them. They didn't seek her, so she won't reveal herself to them. Eventually it will be too late to repent. There's no second chance once final judgment is cast. If you continue to reject the kindnesses of Jesus—even his kindness of letting you ruin your life in foolishness right now—eventually it will be too late. Once final judgment is rendered, there's no turning back.

Today is the day of salvation. That's Wisdom's purpose in this sermon. She wants to move the audience to present action. Wisdom doesn't want you to wait until you wreck your life. Jesus wants you to repent now and turn to him because he knows where you're heading, and he wants to save you from the ruin.

This happened to them because they despised knowledge and didn't choose to fear Yahweh. They had their chance, and they refused. They rejected the wisdom of this book, and that means judgment. Wisdom tells us plainly here that rejecting Wisdom is the same thing as rejecting the Lord. All of the practical wisdom this book exhorts you to do and all of the foolishness it warns you to avoid is ultimately about whether or not you've accepted the Lord. The reason you are caught in that sexual sin, can't finish your homework on time, or shoot off at the mouth and get yourself in trouble is not just because you're an idiot. Ultimately it reveals that you have rejected Jesus. You're not in right relationship with God, so you are not walking rightly through his world. This will ultimately mean judgment. Your failure is not a failure of effort or desire; it's that you've missed Jesus. Wisdom—Jesus—is the mediator who brings us into right relationship with God and the world around us. Choose humble faith in the Lord over your own way that seems right to you but leads to death.

These men would have none of Woman Wisdom's ways, so they face the judgment. C. S. Lewis said there are two types of people in the world: "Those who say to God 'Thy will be done,' and those to whom God finally says 'Thy will be done'" (Lewis, *Great Divorce,* 72–73). Ultimately God will give us what we've chosen. Proverbs presents judgment as reaping what you have sown. If you reject Wisdom (Jesus), you will eat the fruit of your own way. The Lord built the world in such a way that certain consequences are inherent in certain actions. Bad actions will reap bad consequences; good actions will reap good consequences. If you are lazy, you will be poor. If you cheat on your spouse, you will lose what you have. If you are hasty with your words, you will lose friends. This is the way the world works; and if you ignore that, you will wreck your life. God made everything, he knows how it works, and he reveals that to us because he loves us and wants what it best for us. The things he lays out in Proverbs are not his way of raining on our parade but rather his way of telling his beloved children how life works best. We end up hurting ourselves, this text says, when we choose autonomy from God. It's not just that sin is wrong, although it is, but sin is also destructive. In the end, the Lord will see to it that his order works out. Proverbs 24:12 says, "Won't he repay a person according to his work?" So refusing the wisdom of this book (i.e., refusing Jesus), as we all have, will wreck your life now and/or later.

The wages of foolishness is death. The judgment for unfaithfulness to the Lord is death (1:32). The "apostasy" (abandoning of the Lord) of the inexperienced will kill them. This word *apostasy* is used in Jeremiah and Hosea for cheating on the Lord (Jer 2:19; Hos 14:4). Foolishness isn't about mental capacity; it's rebellion against God. The sentence for that is death. In the immediate context of Proverbs 1:32-33, this means the "death" of exile for Israel. And for us, in the scheme of the whole Bible, it means eternal banishment in hell. The really sad part of verse 32 is that it talks of the "complacency" of fools. We can be lulled into a false sense of security thinking that everything is fine. We can think that our folly is not that big a deal. "This isn't something I need to worry about right now; I've got plenty of time to address that." We often don't recognize that our behavior, which we think may just be a minor character flaw, is a rebellion that will ultimately destroy us.

## Accepting Jesus Leads to True Life

### PROVERBS 1:33

While the complacent fool will have his feet knocked out from under him, those who accept Wisdom—those who listen to her and are in a personal relationship with her—will live securely and be unafraid of danger. Again, in the immediate context of the life of Israel, this refers to safe dwelling in the land without fear of enemies or exile. In the context of the whole Bible, this refers to living with God forever in the homeland he has provided for us, the new creation. We experience something of this confidence now because we know that our ultimate enemies—sin, Satan, and death—can't ultimately destroy us when we are in Christ. This knowledge should enable us to sleep at night without nightmares that our worst fears will be realized.

## Conclusion

We've all been foolish. At times we have all failed to walk in wisdom. The good news is that wisdom isn't a thing; Wisdom is a person we can trust. He will forgive your failures and enable you to be wise. But he warns you not to be complacent because today is the day of salvation.

## Reflect and Discuss

1. Have you ever encountered a hellfire and brimstone preacher? How was his message received? Is it strange that Solomon presents Lady Wisdom in this way?
2. Why did Solomon choose to personify wisdom? What does it add to the text?
3. Why is Wisdom presented as a woman? What may have been the reasons Solomon did so?
4. The wisdom in Proverbs is not just Solomon's personal wisdom. What does God reveal in time through his wisdom?
5. Lady Wisdom extends an invitation to her hearers. So also did Jesus to his. What are the two options presented?
6. What is ultimately the only way to become wise?

7. Solomon says that if you reject Wisdom, Wisdom will laugh at your calamity and terror and distress when it comes like a storm. Is this fair? Loving? What did Jesus say about this? What did he say would happen to people who reject him and his teaching?
8. Solomon warns about the complacency of foolishness. About what acts of foolishness in your life are you complacent? Why is complacency in this life so eternally deadly?
9. How are rejecting Solomon's wisdom and rejecting Jesus connected?
10. What is the immediate promise Solomon makes to those who obey wisdom? What did that mean for the nation of Israel? How does this promise apply to us in the context of the entire Bible?

# I Hear Voices All the Time

## PROVERBS 2:1-22

**Main Idea:** Listen to the voice of Wisdom.

---

**I. Make a Decision for Wisdom—Jesus Christ (2:1-11).**
**II. Wisdom—Jesus—Will Save You from Evil (2:12-22).**

---

When I (Jon) was five years old, my parents volunteered to clean the church building once a month on Saturdays. On the Saturdays that they cleaned, they brought their four sons with them and told us to play on the playground. There was a bridge on the church property that overlooked a creek. My dad sternly warned us not to go down to the bridge or play in the creek or we would get a spanking. We were to stay in the playground only. Well, we didn't listen to my dad. We went to the bridge to throw rocks into the creek. Once we had thrown all of the rocks, we started to frantically look for more rocks to throw. I saw one on the ledge on the other side of the bridge rails, so I decided I could climb over, hold onto the rail so I wouldn't fall, and grab the rock to throw. My plan didn't work. I fell into the creek, almost breaking my ankles. My brothers helped me up to the building, where I entered the room my parents were cleaning, soaked to the bone. My dad made good on his threats!

The reason my dad warned us not to go down to the bridge or the creek was because he wanted what was best for us. He didn't want us to get hurt. At the time I thought he was trying to keep me from having fun, but that wasn't true. He knew that the most fun we could have was on the playground. And he knew that even though the bridge looked fun at the time, there was danger there. I should have listened to his voice.

In life we are bombarded with all kinds of voices and messages. These are human voices. They might be a parent, a teacher, a coach, a coworker, a friend, or a commercial, but these human voices have spiritual voices and messages that stand behind them. There are godly messages, and there are evil messages. These messages instruct us, exhort us, warn us, and make promises to us. The questions we must ask are,

Whose voice will I listen to? What message will I trust as good and helpful? What message will I reject as bad and harmful?

God warns us and instructs us to keep us from harming ourselves—not to keep us from having fun. He wants what is best for us, and he doesn't want us to hurt ourselves. Will you listen to his voice? Or will you listen to the voice of another because it seems to offer more happiness at the time? The difference between the good life and the foolish life is the voice you heed. This is the key to Proverbs. Wisdom is a person—Jesus. Will you listen to him? If you will, he will make you wise. But we learn in Proverbs 2 that foolishness is also personal. There are voices in your ear, in your head, and the person Folly often stands behind them trying to get you to yield. Will you? Notice the competing voices in Proverbs 2:1-22.

## Make a Decision for Wisdom—Jesus Christ

### PROVERBS 2:1-11

Proverbs 2:1-11 motivate the son to get wisdom, and verses 12-22 tell him the dangers that wisdom will deliver him from. Verses 1-4 give a conditional clause. If you do this, then this will happen as a result. Again, Solomon is a masterful teacher. We can't just tell our children what to do; we must tell them why they should do it. Verses 1-4 pose the condition for the son—if he will pursue wisdom—then verses 5-11 tell him the helpful outcomes it will produce in his life, such as a right relationship with the Lord who grants the gift of wisdom and a new ability to walk in righteousness (as promised in the introduction; see 1:1-7).

Solomon appeals to "my son" (v. 1). The father—King Solomon—is teaching his son—the crown prince—wisdom. Again, Solomon is obeying the exhortation of Deuteronomy 6 to teach the law to his children, and he is obeying Deuteronomy 17 that says the king is to be a man of the law in order to establish his kingdom. He wants his son to receive his sayings and hide his commands within his heart. The son will only do this if he trusts that the wise sayings are true. Solomon wants his son to commit to and embrace his teaching. His teaching is the rest of the book. Proverbs 2 seems to imply that the wisdom of Proverbs is the law of Moses fleshed out in daily life. That's why the teachings are repeatedly called "laws" or "commandments." That's why wisdom starts with the "fear of the Lord" (i.e., love God, which is the greatest command) and leads to how you treat others (i.e., love neighbor, which is the second command; Matt 22:34-40). In order for the son to live them out, he must internalize them. The law needs to be written on the heart. But how? Words can go in one ear and out the other. But words can also go in the ear and down into the heart to produce inward-out transformation (Prov 2:2).

Solomon exhorts his son to call out for understanding (i.e., call out to Wisdom like she called out to you; 1:20-33). If the son will call out to her, she will save him from evil (vv. 12-19). Solomon tells his son to seek wisdom like a hidden treasure. Go on a treasure hunt for wisdom because wisdom is more precious than silver or gold (8:10). Nothing you desire can compare with wisdom.

If the son will commit to Solomon's teaching—if we will commit to Christ, the embodiment of Solomon's teaching—then we will understand the fear of Yahweh and know God. Wow! Wisdom—Jesus—is the mediator who brings you into right relationship with God.

There is a reciprocal cycle laid out here in Proverbs 2. Seek Wisdom, and you will find God. Find God, and you will gain wisdom. A right relationship with God will make you wise. Knowledge implies an intimate relationship. This happens by faith. Oftentimes allegiance precedes understanding. I was counseling with an unbeliever whose marriage was ending because of his addiction to pornography. This man was a confessed atheist, yet he came to me for counseling. I tried to lay out, as best I could, the wisdom of God's design for sexuality. But I constantly told the young man that this won't work—these things won't make sense to you—unless you first believe Jesus is Lord and his ways are best. And they didn't end up working for him. This is the cycle we see here.

So we should pursue wisdom by studying Proverbs and calling out to Wisdom (Jesus) because that will lead us to know God. This is essential because the Lord is the one who gives wisdom; it comes from his mouth (2:6). There is a paradox here. Wisdom—like salvation—is both a gift to be received and something to work out with fear and trembling (Phil 2:12-13). Wisdom is a pursuit (Prov 2:1-4) and a gift (vv. 6-7) (Goldsworthy, *Tree of Life*, 52–53). So we need to be diligent and work at wisdom. As Solomon does, we need to observe the world around us and see how it works. Solomon looks at ants and is instructed (6:6-8). We need to do this as well, but we do it through the fear of the Lord—through dependence on God and his Word. And as we seek, God grants more to us. James 1:5 says that if we lack wisdom we should ask the Lord for it because he gives it generously. Solomon already knows this because he asked the Lord for it (1 Kgs 3). The gift of wisdom is found in God's Word. Solomon's words are God's words, and we should commit to them because wisdom is found here.

Proverbs 2:6-9 clearly states that the Lord gives wisdom as a gift to his faithful covenant people, and he thereby guards them from the temptations that might destroy them (we will see this later). Commit to the Lord's wisdom, and you will understand righteousness and the good path (v. 9). We see in Proverbs 2 the same words used to describe multifaceted wisdom in 1:1-7. So pursuing wisdom and receiving it from the Lord will give you what the introduction to Proverbs promised. Again, wisdom is not a high IQ; it's moral discernment of good and evil. It is the ability to see life from God's perspective and then to act accordingly.

How does God produce morality in us? Proverbs 2:10 says that wisdom will enter our hearts. For us to walk the path of righteousness and wisdom, we must have the law written on our hearts and experience an inner transformation. That's the only way we can obey God (see Jer 31; Ezek 36). Proverbs is not teaching tips for behavior modification. That won't work. You can't obey the Lord until you know him intimately in a personal relationship and his law is written on your heart. When that happens, discretion will keep a protecting watch over you (v. 11). This is essential to wisdom in daily life. You must listen to the voice of the Lord (vertical relationship) in order to live wisely before others in the world around you (horizontal relationships). He will protect you. That raises the question, What do you need protection from?

## Wisdom—Jesus—Will Save You from Evil

### PROVERBS 2:12-22

Wisdom will save you from the path of evil that leads to death. There are two groups mentioned in verses 12-22—two sets of voices that can pull you toward ruin and death: (1) evil men and (2) an evil woman.

First, wisdom will save you from the men who speak perversely (v. 12). These people, similar to the gang of Proverbs 1:8-19, are rivals to the voice of the father and the voice of God. And as we will see later in Proverbs, there's a personal being that stands behind these human figures. Like Satan in the garden, these men distort reality and try to get you to follow the distortion. They seduce you. That's what it means to speak perversely. Perverse speech distorts ultimate reality. The people who are saying this may genuinely believe that what they are saying is right and true and helpful, but it goes against the created order. Their words go against the way things really work. For example, a woman may genuinely think that marriage is just about two people who really love each other instead of a covenant relationship between one man and one woman for a lifetime. But that goes against the natural and God-ordained order of things. A man may think that not being happy with his wife is a legitimate ground for divorce, but that goes against the order of things as established by God. A boy or young man may genuinely think that fooling around with his girlfriend before marriage just helps you know what you like and don't like, but that goes against the order of things and God's call to be holy.

Perverse speech calls sin "good" and rejoices in evil. Proverbs 24:24 states, "Whoever says to the guilty, 'You are innocent'—peoples will curse him, and nations will denounce him." Justifying someone's sin or saying that it's not a sin is perverse speech. For example, it is perverse speech to tell someone their grudge is warranted because the hurt perpetrated against them was very severe. It is not right in the eyes of God. Proverbs 30:20 says, "This is the way of an adulteress: she eats and wipes her mouth and says, 'I've done nothing wrong.'" People can find all kinds of ways to justify their sin as if it's not wrong. "It's OK for me to flirt with this woman at work because my wife doesn't respond to me the way that she should." With our mouths we justify and rationalize and minimize our sin or the sins of others. Any person who will counsel you in such a way as to justify sin in your life is someone of perverse speech that should be avoided. They are leading you down dark paths, and they rejoice in evil (2:13-14).

Wisdom will deliver you from them. What are the harmful consequences for listening to counsel like that from yourself or someone else? They will take you down the twisted path toward death.

Wisdom will also save you from the "forbidden [or foreign] woman" who is smooth-tongued (v. 16). This is the first time we meet the forbidden woman in Proverbs; she will be a major character in this book. She is the subject of the father's warning many times. She is clearly presented as Solomon's competitor for his son's affection and attention because her "flattering talk" (v. 16) rivals his words (v. 1) and the Lord's words (v. 6). Her flirtatious words mimic the dad in order to get the son to listen. Who will he listen to?

Here she refers to a literal person with whom the son can commit sexual sin. But later she will be personified as Woman Folly—the rival to

Woman Wisdom (Prov 9). Folly will be described in the same way as this woman. They are both flatterers who lure their prey to death (cf. 5:3; 7:14-21; 9:13-17 and 2:18; 7:27; 9:18) (Murphy and Huwiler, *Proverbs*, 21). If the son begins an affair with this forbidden woman, it will reveal that he has rejected his father, Wisdom, and the Lord. Embracing the human forbidden woman by means of sexual sin reveals that spiritually he is in a relationship with Woman Folly instead of Wisdom (i.e., Jesus). This is not shocking since sexual sin and spiritual sin are tied together throughout the Bible. Already in Proverbs 1:32 rejecting Wisdom is described with the same word as unfaithfulness to the Lord in the prophets. Adultery is the distortion of the most intimate human relationship, and 1 Corinthians 6 reveals that it is also a distortion of the most intimate spiritual relationship. The whole point of Proverbs 1–9 is that if our horizontal relationships are off, our vertical are as well, and vice versa. Solomon knows this full well because he fell for forbidden "foreign" women who led him to idolatry and destroyed his dynasty (1 Kgs 11:1-5). Falling for the forbidden woman would reveal that the son is being led away from the Lord (Wisdom) and is instead embracing Folly.

How does this woman work? She flatters with her words. This is perhaps shocking to some. Most of us think of unfaithfulness as starting with looks, but that's not the case in Proverbs. Adultery and sexual sin start with flattery. One of the top needs that men have is respect and admiration; so if a woman inflates the male ego, he will usually respond. They are suckers for flattery. This may start in a subtle way that the man doesn't recognize as unwise. His coworker might lend a sympathetic ear, or she may laugh at his jokes. He may think of their conversations as just "harmless flirting." Or perhaps he justifies his flirtation with, "I'm not happy at home." Before long, he starts to look forward to work events that she will be at, or he begins to send secret messages to her on Facebook. Before he knows it he's cheating on his wife, and it all started with what many looking on would justify as "harmless conversation." This can happen with women too. Solomon is teaching his son, but if he was teaching his daughter he could warn about forbidden men that flatter with their words to get women to do what they want!

Any sexual activity outside marriage's covenant commitment before God and witnesses to your heterosexual spouse is sinful, foolish, and deadly. This woman forsakes her husband and the vows she made to her God, and she will lead you to do the same. She violates the covenant law of God, and so would you by your foolish embrace of her. Her house sinks down to death, and those who enter never return to life. This destruction may happen now with the loss of your family, your reputation, or your money in alimony, or it may happen later at judgment. But, mark it down, it will happen. The wages of sexual sin is death with no hope of return. What is the antidote? Proverbs 2 says that it's a right relationship with God through Wisdom (vertical relationship), and Proverbs 5 says it's an intimate relationship with your wife (horizontal relationship).

So listen to the father and get wisdom so that you can walk righteous paths that protect you from derailing. The upright—those who are connected to the Lord through Wisdom (Jesus)—will inhabit the land (i.e., Israel in that context and the new creation for us in Christ). This is a reference to the eternal life with God in the homeland he provides for us. But the wicked—those following after Folly as evidenced by their distorted worldview and sexual sin—will experience the "death" of exile (i.e., Israel's exile in that context, and ultimately hell for those outside of Christ).

## Conclusion

Jesus is not only the Wisdom of Proverbs, but he is also the Son who perfectly listens to his Father, perfectly keeps the covenant, and avoids immorality. However, in the end, Jesus takes the penalty that covenant-breakers like us deserve. He went down into death for sexual sinners like us, but three days later he triumphantly returned to the paths of life! Through his life, death, and resurrection he has defeated all of our enemies. It is not inevitable that they will drag you down to death. He can rescue you from them by empowering you to walk in wisdom. It is not inevitable that they will cause your exile from God forever. Jesus came out of death to inherit the whole earth, and you can be his coheir if you are united to him by faith. If you find yourself giving in to evil, consistently rationalizing your sin, or being enslaved to sexual sin, then circumstances may be revealing to you that you're not listening to the voice of Wisdom. You have, instead, been seduced by the voice of another. If that's true, come to Jesus—the Wisdom of God—and follow his leading voice! Listen to him. He has the words that lead to life.

## Reflect and Discuss

1. Are there times when you can still hear an authority figure from your past (parent, family member, teacher, coach, etc.) warning you about a certain action?
2. How will viewing the voices in our lives (people, commercials, etc.) as having spiritual voices and messages that stand behind them change the way we make decisions? How should it affect the voices we are allowing to speak into our lives?
3. Did you have an authority figure growing up who never told you why something was off-limits but only said, "Because I said so"? Why is that so maddening? How does Solomon model proper parenting/adult leadership in Proverbs?
4. What are some specific ways that the wisdom of Proverbs is the law of Moses fleshed out in daily life?
5. What is the "reciprocal cycle" in Proverbs? How should this cycle change the focus of our lives, the priority of our pursuits?
6. Is wisdom a gift from God or something to be worked for?
7. According to Proverbs 2:10, what is foundational to living in wisdom?
8. How is "anyone who says perverse things" (Prov 2:12) a rival to the voice of Wisdom? What tactics does this person use?
9. What does Proverbs tell us is the first step to sexual sin and adultery? How is this different than what we would normally think?
10. While Proverbs is not about behavior modification, what does it say that your behavior reveals? If you find yourself giving in to sin, what does it say about more fundamental issues?

# Does Proverbs Preach a Prosperity Gospel?

## PROVERBS 3:1-12

**Main Idea:** You can be a blessed covenant-keeper through faith in Jesus.

---

**I. We Should Keep the Covenant (3:1,3,5,7,9).**
**II. God Blesses Covenant-Keepers (3:2,4,6,8,10).**
**III. This Is Generally True Now and Will Always Prove True Later (3:11-12).**
**IV. Jesus Kept the Covenant for You.**

---

In high school I (Jon) lettered in two sports and competed all year round, so I was in great shape. But once I graduated and ceased to play competitive sports, I no longer had any motivation to work out and stay in shape. The results were not good! Solomon understands our need for motivation. He wants his son to be wise, but he knows that he needs to motivate him in order to get him to train in wisdom.

Proverbs 3:1-12 is about being in a faithful covenant relationship with God. Israel was in a covenant, marriage-like relationship with the Lord that was established at Sinai during the exodus. This covenant involved commitments that were to be upheld by each partner. We see this laid out here. In our modern translations, the odd-numbered verses give the obligations of the human partner in the covenant, and the even-numbered verses give the obligations of the divine partner.[6]

## We Should Keep the Covenant

### PROVERBS 3:1,3,5,7,9

The odd verses give the obligations that we are called to live up to if we are in a covenant relationship with the Lord. Solomon starts in verse 1 by saying, "My son, don't forget my teaching, but let your heart keep my commands." Again, the father is King Solomon, and the son is the crown prince. He exhorts his son to obey the law—his teaching (Hb

---

[6] This insight came from Bruce Waltke, and the entire sermon is built on this premise (*Proverbs, Chapters 1–15*, 238–50).

*torah*) and commands. We've seen throughout the Proverbs that there is a strong connection between the law and wisdom. Deuteronomy 4:6 says that keeping the laws is the wisdom of Israel. Deuteronomy 6 commands parents to teach the law to their children, and Deuteronomy 17 commands the king to be a man of the law. Solomon is obeying all of this in Proverbs by showing how wisdom is obeying the law in daily life. He is training his son in this so that he can establish the messianic kingdom.

But the law must be internalized in order to be obeyed. There has to be inward transformation where the law is written on the heart (Jer 31; Ezek 36). Theologians call this "regeneration." We see this not only in verse 1 with "let your heart keep," but we also see it in verse 3: these teachings must be written on the "tablet of your heart." This is covenant language. "Loyalty and faithfulness" are words that are associated with the covenant and the royal rule of the king (Prov 20:28). The covenant must be written on the heart of the king and the people for the kingdom to flourish. Solomon says to "tie them around your neck" (v. 3), which recalls the language of Deuteronomy 6 where the law was to be bound on the hand and inscribed on a frontlet for the eyes. And the command to write it on the "tablet" of your heart connects much Old Testament expectation. The Ten Commandments were written on stone tablets, and the people didn't obey them (Exod 20; Deut 5). But Scripture promises that a day is coming when the covenant will be written on the tablet of the heart so that one can obey. The Lord will perform this. In Jeremiah 31:33 the Lord says,

> *"Instead, this is the covenant I will make with the house of Israel after those days"—the Lord's declaration. "I will put my teaching within them and write it on their hearts."*

So, as anticipated by the rest of the Old Testament, Proverbs recognizes the need for inward-out transformation, not behavior modification. Proverbs isn't exhorting us to behavior first and foremost; it's advocating our need for regeneration before these things can be followed.

How does this happen? Verses 5 and 7 say you should trust the Lord instead of trusting yourself. One could boil the whole of Proverbs down to this truth. Obedience to the law starts with faith. This is the key to wisdom, as 1:7 already stated. Trust in Yahweh with all your heart and don't lean on your own understanding. Trust God, not yourself. Foolishness is trusting in your own mind and heart (28:26). Wisdom starts with recognizing that you don't have it and looking to God in humility for it. The way that seems right to humans ends in death. We think that what is best for us is autonomy and the power to choose what to do with our own lives, but Proverbs says that is suicidal. What seems right to us usually ends up wrecking us.

There is the wisdom of God, and there is the wisdom of humans. The world says that it's wise to live together before marriage, but God says that you can't practice true intimacy without a covenant commitment where you're actually connected to each other. The world says it's wise to hoard your possessions, but Proverbs 11:24 says, "One person gives freely, yet gains more; another withholds what is right, only to become poor." The world says that it's OK to hold a grudge—after all, how will the person know that what they did hurt you so badly if you let it go? But the Bible says forgive your enemies. The world says it's wise to promote yourself, but that's not true in God's economy (27:2).

Here's the key: don't be wise in your own eyes. That's the root of foolishness going all the way back to the garden of Eden. Instead, you should fear Yahweh. Thinking that you are wise is foolishness. Wisdom and folly boil down to humility and pride. Submit every area of your life to the Lord, and he will produce wisdom in you. If you do veer off the right path, Proverbs 3:7 says repent—turn away from evil. Recognize your sin and foolishness and turn from it to God.

Solomon gives one practical example of how inward piety leads to outward obedience to the law. Verse 9 speaks of generosity: honor the Lord with your possessions and your first produce (cf. Lev 23:10; Deut 18:1-5). Again, this is covenantal language (i.e., obedience to the law). Give back to Yahweh out of what he has provided for you. Give the firstfruits; give your best and your first to God, not the leftovers. This means giving should be set out at the top of your budget, not at the bottom "after everything else is covered." This practice demonstrates gratitude for what God has given and confidence that he will continue to provide (see 2 Cor 8–9).

## God Blesses Covenant-Keepers

### PROVERBS 3:2,4,6,8,10

The even verses give the divine partner's obligations. He will be the faithful rewarder. Verse 2 starts with the word *for*, which gives the why, the motivation. Following this law will add days, years, and peace to your life. Just like the fifth commandment, Solomon says to obey your dad, and in return you will live a longer life and a better life (cf. Eph 6:1-3). In Proverbs, Solomon does give guidelines for healthy living that will generally increase your chances of a full life. If you unwisely get into drugs, illicit sexual sin, greediness for gain, or any number of follies outlined in the book, it can cut your life short.

Ultimately, what is being taught here is eternal life and abundant life. This is picturing a return to Eden, to shalom, to the way things are supposed to be. There will be complete harmony with God, other people, and the world around you. That's what all the even verses are picturing.

Proverbs 3:4 gives the reward for covenant loyalty, and that is acceptance and a good rapport with God and people. Again, wisdom is about right relationship with God and others. Verse 6 gives the promise of the Lord to make our paths straight. He will give divine direction and divine protection to our daily lives on the right path. Verse 8 gives the reward for fearing the Lord and not being wise in our own eyes, and that is health. A well-ordered life leads to health (by contrast, sexual sin can lead to disease according to Prov 5). The picture of all of these verses is that wisdom reverses the curse of sin, death, and sickness. Wisdom is a return to paradise. Leviticus 26:16 taught that breaking the covenant would lead to disease. Proverbs shows that faithfulness to the covenant will lead to the blessing of health.

Finally, Proverbs 3:10 gives the reward for generosity to the Lord, and that reward is full barns and vats that overflow with new wine. God will bestow wealth on those who are generous. Again, this is covenant language. Deuteronomy 7:12-15 says that covenant faithfulness will lead to God blessing the fruit of the ground and taking away disease. If Israel obeys God, things will go well. The rain will fall, and the crops will grow (Deut 11:14; 28:8; Mal 3:10). When Israel disobeys, the reverse will happen (Deut 28:51). So it seems clear that obedience will lead to God giving us more. This shouldn't surprise us. Good stewards can be trusted with more.

My (Jon's) parents paid for me to go to the University of Kentucky my freshman year. But if I had partied every night, shown up late to classes, and flunked the first semester, do you think they would have continued to pay for my college? No! But since I went to class, finished assignments on time, and made good grades, they were happy to continue to pay my tuition. A good steward will be trusted with more, and a bad steward will lose what he's been given.

So obey God by doing the odd verses and in return you will get the rewards of the even verses. But this raises an important question: Is this really true? What about instances where things don't work this way?

## This Is Generally True Now and Will Always Prove True Later

**PROVERBS 3:11-12**

Are these verses teaching a prosperity gospel? Are they teaching that we should trust and obey the Lord and in return he will give us health, wealth, and happiness? The answer is, "Yes, of course!" But there's a problem. This doesn't always work out immediately in a fallen world. Sometimes you can believe and obey, and things go bad for you. You get cancer instead of health. Despite your great generosity to the work of the Lord, you get laid off. Sometimes we suffer now and receive the rewards only in the next life. So it's not your best life now; it's your best life later and forever.

The proverbs are generally true now, but they are always ultimately true.[7] In the new creation we will experience every spiritual and physical blessing that has been promised to us. Proverbs 3:11-12 helps us understand this interplay. Solomon tells his son to accept Yahweh's discipline and not reject it. Don't get mad at Yahweh when he allows discipline in your life because he does so for your good. In order to be truly wise, one must have correction and discipline. That is key to the book because left without discipline we will go down the wrong path to destruction. That's our sin nature.

The Lord certainly disciplines his children by holding their sin accountable to rid it from their lives; but he also might allow suffering into his children's lives, not as a punishment for sin but rather to produce maturity in their lives. While a parent disciplines a child for breaking rules, discipline is also what we do to our bodies when we excercise. You put your body under hardship so you can get in better shape for later. We voluntarily let hard things into our lives to prep us for something much better later. For example, when our older daughter, Maddy, began learning to read, it frustrated her a great deal. She got very upset that she couldn't read right away. She wanted to quit and play with her

---

[7] Mark Dever says, "Individual proverbs are always *ultimately* true. . . . Individual proverbs are *normally* true now" (*Message*, 510, emphasis original).

toys. But as she labored through the hardship she became a great reader and began to enjoy reading. God often operates in this way. He will allow hardship in our lives to produce something in us. In Deuteronomy 8 he tells the children of Israel that he let them endure lean times so that when they had plenty they wouldn't forget him.

Why does he do this? Because he loves us just like parents who discipline their child out of love. He loves you enough to allow hardship at times to prepare you for something greater later. He loves us and wants to make us like Jesus, so that means discipline (cf. Heb 12—he allows suffering to produce holiness). So yes, God will reward us, but he doesn't always give us what we want when we want it. Instead, he gives us exactly what we need when we need it. He will conform you to the image of his covenant-keeping Son so that you are the kind of person who can rightly experience the covenant blessings. Sometimes you will suffer now and not receive an immediate reward because the Lord is molding you for a greater glory later.

The problem with smiley prosperity preachers on TV is that they assume godly people will never suffer in this life. That's unbiblical (see 2 Tim 3:12). Godliness through Jesus Christ is no guarantee that things will always go well for you in this life (see Job). After all, our righteous King suffered in this life. But even if things go badly for you now, they will go well for you ultimately in the next age and be far better than any good life here.

Finally, the last problem with the prosperity gospel is that it bypasses Jesus. The question must be asked, Who keeps the covenant?

## Jesus Kept the Covenant for You

The false gospel of the prosperity preachers misunderstands that none of us are faithful covenant-keeping sons. None of us have been perfectly obedient to the Lord. None of us have perfectly trusted God instead of ourselves. None of us have perfectly turned from evil or been completely generous as we should be. This covenant relationship between the Father and the Son is not kept by God's firstborn son Israel, nor is it kept by David, Solomon, or Solomon's sons. Jesus is the Son who finally keeps it. Luke 2:52 shows that he is the Son of Solomon who grew in wisdom and in stature and in favor with God and people (cf. Prov 3:4) (Goldsworthy, *Tree of Life*, 57–58). He is the King with the covenant on his heart (3:3; cf. 20:28). So he is the one who gets the blessing, not us.

The good news is that he represents us before the Father in this covenant relationship. He lived up to our obligations for us, and then he took the curses of covenant breaking in our place. He experienced sickness, sorrows, enemies, and a premature death for us (see Isa 52:13–53:12). He offers full pardon to all covenant-breakers who believe in him. His righteous record of keeping the covenant is credited to the account of all who are united to him by faith, and as a result they will experience the blessings of covenant faithfulness by his merits not their own! And if you are joined to him by faith, God will do the work by the power of the Spirit to conform you into the image of his covenant-keeping Son—sometimes through discipline.

As sons of the Father in Christ Jesus, this is how we are to live—this is now how we can live. Your Christianity has never been about keeping the rules in order for God to save you. Christianity is about how God saves you through his Son and then molds you into his image so you can live out the life God meant for you to live. As we live out this covenant by the power of Jesus's Spirit—obeying the law, trusting in the Lord, looking away from ourselves, and being generous to those in need—we recognize that the rewards will work out now or later. This is about faith, not effort. Faith is the key to obedience. Radical confidence in our rewarding God will be the means by which you keep his commands. You will give because you trust him to continually provide. You will forgive because you trust him to be a good and fair judge. That's how God's Son lives. That is how we live in him.

## Conclusion

The problem with the prosperity gospel is not that it wants us to be physically blessed. God has promised that we will be. The problems with this false gospel are (1) it misunderstands life in a fallen world where the righteous suffer, (2) it bypasses Jesus who is the only one who has fulfilled these obligations, and (3) it doesn't promise enough prosperity. The true gospel says that the faithful Son had his life cut short in the short run, but he was raised to an indestructible life to inherit the cosmos. That's a prosperity worth having, and it's available in Christ.

## Reflect and Discuss

1. Has there been a time in your life when you were working toward a set goal? How was your motivation before you reached the goal, and how did it change after you reached it?
2. When Proverbs 3:3 says these teachings must be written on the "tablet of your heart," how does it connect with the covenant God made with Israel?
3. What is the one truth that could boil down the whole of Proverbs?
4. In contrast, what is the root of foolishness? How does it connect back to the garden of Eden?
5. What is the one practical example Solomon gives in Proverbs 3:9 of how inward piety leads to outward obedience to the law? How should this truth affect your life?
6. Does Proverbs teach that we should trust and obey the Lord and in return he will give us health, wealth, and happiness? How does this play out in the short term? How does this play out ultimately?
7. How does the reward for generosity to the Lord in Proverbs 3:10 connect back to the covenant between God and Israel?
8. What are the two types of God's discipline? How have you seen his discipline in your own life?
9. One problem with prosperity preachers is that they assume godly people will never suffer. How does Proverbs answer the question of suffering in this life?
10. How does the false gospel of the prosperity preachers bypass Jesus?

## I'd Rather Have Wisdom than Silver or Gold

### PROVERBS 3:13-35

**Main Idea:** Wisdom (Jesus) is the superior treasure above all else.

---

**I. Wisdom Will Give You an Abundant and Eternal Life (3:13-18).**
**II. Wisdom Will Give You a Perception of How the World Works (3:19-20).**
**III. Wisdom Will Give You Peace of Mind (3:21-26).**
**IV. Wisdom Will Give You God's Blessing Instead of His Judgment (3:27-35).**

---

When my (Jon's) girls see commercials for toys or dolls or new Lalaloopsies, they exclaim, "I have to have that! Mom, can I get it? Dad, can I get it?" At Christmas time or for their birthdays, we have a hard time getting them to narrow in on a few items they want. We have to ask them things like, "If you could only get one thing, which would you want?" We want to determine what their heart is set on above all else.

What about you? What one thing do you want most? What in life do you have to have? Often commercials can awaken us to our desires. Maybe there are things you just have to possess, foods you just have to consume, or relationships you just have to have. What's the superior treasure in your life that you wake up thinking about, go to sleep dreaming about, and spend your day planning to get? It may be money, stuff, sex, success, or any number of things.

Wisdom—Jesus—is the treasure that is superior to all that we can set our hearts on. Solomon will tell us in Proverbs 3:13-35 to seek Wisdom first, above all else. When Solomon wrote these words he was encouraging his son to commit to study this book—Proverbs. But in the fullness of time, the Spirit has revealed to us that Wisdom is a person—Jesus Christ. We are to seek him—the pearl of great price—above all else, and all these other things will be provided for us (Matt 6:33). If we set our supreme desire on things—even good things—it will prove disappointing. It may even wreck our lives. But when we set our supreme desire on Jesus, we are able to enjoy these other things as gifts that cause our hearts to praise Jesus for providing them.

## Wisdom Will Give You an Abundant and Eternal Life

### PROVERBS 3:13-18

Proverbs 3:13-18 is a poem or a hymn about the supreme value of wisdom. As we've seen, Solomon has personified his wisdom as a beautiful woman. He says to get her above anything else. Again, in the fullness of time (Gal 4:4), the New Testament revealed to us that this personification pointed to a real person—Jesus of Nazareth—whom we can know and pursue and treasure above all else. The benefits of wisdom are given here to motivate us to be with her at any cost. The idea is to get wisdom because it leads to a happy and blessed life. We see that this idea brackets the poem ("happy" in vv. 13 and 18). This is called an *inclusio* (Garrett, *Proverbs,* 257). Garrett points out that this passage is a hymn and is bracketed by "blessing" at the beginning and end. Solomon gives a beatitude: Blessed or happy will be the one who gets Wisdom—Jesus.

Wisdom's profits are better than silver, gold, or jewels. Wisdom is better than money and stuff. Wisdom is better because it cannot be lost or destroyed (see Matt 6; moth and rust destroy money and stuff). Wisdom is better because, as we saw in verses 1-12, it shapes you into the kind of person who can enjoy these things in the proper context. To paraphrase Waltke, money can put food on the table but not fellowship around it. Money can buy you a house, but it cannot produce a home. Money can give a woman jewelry, but it cannot buy her real love (*Proverbs, Chapters 1–15,* 257). Wisdom is better than that. Wisdom gives physical, spiritual, and relational blessings. Proverbs teaches us that wisdom creates happy homes, loving marriages, and treasures that cannot be valued by marketplace prices. Riches won't ultimately make you happy, but Solomon says that wisdom will. The main reason is that wisdom is ultimately not a thing; Wisdom is a person you can have a personal relationship with—Jesus.

So get Jesus at any cost because nothing you could ever desire compares with him. Wisdom is better than anything you can desire, so grab her and don't let her go. Jesus—like the kingdom of God, the pearl of great price, the treasure in the field (Matt 13:44-46)—is worth selling all that you have to get him. Is there something that you desire more than Jesus? What is supremely valuable to you? Even if you wouldn't say it out loud, in your mind do you think, "Well, for me to be happy, of course I need Jesus, but I also need a happy marriage. I need Jesus plus ______." What is it that you have to have in addition to Jesus? I need Jesus plus a promotion. I need Jesus plus the right car. I need Jesus plus a house in the right neighborhood. I need Jesus plus romance. I need Jesus plus financial security. I need Jesus plus the perfect Christmas card photo of a family. Whatever you put in that blank is what you treasure most, since you've given it the same status as Jesus.

Solomon exhorts us through the Spirit that if our heart is set supremely on the stuff of this life as the means to happiness, then we may lose those things, and happiness will certainly elude us. But if you set your heart supremely on Jesus, then you will certainly get true happiness, and he may provide you other things to enjoy in their proper context. But true happiness can only be found if Jesus is our supreme treasure. Seek wisdom above all else, and these other things will be provided for you. Solomon knows this. In 1 Kings 3 the Lord told Solomon he would grant whatever Solomon asked for. Amazing! If you could ask God for one thing, what would it be? Solomon could've asked for riches, long life, victory over his enemies, or the most glorious empire any king has ever ruled; but instead he asked for wisdom above all else. So the Lord gave him supreme wisdom; and the Lord also provided long life, money, and victory over his enemies.

So Solomon tells us in Proverbs 3:16-17 that getting wisdom above all else will add long life, riches, a good reputation, and a pleasant course of life. Wow! You get to live longer because the wise and pleasant paths you are walking help you avoid the pitfalls that lead to an early death, and you receive honor because those paths help you avoid things that will damage your reputation. Living a life of risky and foolish behavior as laid out in this book—whether it be sexual sin, violent behavior, or not being able to control your tongue—may lead to an early death or at least a ruined reputation. On the other hand, heeding the wisdom of this book will lead to wealth since hard work instead of laziness, spending wisely rather than frivolously, and saving for down times will ensure that you have the provision you need. Again, following the wisdom of this book will generally lead to these blessings right now, but they will always ultimately lead to these blessings. Proverbs are promises that are generally true now, but they are always ultimately true.

Wisdom—Jesus—is the tree of life (see Gen 2). The tree of life is only mentioned in Genesis, Proverbs, and Revelation. Eating from this tree will give you immortality (Gen 3:22). Wisdom (Jesus) is the path to eternal life. This entire poem is calling us back to paradise at creation. Proverbs 3:13 said that happy is a "man" who finds wisdom, but the Hebrew word used there is "Adam." Solomon reveals that what was lost in Eden by human sin and what separated humanity from Yahweh is now available again through Wisdom. Indeed, in the garden humankind reached for knowledge apart from God and his Word. Adam and Eve sought to determine for themselves right and wrong. As a result, they became unwise and inherited death. But if we will humble ourselves and take hold of Jesus, we will receive back what was lost in Eden. We will be given the knowledge of good and evil, the tree of life, and the shalom of the untarnished creation. That is a happy life indeed (v. 18).

So seek Wisdom—Jesus—first, and all these other blessings will be provided for you!

## Wisdom Will Give You a Perception of How the World Works

**PROVERBS 3:19-20**

Yahweh created the whole world by wisdom, so there's a wise order to the world. The mention of the earth and the heavens in verse 19 is what scholars call a "merism." A merism is where the whole is communicated by mentioning its extremities (Murphy, *Pocket Dictionary*, 107). For example, earth (the ground) and the heavens (the sky) are used to talk about the whole of creation. Or consider, "as far as the east is from the west, so far has he removed our transgressions from us" (Ps 103:12). This communicates that as far as our sins could possibly be removed from us, they have been. Solomon says the Lord created the whole of the cosmos by means of wisdom. This is not surprising because wisdom is a skill used for building in the Old Testament (e.g., the tabernacle in Exod 31; the temple in 1 Kgs 7; and now creation itself, which was the original sanctuary of God).

This is why wisdom is so valuable. There is a wise order to the world. The world works in a certain way—according to the pattern of wisdom—so you can know the order and live by it if you possess wisdom. In a fallen world that has been broken by sin, this order generally works out now; but it will always work out later. Wisdom gives you the ability to perceive God's order and live by it. You must live by this order. Don't try to live against the grain because that is ruinous. Microwaves were designed to work in a certain way. Certain materials are not supposed to go into them. One time my (Jon's) youngest brother was eating something from Taco Bell, and he had some sauce packets he had saved in the fridge. He wanted to warm the sauce up, so he put the packet in the microwave. What happened next? A light show on par with the Fourth of July went off in our microwave! That's true with creation as well. If you live against the grain of how things work or how wisdom has ordered the world, it will go badly for you. Solomon tells us in Proverbs 6 that we can observe ants and deduce that hard work will lead to provision and laziness will lead to poverty. You can observe that a soft answer cools fury. Dishonesty in the justice system will destroy a society. That's just the way that the world works, and trying to live against its order is suicidal.

This wise order is also Christ-centered. It points to him. God created the world through Jesus (John 1; Col 1), and Jesus is the one who upholds the world right now by his Word (Heb 1). Also, all things are being united in Christ (Eph 1), so all things are centered on him, including the created order. For example, the seasons point to Christ. There's a reason God created the seasons to work in such a way that flowers and plant life die in the winter and come back to life in the spring. That reason is Jesus of Nazareth—to point to his death and resurrection. Since the created order is centered on Christ, you must know him in order to perceive and live according to the order. The order is personal because he is the one who created and upholds the world.

## Wisdom Will Give You Peace of Mind

### PROVERBS 3:21-26

Solomon appeals to his son to not let wisdom and discretion depart from his sight because they are life (vv. 21-22). Keep the wisdom of this book through Jesus, and it will keep you secure from the ruin of the wicked when that comes (v. 25). Solomon's point is that wisdom keeps you safe from sudden trouble. That's why you should get wisdom above all else. You will walk safely during the days of your life, and you will sleep peacefully at night. This is an appeal from a parent who desperately wants his child to be safe. Don't we all? He says you won't stumble if you keep walking on the wise path (again, this is generally true now but always ultimately true).

Wisdom will give you a good night's sleep without worry (v. 24). You will sleep well because you haven't done the foolish things that cause you to stay awake worrying. You won't be afraid that you'll get caught or be found out. You won't have to lie awake thinking to yourself, What if she reads that e-mail? What if he runs into that person? Who else knows about this? How can I make sure this never gets out? Walking in wisdom and avoiding the foolishness of sin will keep your conscience clear and your mind free from worry. And if you get wisdom, you will ultimately be safe because Yahweh is the one who watches over you all day long (v. 26). God Almighty will be looking out for you! The fear of Yahweh is the beginning of wisdom, and he will keep those who fear him safe.

## Wisdom Will Give You God's Blessing Instead of His Judgment

### PROVERBS 3:27-35

Solomon moves from our vertical relationship with Yahweh (v. 26) to our horizontal relationships with others. Wisdom teaches that if your vertical relationship with the Lord is right your other relationships will be right in everyday life. One practical example of keeping this wisdom as Solomon has exhorted is being a good neighbor. You are not wise or in a right relationship with the Lord if you're not a good neighbor. If you love God, you will love your neighbor.

Solomon first mentions two sins of omission (failing to do good), and then he mentions two sins of commission (doing something bad). Solomon says to not withhold good from those to whom it's due when it is in your power to do it (v. 27). This refers to giving something good to someone who deserves it or needs it when you have the means. This could be giving a fair wage or money to a person in need. This could be a meal, clothes, a tool your neighbor is lacking, or some other physical aid. The wise are attentive to the needs of their community. They are the neighbors everyone wants to have.

There was a communal life in the Old Testament, where the people of Israel were called to care for each other's property. This is true in the body of Christ as well. First John 3:17-18 says,

> *If anyone has this world's goods and sees a fellow believer in need but withholds compassion from him—how does God's love reside in him? Little children, let us not love in word or speech, but in action and in truth.*

Proverbs 3:28 fleshes this out. Don't delay in doing good if you have the means. Don't put it off because you're lazy, and then forget. Don't put it off because you are indifferent or selfish. Don't just try to get rid of the person with an excuse like, "I don't have any cash on me." Right then, go the extra mile to meet the need. Failing to do good to your neighbor when it is in your power is foolish and wicked. It is sin.

Solomon moves from failing to do good to actively doing evil. Don't plan evil against your neighbor who lives trustingly beside you (v. 29). Don't accuse your neighbor without reason if they haven't wronged you (v. 30). This can refer to a false accusation for gain. You accuse them out of jealousy, or you do so in order to get something that belongs to them. Solomon acknowledges that it's OK to seek justice if there is an appropriate cause. You may have to take a neighbor to court to stop some injustice against your family, but you don't do it out of spite or to get even with them. And Paul makes clear that within the body of Christ this is not appropriate at all (1 Cor 6).

Finally, Solomon exhorts his son not to envy the violent person who seems to prosper because of his schemes. There are times when it looks like following Wisdom—following Jesus—doesn't work like we think it should, and following the ways of evil can lead to short-term success. I mentored a guy several years back who was distraught when he came to meet me for breakfast. I asked him what was wrong, and he told me that a guy he worked with came into work cursing because he had accidentally gotten his girlfriend pregnant. This crushed my friend because he and his wife had begged God for a baby and it wasn't happening for them, but this guy was sinning and got a baby that he didn't want! There are times in this fallen world when it may look like the path of sin is the path to getting what we want. Solomon acknowledges that some people do use their power to manipulate and abuse others to get what they want, and they get it. You might be tempted to jealousy and to adopting their ways when you see their success. Solomon pleads with his son not to envy these people because in the end the tables will turn. In the end, they lose.

Judgment will fall. God opposes these people, so they will not prosper forever. And God is for you if you belong to his Son; and that means even if you don't prosper right now, you will later. Yes, there's an order to the world where things work out in a certain way. Yes, in a fallen world it doesn't always work out immediately. But God stands behind the order upholding it, and he will call for a reckoning on the last day. There will be a judgment. When the order works out in the here and now, when fools are struck with poverty, lose their family, or irreparably damage their reputation, that is merely a foretaste of the ultimate reckoning they will receive on the last day. And when the wise have plenty, a happy family, and a good standing in the community, that also is merely a foretaste of the glory to come. But even if these things don't work out immediately, God will see to it that they do in the end.

Wisdom has its rewards, and Solomon holds them out to his son as a motivation to get wisdom. If you believe that Wisdom—Jesus—can make good on these rewards, then you will walk in these ways. The devious person—the person who goes against the created order—is detestable to Yahweh (3:32). And judgment will fall on you if you do not follow the golden rule to do unto others as you want them to do unto you. Solomon says there's a curse on the house of the wicked but blessing on the house of the righteous (v. 33). This encourages and warns us that our actions affect more than just us. The sins of the parents will affect the children, and the righteousness of parents trying their best to walk after Jesus will affect them positively. This is language from Deuteronomy 27–30. There is a choice between blessing (life) and curses (death) in obedience and disobedience. There is a choice between honor and dishonor here (Prov 3:34-35). Don't mock or you'll be mocked. Humble yourself to receive grace from the Lord.

## Conclusion

Jesus is the Wisdom of God, but he's also the wise son of Proverbs who humbled himself, took on the curse for us, and offers us the blessings of wisdom. He truly is more precious than silver, more costly than gold, and more beautiful than diamonds. As George Beverly Shea used to sing,

> I'd rather have Jesus than silver or gold;
> I'd rather be His than have riches untold;
> I'd rather have Jesus than houses or lands.
> I'd rather be led by His nail-pierced hand
> Than to be the king of a vast domain
> Or be held in sin's dread sway.
> I'd rather have Jesus than anything
> This world affords today.
> (Rhea F. Miller, "I'd Rather Have Jesus," 1922)

Yes, riches can be great, long life is something we all hope for, having a good reputation is precious, being able to sleep in peace at night is priceless, but Jesus is better than any and all of these things. Seek him above all of these, and you might just find that he adds these other things to you in the process.

## Reflect and Discuss

1. Are you seeking or chasing after the wisdom that is Christ? Or are you in pursuit of the misunderstood prosperity that is believed to be included in the blessings of wisdom?
2. How does the prosperity gospel, often preached in today's culture, affect the true pursuit of wisdom (Christ)?
3. What efforts do you take to protect your family or yourself morally?
4. Walking in wisdom can protect you from sin. What efforts are you making to have this peace of mind?
5. Solomon exhorted his son to be a good neighbor. We should follow this exhortation, but it is good to ask, who is my neighbor? How is being a good neighbor somewhat countercultural in today's society?
6. As followers of Christ, what often prevents us from meeting known needs? What part of the culture today tells us to ignore the needs of others?
7. Solomon refers to two types of sin: omission and commission. Is one more detrimental to the Christian life than the other? In what ways can you avoid the pitfalls of each one?
8. How does the pursuit of wisdom keep you from chasing the things of this world when you see others who are not pursuing wisdom have earthly gains that you may miss?
9. Do the promised rewards of wisdom provide comfort or worry, since they may not come until you are in glory? Why?
10. Personified Wisdom changes the outlook of seeking wisdom. Instead of seeking knowledge, you are now seeking someone. How does this affect your pursuit of wisdom?

# You've Got a Problem with Jesus

## PROVERBS 4:1-19

**Main Idea:** If you walk in foolishness, you are walking away from Jesus.

---

**I. Have a Relationship with Wisdom (4:1-9).**
**II. Grow Progressively in Wisdom (4:10-19).**

---

I love Proverbs because it corrects our misunderstandings about spirituality. We tend to compartmentalize spirituality and push it to the margins of our lives. We divide our lives into our spiritual activities (Sundays and maybe Wednesdays) and secular activities (the rest of the week). We think of most of life as morally neutral. We think God is more concerned with the "spiritual" things we do than he is with the rest of our lives. We think that God really cares about us having a good devotional time; but he's not necessarily concerned with our jobs or our schools, outside of us trying to be a good witness in those places. We think God is really concerned that I be a witness but he is not as concerned that I show up on time or that I complete my assignments by their due date.

Solomon blows this paradigm apart in Proverbs. The nitty-gritty details of your daily life are not morally neutral. That's the whole point of Proverbs. Wisdom isn't first and foremost tips for daily living that you follow; Wisdom is a person that you know and a path that you then walk. If you lack wisdom in a practical area of your life, it's not just that you are a fool in that area, although you are; you are demonstrating that you have a problem with Jesus.[8] If you walk in foolishness, you are walking away from Jesus. If you have a temper problem, you love to argue with people, you go too far with your girlfriend, or you can't see a task your boss assigns you through to completion, those are not just minor character flaws. They reveal that you have a problem with Jesus. If you find yourself walking down the wrong path, it reveals you are following the wrong person, and that's deadly! That's exactly what Solomon teaches us here through the Spirit in Proverbs 4:1-19.

---

[8] Much of this section is built on Russell Moore's insights into the wisdom of Proverbs.

## Have a Relationship with Wisdom

### PROVERBS 4:1-9

The father again appeals to his son to listen to his instruction in order to gain understanding (wisdom). Wisdom is dispensed from a parent to a child. He says, "Listen to me because I have good instruction. Don't abandon it." Not only is the wisdom parental, but it is multigenerational. This was passed down from his father and mother (i.e., David and Bathsheba). In effect, Solomon says, "My dad taught me the law as the means to life and establishing the kingdom (see 1 Kgs 2), and now I'm teaching this to you!"

Instruction in wisdom should be a multigenerational thing. Parents have been entrusted with the responsibility of passing this down to their children. We can pass down patterns of foolishness like laziness, addiction, abuse, or passivity. Or we can pass down patterns of wisdom like humility, a good work ethic, and responsibility. Proverbs 3:33 teaches us that we can bring blessing or cursing on our house. The good news is that the chain of wickedness can be broken with one generation that pursues the Lord, but the bad news is that a chain of faithfulness can be broken in one generation as well. The goal of Christian parenting is to pass down godly wisdom so that the chain will not be broken by your children or grandchildren. As my friend Jimmy Scroggins has said, "The goal of Christian parenting is not just Christian children; it is Christian grandchildren."

Solomon says that David told him to let his heart keep his commands and live. Again, wisdom is tied to the law, and it must be obeyed from the inside out. It must be written on the heart (Jer 31:33). Practically, wisdom prolongs life because it avoids the risky behaviors that bring premature death like addictions, disregarding governmental laws, or disregarding parents by running into traffic. The life that will not heed authoritative counsel will often end early. Eternal and abundant life is found in obedience to the law (Lev 18; Jesus is the fulfillment).

So David told Solomon to get wisdom and not to forsake her (4:6). Again, Wisdom is personified as a woman (i.e., Lady Justice) to get his son to make a decision for wisdom. Ultimately, we New Testament Christians know that this is fulfilled in Jesus. Jesus is the wisdom of Solomon—the Wisdom of God or the law of God—in human flesh. He fulfilled the Proverbs. David exhorts Solomon to begin a relationship with wisdom (i.e., marry her) and never abandon her (i.e., don't be unfaithful to her). He says that she will keep him safe and preserve his life, so he should love her. Again, wisdom is first and foremost a person to be in relationship with, not a set of ideas to live out.

Then, according to many English versions, David makes a statement in verse 7 that seems odd. He says, "The beginning of wisdom is this: Get wisdom" (ESV). OK? So you are saying that the first step to getting wisdom is getting wisdom? That's strange. That does not seem all that wise, to be honest. But again, what this means is that the first step to being wise is making a faith decision to commit to Wisdom—Jesus. Other English versions say something like, "Wisdom is supreme—so get wisdom" (CSB). The point is the same: Wisdom—Jesus—is the most important matter in all of life, so commit to him.

So the multigenerational task is to introduce our children to Jesus first, then introduce our grandchildren to Jesus. This is most important. Read the Bible to your children, pray with them, bring them to church, have family devotional time, share your testimony with them, let them see you worship Jesus in gatherings, let them see you participate in the ordinances, and share Jesus with them so they can know him intimately. Then, based on that relationship with Jesus and in that framework, teach them practical wisdom like how to be honest, how to fight anxiety, how to handle money, how to avoid get-rich-quick scams, how to receive a rebuke, how to lovingly give a rebuke, how to complete tasks like chores, and a thousand other things.

Wisdom begins with a personal relationship with Jesus Christ because wisdom is not principles to learn. Wisdom is a person to know and follow—infinitely superior to Dear Abby tips. Jesus is the pearl of great price. He's the one worth forsaking all else to get. David says to prize Wisdom highly, and she will exalt you, just like the Lord in due time exalts the humble (v. 8). David uses the metaphor of the crown (v. 9) to say that she will honor you (cf. Rev 4:4). She will give you a good public reputation. Wisdom is Jesus Christ, and you have to relate to him above all else! Prize him and he will honor you.

## Grow Progressively in Wisdom

### PROVERBS 4:10-19

In verses 10-19 Solomon again exhorts his son to listen to his wise teaching in order to prolong his life (v. 10). We have seen this throughout

Proverbs. Solomon says, "I am teaching you the way of wisdom; I am guiding you on straight paths" (v. 11). This refers to the wise course of life. It's the ethical course to take because it is the "straight" path. Wisdom is a person to know and a path to walk. Solomon says that since his son has embraced Wisdom, now he must stay on the path of wisdom, that is, the path of morality and the safest course (v. 12). Keep hold of Wisdom, and she will be your life (v. 13). Do not walk on the wicked path (v. 14). Again, wisdom is not intelligence, and foolishness is not morally neutral. The idiot friend on every sitcom is not the biblical picture of folly. Solomon lays out the "doctrine of two paths" (Fox, *Proverbs 1–9*, 128–31). There are two roads or ways: (1) the wise, righteous path that leads to life and (2) the foolish, wicked path that leads to death.

Wisdom is a path or course of life. Wisdom is a progressive thing; it is not something you arrive at. This is very similar to the New Testament idea of sanctification, where we "walk" in the Spirit (Gal 5:16,25). You are being conformed into the image of Christ, and this will take your whole life. You start down the path through Jesus; after all, he is "the way" (John 14:6). You must know the person of Wisdom to walk in the way of wisdom (Prov 4:13-14).

However, the path that you progressively walk reveals whom you are embracing. Your daily life decisions reveal whether you are following Jesus or walking away from him. The fact that you cannot control your temper with your children, constantly want to argue with your coworkers, go in and out of dumb dating relationships, spout off at your parents, or cannot follow through on school work has everything to do with Jesus. It reveals that you've gotten off the path of wisdom and are walking down the foolish path (vv. 11-14). It reveals that you aren't holding onto Wisdom—Jesus (v. 13).

Walking the path of wisdom is a lifestyle that avoids the things that lead to an early death. We see this repeatedly. Solomon says when you walk this path you will not stumble (v. 12). There is safety and security on this smooth path. You avoid the obstacles of foolishness. Fools don't see the connection between their foolishness and the consequences. They do not see that their laziness has led to them not having a job. They think their employer mistreated them. The fool does not see the connection between his porn problem and the train wreck of his marriage. He thinks his wife wasn't as responsive as she should have been. The fool doesn't see how his actions led him to stumble.

Solomon warns his son not to enter the path of the wicked. He says to avoid it. Do not go on it. Turn away from it (v. 15).[9] When you come to a road that seems right but that will take you off the path that God has revealed, then move on and do not take it. Solomon is setting his son up here in the introduction (Prov 1–9) for the sentence sayings that will come later (Prov 10–31). These sayings will contrast the way of wicked foolishness with the way of righteous wisdom. He says there will be things that seem like the right course in life but they are not. It will seem like withholding discipline from your child is loving, but it isn't. It will seem like hoarding your possessions will give you financial security, but it won't. It will seem like holding your tongue instead of rebuking a friend who is going down the wrong path is the easier and better thing to do at the time—after all, we aren't supposed to judge—but that isn't wise or loving.

Don't follow the wicked way that seems right at the time because those on the way of evil eat, drink, and sleep foolishness and wickedness—and they want others to join them (vv. 16-17). They will tempt you to follow them into laziness, gossip, quick-temperedness, and other degeneracy. In contrast, the path of the righteous is like the light of dawn, which shines brighter and brighter until full day (v. 18). The righteous way is a path of progressing in holiness until the last day. Just like the sun is seen at dawn and then gets brighter and brighter until it reaches its zenith, so those who walk on the path of wisdom will see more and more of the path and walk in greater and greater wisdom until the day they are made truly wise in the presence of Jesus. The way of the wicked is a path of deep darkness where they do not know what they stumble over.

I (Jon) often get dressed in the dark so as not to wake my sleeping family. It is quite possible for me to leave the house with the wrong socks or some other wardrobe mishap. Solomon says wisdom is the remedy for that. Foolishness is trying to live your life in the darkness. You can't see the way things really are, so you keep ruining your life and falling into misery. But wisdom is like the light of the sun that shows you how things really are, so that you can follow progressively the right course in life. The wise path is lit so you can see where you are walking, and the foolish path is dark so you stumble. Wisdom is a lamp—Jesus is the light of the world (John 8:12)—so you can see the right path to take. But if

---

[9] "Stay as far away from it as you can!" (Wiersbe, *Be Skillful,* 52).

you do not have the light, you cannot see where to walk. You stumble. Eventually, you fall.

Foolishness keeps you from seeing rightly. You may think you are taking the right step. It may seem right to you, but you do not see that you will stumble. Wisdom is progressive like the soft light of dawn growing into full midday brightness. One day we will see completely clearly (resurrection day; see Dan 12). We get a taste of that now through wisdom. We will get the fullness later.

## Conclusion

Jesus is wisdom, righteousness, and sanctification for us (1 Cor 1:30). He is the way, the truth, and the life (John 14:6). Wisdom is found in Jesus and in walking with him. If part of your life is moving into foolishness, that's not just dangerous because of the temporal consequences that you may face. That's dangerous because it reveals you are moving away from Jesus. You can have an amazing quiet time; but if you can't control your tongue, you've got a problem with Jesus. You can raise your hands high during praise songs; but if you can't clean your room when your mom tells you to, you've got a problem with Jesus. You can be in three different Bible studies throughout the week; but if you nag your husband constantly, you've got a problem with Jesus. You can teach a Bible study class every week; but if you can't take the trash out for your wife, it reveals that you've got a problem with Jesus. Jesus is concerned with every area of your life. If you have areas of foolishness in your life, you are walking away from Jesus.

## Reflect and Discuss

1. Are there things in your everyday life that you think are morally neutral that are off-kilter? What are they?
2. Does God's care of the everyday details change your approach to your everyday life?
3. Since Wisdom is Christ, what does it mean to marry Wisdom?
4. Wisdom is not just a characteristic; it's a person you can be in a relationship with. What does the "wise" life look like in light of this?
5. How is Solomon's exhortation for his son to listen to him different from what we hear in today's culture? How can you as a parent go against the flow?

6. How can you grow progressively in following Christ? Are there still areas in your life where you embrace something other than Christ? What are they?
7. There are two paths that are revealed here, the wise path and the foolish path. Are there foolish areas you need to redirect? What steps need to be taken to make this course correction?
8. What outside factors push us off the wise path or pull us toward the foolish path? How can we avoid these lures?
9. Sinful/foolish areas in life reveal a problem with Jesus. How does this challenge you when you take inventory of your life? What is the right response to them?
10. What is the difference in the wise life and the foolish one?

# You Need a Change of Heart

## PROVERBS 4:20-27

**Main Idea:** Your heart is the command center for your life.

---

**I. Messages Affect Your Heart (4:20-22).**
**II. Your Heart Is the Command Center for Your Life (4:23).**
**III. Your Behavior Reveals the Condition of Your Heart (4:24-27).**

---

Many people think of God like they think of Santa Claus. He judges you if you're naughty, and he rewards you if you're nice. Because of that misconception, much of modern Christianity consists of behavior modification. Many people think the main message of Christianity is "Stop doing bad things so God will like you, bless you, and take you to heaven instead of hell when you die. Heaven is for good people, and hell is for bad people; so be a good person and go to heaven not hell."

There are lots of problems with this understanding of Christianity. One, it is not biblical. Another is this: We cannot stop sinning. We cannot perfectly modify our behavior. Isn't this clear? When I (Jon) was a boy, my mom was really concerned about my habit of chewing my nails, and she wanted to rid me of it. So she bought some stuff to rub on my nails that would make them taste yucky so I wouldn't put my fingers in my mouth. She wanted to modify my behavior. But instead of helping me quit, over time I began to like the taste of what she rubbed on my nails. Has there ever been something like this in your life? A habit you can't seem to break? It does not matter how many patches for tobacco they come out with or how many paleo diets you see, you cannot seem to change over the long haul. You do well for a while, but then you go back again to those old habits and lifestyles. After a month or two all the weight is back, or you are back to a pack of cigarettes a day.

In the same way, has there ever been a sinful or foolish behavior in your life that you just could not stop? You may have even begged God to take it away. You know it's wrong, destructive, sinful, and unwise, but you just can't stop. It's a continual struggle. There are sin patterns that we try to break but can't. We try to modify the behavior. We say, "It's bad, so stop it!" We may even put guards in place that help for a little while, but eventually the guards are not enough. For example, you recognize that you have a porn problem so you put guarding software on your computer to keep you from going to those sites. Things go well for a little while, but then you learn to get around the software, or you look at it on your phone. Or you've got a problem with your temper. You explode in anger at your children. So in order to modify the behavior, you decide you'll count to ten before responding to anything. But sometimes you forget to count because you're just so angry.

Why don't these things work? As one pastor said, behavior modification is like mowing dandelions. You can mow over the dandelions, and your lawn will look good; but a day or two later the dandelions have popped up again because you didn't address the root. Behavior modification treats the surface issue, but it does not dig down to the source. The problem is in our heart—that is the source. If we do not deal with sin and foolishness at the heart level, then even if we mightily try to modify the behavior, it will find new ways to pop out in our lives. So if you have a problem with addiction to alcohol, your primary problem is a lack of self-control. You may modify the alcoholism, but if you do not address the root issue of self-control, the alcohol problem will come back or the self-control issue will resurface with smoking, overeating, or taking painkillers.

This is a problem for all of us. We are all sinners by nature, so we are all broken at the heart level and bent toward sin. That means we love things that God hates, and we hate things that God loves. So we can try to modify the behavior, but it won't bring lasting change because we are only treating the symptoms and not the source.

The behavior modification approach to Christianity has brought a lot of heartache. Behavior modification can either lead to depression when you can't fully address your problems or pride if you are able to solve your problems. These are both problematic. The answer for us according to Proverbs 4:20-27 is not behavior modification; it's that we need a new heart because the heart is the command center for life. The heart is the source for every behavior in your life, so in order to address sin and foolishness we must address them at the heart level. For us to obey God and walk in wisdom, we need a change at the heart level.

## Messages Affect Your Heart

### PROVERBS 4:20-22

Proverbs continually teaches us that Wisdom is a person to love and a path to walk. The father continues to encourage his son to stay on the right path. The son must daily live the law by walking in righteousness. But he must have a new heart with the law written on it to do so.

The father again appeals to his son to embrace his teachings. He emphasizes body parts here (Waltke, *Proverbs, Chapters 1–15*, 294). He says, "Give your ear to my sayings, don't let them escape your eyes, and keep them in your heart" (vv. 20-21; authors' translation). The "sayings" refer to the teaching of Proverbs. Solomon is advising his son, and us through the Spirit, to learn the doctrine of Proverbs (i.e., control your tongue, have a good work ethic, save money, do good to your neighbor, etc.).

Wisdom is a process of receiving the right words and listening to the right voice. There is a necessity of belief because you will continue to listen to the one you trust. Whose voice and what messages do you listen to? There are so many competing messages for Solomon's son. There are messages coming from the mouths of God, his father, counselors, peers, the forbidden woman, and others. They are all competing for the son's attention. They all want his heart. The same is true for us. There are songs, movies, shows, books, peers, neighbors, coworkers, parents, and family members speaking into our lives. They try to tell us what to do, how to think, and what decisions will be wise. It can be anything from what product to put in your hair to what relationships you should pursue.

But which ones you listen to is of vital importance because messages go in your ear and then down into your heart (Waltke, *Proverbs, Chapters 1–15*, 295–96). Your ears and eyes are the gates to your heart. This is why what you listen to and what you look at are so important. The songs you hear, the sermons, the sitcoms, and many other sources shape you. They are powerful, and they can capture you and get you to believe things. Are you listening to the voice of God mediated through Solomon? Is God's Word the ultimate authority and final word on the matters of your life? Or are you listening to the voice of Folly? Are you listening to messages that have the influence of Satan standing behind them? Are you listening to what will lead you astray?

This is true of listening with the ear, but it is also true of seeing with the eye. What you see will also go down into your heart. So commit yourself to listen to and read wisdom so that it will shape your heart. Don't just hear or read it; work it down into your heart so it can bring lasting change. This means that you must know wisdom, memorize wisdom, and meditate on it. Meditate and identify what idols or values in your heart are keeping you from walking in wisdom. Yes, the work of God is necessary to change your heart as we will see, but there is also work for you to do on your heart.

Words must go in your ear or eye and down into your heart for you to obey the wisdom of God. The law—wisdom—must be written on the heart. This is a constant theme in Proverbs. Wisdom must enter your heart to keep you from evil (2:10; 3:1; etc.). Proverbs 3:3 and 7:3 say the wise teaching must be written on the "tablet of your heart." Like the Ten Commandments were written on stone tablets, the wisdom of Proverbs must be written on your heart in order for you to walk in it (cf. Jer 31).

Why should you listen to his words and receive them in your heart? You should receive them because they are life and health (Prov 4:22). Wisdom reverses the curse of death. We've seen this before: wisdom is a return to Eden—to paradise. Wisdom reverses the curse's effects on the course of your life. But these things must be written on your heart for you to obey these commands and receive these benefits because the heart is the command center for your life.

## Your Heart Is the Command Center for Your Life

### PROVERBS 4:23

This is one of the key verses to understanding Proverbs and all of life. Guard your heart because from it flow the springs of life. The heart is the key and source to everything in your life. The heart is the source of the river of your life; it's the command center. Everything you do flows from your heart. The way you think, talk, and act flows from your heart. The heart is the agent governing all your body's actions.

But we have a problem. We have broken and sinful hearts that lead us astray. We inherited this heart from Adam. Proverbs 22:15 says, "Foolishness is bound to the heart of a youth." Proverbs 20:9 says, "Who can say, 'I have kept my heart pure; I am cleansed from my sin'?" The answer is, no one! Proverbs 28:26 makes clear, "He who trusts in his own heart is a fool" (NASB). Your heart will lead you astray, so "follow your heart" or "trust your feelings" is stupid advice.

The reason we have bad behavior is because the source of our behavior—our heart—is bad. Jesus teaches this in Matthew 12:33-37.

> *Either make the tree good and its fruit will be good, or make the tree bad and its fruit will be bad; for a tree is known by its fruit. Brood of vipers! How can you speak good things when you are evil? For the mouth speaks from the overflow of the heart. A good person produces good things from his storeroom of good, and an evil person produces evil things from his storeroom of evil. I tell you that on the day of judgment people will have to account for every careless word they speak. For by your words you will be acquitted, and by your words you will be condemned.*

Proverbs and Jesus tell us that sin starts in the heart before it manifests itself in our behavior. All throughout Proverbs Scripture tells us that lust, perversion, deceit, anxiety, backsliding, pride, jealousy, and wrong speech reside first in the heart. Jesus makes this clear again in Mark 7:20-23.

> *And he said, "What comes out of a person is what defiles him. For from within, out of people's hearts, come evil thoughts, sexual immoralities, thefts, murders, adulteries, greed, evil actions, deceit, self-indulgence, envy, slander, pride, and foolishness. All these evil things come from within and defile a person."*

Behavior modification is a joke that is not funny. The Pharisees were good at it, and Jesus called them evil. Why? Because Jesus is concerned with the heart—with our motives and attitudes—not just our outward actions. Jesus says in the Sermon on the Mount that sexual sin does not start with the outward act; it starts in the heart, and we will be judged for that! But not only will we be judged for it later; we also will not be able to see lasting change now. If all we do is modify behavior but leave the source issue untouched in our hearts, it will spring up and break out elsewhere. What's in the heart will come out in words, actions, and course of life. It is inevitable. Both Solomon and Jesus are clear on this.

Your behavior reveals the state of your heart. Outward gossip can reveal jealousy, bitterness, or pride in the heart. Adultery or pornography reveals lust in the heart. For real and lasting change to happen in your life, you need to assess what's happening in your heart. Maybe your money problems can be traced back to a lack of contentment in God in your heart. Maybe the lies you tell reveal insecurity in your heart where you worship the approval of others. Examine your heart to figure out the motivations for your behavior.

Since we all have heart issues, we need new hearts for real and lasting change. Deuteronomy said that we fail to obey the law because we lack the hearts to obey (Deut 5:29; 10:6; 29:3). But it also promised that one day the Lord would perform an inner transformation of the heart that would enable obedience (Deut 30:6). This promise is repeated in Ezekiel where the Lord says he will give his follower a new heart (Ezek 36:26) and in Jeremiah where the Lord says he will write the law on our hearts (Jer 31:33). Proverbs promises the same—a new heart with the law written on it (Prov 3:3; 7:3). Foolishness, or "lacking sense," is described in the Hebrew of Proverbs as literally "lacking a heart" (6:32; 7:7; 9:4; 10:13; 11:12; 12:11; 17:18; 24:30; cf. Deut 5:29). The adulterer lacks a heart (Prov 6:32; 7:7). Woman Wisdom and Woman Folly seek the affection of the one who lacks heart (9:4,16). The one who lacks heart will die (10:21). The lazy fool is one who lacks a heart (24:30). In contrast, the wise person who listens to wisdom "acquires" a heart (15:32; cf. Ezek 36:26).

So we need to be born again with a new heart—a new source of power we did not have before. This happens through belief in Jesus. Once you trust Christ for salvation, you are born again and given new appetites for God, his Word, his church. You're not given perfection—yet—but you are being changed. Solomon warns us to guard our hearts. Guard what you hear and see—what you allow into your heart—because it will have a tremendous impact on the course of your life. After all, the heart is the command center for your life.

## Your Behavior Reveals the Condition of Your Heart

### PROVERBS 4:24-27

In the last section of Proverbs 4 Solomon says that our actions reveal what is in our hearts. He starts in verse 24 with our words. Your mouth reveals the state of your heart (Wiersbe, *Be Skillful,* 53). He tells his son to put away devious speech. This is a command for good behavior, but the son will only be able to obey it if he has guarded his heart. You must have a new heart—and guard that heart (v. 23)—to keep your tongue in check (cf. Jas 3). Evil speech reflects an evil heart. If you use your speech to hurt others, deceive others, gossip about others, or falsely flatter others, then it's the overflow of a sinful heart. Again, Jesus told us this clearly in Matthew 12:34—"The mouth speaks from the overflow of the heart." Jesus says that our words will justify or condemn us on judgment day. That's not because good works—or good speech in this case—gets us to heaven. It is because your speech reveals whether or not Jesus has changed your heart!

This is also true of our actions—the course of our life (Prov 4:25-27). You must have the right heart to stay on the right path where things will go well. Solomon exhorts his son to keep his eyes on the path (v. 25) because if he gets distracted, he will swerve off the path and injure himself. When my twin brother and I (Jon) were very little we lived in a parsonage across the street from the church where our dad was on staff. We were poor and could not afford even a plastic pool, so on warm days our mom would turn on the sprinkler, and we would strip down to our birthday suits and run through the water. One day we were doing this when a ladies' Bible study let out at the church. A lady was so distracted by the naked jaybirds across the street that she walked into a telephone pole and split her head open. Solomon warns his son not to get distracted and go off the path into the danger zone. If you do find your foot slipping, then repent—turn away from evil (v. 27). Again, we will not be perfect in this life. That's not the expectation. But there should be gradual, sanctifying change in the course of our lives. If there is not, there is the danger of judgment.

Solomon is very concerned that his son get this—and we need to get it too—because we cannot walk in the wisdom of Proverbs 10–31 that leads to life if we do not have a new heart. If you are off the path of the wisdom of this book, it is because your heart is not right. You can see this in your speech and actions. They will testify for all to see and hear what is in your heart.

## Conclusion

Change must take place at the heart level. That, not behavior modification, is the message of Christianity. You need to be born again by Jesus, and then the Spirit of Jesus will empower you to work on your heart issues. Proverbs hopes for this here, and Jesus gives it. This is absolutely critical because Jesus says that only the pure in heart will see God. That means that we have a big problem because our hearts aren't pure (20:9). But here is the good news: Jesus lived the life you couldn't live, died the death you should've died, and was raised from the dead. He will grant his Spirit and a new heart to all who believe in him. He will account you righteous before God, and then he will begin the work of progressively growing you in righteousness by the power of his Spirit through the Word. So it's OK to not be OK, but it's not OK to stay that way. Ask yourself some probing questions: Do I have a new heart? What do my struggles reveal about my heart? Then ask Jesus to change you at the heart level. He can. He will.

## Reflect and Discuss

1. How has the wrong view of God as being like Santa Claus affected many people's view of Christianity? How has it affected even Christians' view of how to deal with sin?
2. Have you ever had a habit you just could not break? What about a New Year's resolution, diet, or workout routine you could not stick to? What might these superficial examples reveal about a deeper spiritual condition?
3. What is the foundational reason why behavior modification isn't enough? What is the ultimate problem?
4. In Proverbs 4:20 Solomon encourages his son to "give ear" to wisdom. Why is what we listen to so important? How can this truth affect what you listen to as an individual? As a family?
5. What does Proverbs 4:23 show us is key to how we live our life—the way we think, talk, act, and everything we do?
6. What also do Solomon (Prov 20:9; 22:15) and Jesus (Matt 12:33-37) tell us is the source of our sin?
7. According to Deuteronomy (30:6), Ezekiel (36:26), and Jeremiah (31:33), what is the ultimate solution for our sin problem?
8. Instead of isolated actions, what does Solomon say that our sinful behavior reveals?
9. Solomon warns his son not to get distracted and step off the path of wisdom (4:25), but we all sin. What are we supposed to do if we find our foot slipping (4:27)?
10. Jesus tells us that only the pure in heart will see God (Matt 5:8). But Solomon says that our hearts are not pure (Prov 20:9). What is the solution to this big problem?

# Honey Lips

## PROVERBS 5–7

**Main Idea:** Sexual sin is foolish and deadly.

---

**I. Don't Fall into Sexual Sin.**
- A. Words (5:1-4; 6:24; 7:1-5)
- B. Looks (6:25)

**II. Sexual Sin Will Kill You.**
- A. Sexual sin will destroy you with temporal consequences (5:9-14; 6:26-35).
- B. Sexual sin will destroy you eternally (5:21-23; 7:10-27).

**III. How Do We Fight It?**
- A. Horizontally, be satisfied in your spouse (5:15-20).
- B. Vertically, be in a saving relationship with Jesus (7:4).

---

A few years ago a pastor friend of mine walked away from his wife and children for a woman on his staff. When he was confronted about his sin, his response was, "I know it's wrong, but I'm going to do it anyway. I know that God will forgive me." This was obviously devastating to his wife, his children, and his church. It was heartbreaking, but it did not happen overnight. This pastor had developed a problem with porn at the age of twelve. There were times when it was worse than others. There were times that he got caught, repented, sought counseling, and seemed to be freed of it. But something that started out as small as a few looks at a magazine as a pubescent boy ended up destroying his family and ministry.

Sexual sin is so seductive and dangerous because it can start out small and in many cases is seemingly innocent, and then before you know it your life has been ruined. You may think to yourself, "What's the harm in this relationship? What's the harm in a little innocent flirting? I'll never do anything anyway." You will destroy your life, and you won't even see it coming.[10] Sexual sin is appealing; it promises pleasure and

[10] This insight about seemingly innocuous patterns that lead to destruction in the area of sexual morality comes from Russell Moore, "Proverbs 5:1-23—The Horror of Adultery and the Gospel of Christ."

happiness and can even deliver it for a little while, but then it kills you. Sexual sin may cause you to walk away from God, or at least redefine "God" as someone who is OK with your sin. Sexual sin may cost you your family, your reputation, and the respect of your children; or it may just warp your ideas of intimacy in marriage and drive a wedge between you and your wife (or your future wife). There are a thousand different ways that sexual sin can destroy you, but make no mistake—it will.

Sexual sin is not something to flirt with or to keep secret and hope it goes away before someone finds out. It's a killer. Solomon warns us repeatedly about this in Proverbs 5–7.

## Don't Fall into Sexual Sin

Solomon knows this topic well since he repeatedly messed up big time with "forbidden" women (see 1 Kgs 11:3; he had seven hundred wives and three hundred concubines). He warns his son not to fall for the forbidden or immoral woman (i.e., sexual sin). This is a parental responsibility dads and moms have with their children (Prov 6:20). You should have "the talk" with your children; in fact, you should have multiple talks. Solomon speaks continuously to his son throughout this book. Parent, you need to be the expert on sex with your children. Do not abdicate that responsibility to TV, the Internet, or your children's peers simply because talking about it may be "weird." And churches also need to be experts on sex instead of avoiding the subject. God talks a lot about it. Sex is a powerful gift from God, and we need to proclaim the beauty of sex in marriage as Solomon does here (and also in the Song of Songs).

He warns his son because the lips of an immoral woman drip honey; her speech is smoother than oil (5:3).[11] She is a rival to the father (and Wisdom) for the son's affection. Who will the son listen to? Which speech will he heed? Who will you listen to?

Let's note an important caveat. This figure of the immoral woman stands for very real sexual sin that the son can commit with a woman. But Solomon is not absolving the son of his part in this, nor is he making a statement about any predatory makeup of women. This is a father talking to his son, so the figure he will warn him about is a woman. If

[11] Jimmy Scroggins—my youth pastor growing up—referred to her with the nickname "Honey Lips."

he were talking to his daughter, he would talk about an immoral man. The fact is men do this kind of predatory seduction more than women! This section applies to women too. They just need to reverse the image (Longman, *Proverbs*, 164–65).

The son is not an innocent bystander in all of this. We will see that a senseless young man flirts with this (Prov 7). He may loathe his decision later, but he is culpable. And not only can you be preyed on by an immoral man or woman, but you also can be the immoral aggressor or predator. The issue cuts both ways with both sexes.

Solomon is warning his son about any sexual activity outside the covenant of marriage. Any sexual activity that is not with your heterosexual spouse is sin and will destroy you, your marriage, or your future marriage. That includes adultery, lust, fantasies, pornography, fooling around, cohabitation, and homosexuality. Solomon warns his son of two specific ways that he can be tempted to fall: words and looks.

### *Words (5:1-4; 6:24; 7:1-5)*

First, he mentions words. He says in verse 3 her lips drip honey. (*Lips* may imply the desire to kiss her; cf. Song 4:11. Actually, there may even be a triple entendre here; Waltke, *Proverbs, Chapters 1–15*, 308–9.) She's a charmer with her words, and yes, men can do this too. Communication is the first way you are drawn into sexual sin (Prov 6:24). Alluring words pull you away from your marriage vows. This is true for men because they are suckers for flattery and for women because they are creatures of the ear. Sexual unfaithfulness starts with communication. The communication may seem innocent enough at first. The woman in the cubicle beside you laughs at your jokes. The old boyfriend on Facebook interacts with you at a level that makes you feel important. Your friend at the gym seems to understand you better than your wife. You think to yourself that a few text messages back and forth, even if they are a little flirty in nature, are not that big a deal. "Well, I would not be doing this if my husband would just listen to me." "Well, my wife does not admire me like she does." If this is happening in your life, you should hear the *Jaws* theme music in the background. Repeatedly emailing, texting, calling, or meeting up with someone of the opposite sex who is not your spouse is a major issue. It is massively stupid! You may think it is harmless, but you are wrong. You are forging an emotional intimacy through communication that can lead to more.

The smooth words may not be the communication of an individual; they may be messages you are being bombarded with in the culture: "Don't get married too young. Delay marriage as long as you can so that you know you are ready." This causes unfaithfulness to your future spouse as you fool around right now. "It's OK to mess around. How else will you know what you like sexually?" "Guys like girls who are more sexually active. If you don't act somewhat aggressive, he won't want you." Wrong! The lies of culture enter your ear and heart: "Infidelity is hotter than monogamy." "Follow your heart." "Do what makes you happy." Maybe the message is in your own head: "My spouse isn't as romantic with me as she should be, so . . ."

For some women it might be reading romance novels. You read the *Twilight* novels or *Fifty Shades of Grey*. These books cause you to emotionally invest in a man who is not your husband. They cause you to be dissatisfied with your husband. "I wish my husband was more sensitive to my needs like the man in this book." "I wish my husband was romantic like this man in the book." "I wish my husband listened to my inmost thoughts like the man in this book." This is also the seduction of pornography whether in picture or print. Porn offers, to men, women who act more like men (i.e., sexually aggressive) and, to women, men who act like more like women (i.e., emotionally sensitive). This causes you to paint a picture in your mind of the ideal spouse. If that picture is not your spouse, you are in danger!

Guys can talk smoothly to girls to get them into bed. They will feed them whatever line they have to in order to get sex: "If you love me, then . . . No one will find out . . . I love you more than I've ever loved anyone before." Sexual sin starts with communication—with words.

In Proverbs 7 Solomon gives a story that focuses on this woman's smooth words. From his house, Solomon watches a naïve young man. He sees him flirting with sexual sin by going close to this woman's house (7:7-8). So many of us ask those kinds of questions: "Where's the line? How far is too far? How close can I get without going too far?" Solomon tells his son to keep far from her—flee from this temptation (5:8). But he is in the wrong place at the wrong time with the wrong person, so the wrong thing happens. She flatters him with her words: "You're the one for me. I've gotta have you, big boy" (7:13-18). She inflates his ego perhaps in a way that his wife hasn't. She even uses religious talk to ease his conscience (7:14). "God won't be mad; I've already offered sacrifices at the temple. We can be forgiven." She also assures him that no one will find out. "We won't get caught. No one has to know" (7:19-20). This is a lie. This sin is always found out. Someone knows about it. At my first church a guy came to me to confess that he had cheated on his wife. I told him to come clean with her. He said he needed time. I told him that she was going to find out, and it would be worse if he did not confess. He thought there was no way she could find out since only he and the woman knew. But the woman's ex-husband found out and called my church member's wife while their entire family was driving back from vacation. He was busted. This will be found out; and even if it is not in this life, God is watching (5:21). Yet the seductive speech persuades this young man, and he yields to temptation (7:22).

### *Looks (6:25)*

Solomon says that besides words there is a second means that allures you to unfaithfulness, and that is looks. Attraction draws you into sexual sin. Solomon warns his son in Proverbs 6:25, "Don't lust in your heart for her beauty." Lust starts in the heart before the act. Jesus also tells us this in Matthew 5. We see things with our eyes, and it draws us away from our spouse. It starts fantasies in the mind. It might be pornography, inappropriate TV shows, or sexually explicit movies. Porn is a brutal killer right now because you can get it on your cell phone, iPad, or computer with little effort. This should be a warning to parents about giving their children unfettered access to the Internet. Really think before you give your children a smart phone.

Porn is deadly not just because it causes fantasies but also because it warps one's view of marriage and sex. Porn addicts begin to view sex as a completely selfish act that is about my pleasure rather than the pleasure of another. Porn viewing causes you to train yourself to experience stimulation and pleasure outside the covenant of marriage. Then, when you do get married, you bring those fantasies into the marriage. As one author asked, "How would you like it if Hugh Hefner could view your wife's naked body and look it up and down?" That's exactly what's happening when you look at her because you've brought your pornographic viewing into the marriage. You treat her as an object (Challies, *Sexual Detox*).[12] Men especially are creatures of sight, so be on guard about what you look at. Also, we need to say a word to women and par-

---

[12] This is a great ebook on fighting pornography.

ents about modesty. Christian sisters can help their brothers out by following the biblical guidelines for modesty. And parents, especially dads who know how men view women: do not let your daughters dress immodestly. You are inviting disaster! You are not loving your precious daughters as you ought.

The slide toward sexual sin starts gradually by what you hear and look at. And it ends in disaster. It may start out with simply fooling around while dating and assuaging your guilt by saying, "Well, at least we aren't going 'all the way.'" But you are training yourself to experience and enjoy sexual contact outside the covenant of marriage. What makes you think that once you are in that covenant you will be able to keep your vows, since you were not faithful to your future spouse? Facebook in this context can also be a big killer. People rekindle old flames on Facebook. Ashley and I (Jon) have each other's Facebook passwords and can look at each other's stuff anytime we want. This isn't because we lack trust; it's because we have nothing to hide.

Solomon appeals to his son by saying basically, "Listen to me, not her." He says, "Keep your way far from her" (5:8). Paul says, "Flee sexual immorality!" (1 Cor 6:18). Jesus says to gouge out your eyes (Matt 5:29). Do not flirt with this because it is too dangerous. You do whatever you have to do to fight it. Men, do not ever be alone with a woman who is not your spouse. Put blockers on the computer. Get a reporting app on your phone. Be in an accountability group. Get rid of the computer. Get rid of the tablet. Get rid of the smart phone if that is what it takes! Because . . .

## Sexual Sin Will Kill You

### *Sexual Sin Will Destroy You with Temporal Consequences (5:9-14; 6:26-35)*

Solomon warns his son of the temporal consequences of sexual sin. There will be a death, so to speak, right now. You will reap what you've sown. Anyone can see these consequences, even non-believers. Solomon is actually talking in 5:9-14 about the forbidden woman's pimp or her husband taking revenge, but these consequences are generic enough to apply to all of us. They seem very similar to the covenant curses of Deuteronomy 28. When you obey God you will experience blessings that you did not work for, but when you disobey him even what you have worked for will go to another. You will give the best part of you to someone it does not belong to (Prov 5:10). You will waste your time, energy, and resources. Porn is a current example of an incredible waste of time when you could have been producing or providing for your family. Solomon says you will lose your money (in modern cases, alimony and child support). If you fall for this, someone else will kiss your wife and tuck your kids in at night—as Toby Keith sings about in "Who's That Man?"

You may lose your health (v. 11; perhaps an STD). You will be filled with regret that you did not listen when you had the chance (vv. 12-13). It's foolish to not listen to a rebuke. Perhaps your wife came to you with concerns about a new relationship you were developing, and you responded to her in anger. "You're crazy. You don't know what you're talking about. Stop making a big deal out of this. There's nothing there." You attacked her and made her feel like an idiot for her concern. Do you get defensive when confronted on these things? If so, you are the idiot! This is your wife or your husband protecting you. You were convinced they were overreacting, but now you wish you had listened! You may also experience public disgrace and shame in the assembly (v. 14).

Solomon says in Proverbs 6:20-35 that sexual sin may cost you your life. He speaks practically about the cost of adultery. He says the price for a prostitute is like the cost of bread (v. 26). He is not condoning prostitution. He is just saying that it is less costly because it usually destroys just one family whereas adultery destroys two families. He says adultery is more costly because it may cost you your life (v. 34). I heard the story of a man who went into a Sunday school class to beat up a man who had an affair with his wife. Revenge is a reality!

Sexual sin may just cost your life as you know it. You lose the respect of your children or you lose your family. But it may cost you your physical life if the husband wants revenge. You cannot play with fire without getting burned; likewise, you cannot mess with sexual sin without it wrecking your life (vv. 27-28). This wound of shame, disgrace, and possible death is not worth a few minutes of pleasure. And the biggest problem is that these temporal consequences are not even the worst part. They are just a foretaste of hell because the wages of sexual sin is death (Rom 6:23).

### *Sexual Sin Will Destroy You Eternally (5:21-23; 7:10-27)*

Even if you do not die now, you will die later. This sin seems so appealing and sweet like honey, but in the end it is bitter and deadly (5:3-5).

Proverbs 7:22-23 pictures this as an ignorant cow being led along to become a steak for someone's dinner, an oblivious deer that is shot through the vitals by a hunter, or an unsuspecting bird that gets trapped. These poor, stupid animals were just going about their business and did not know that one second later their life would be over!

Solomon says not to be intoxicated with this sexual sin because the Lord is watching (5:21). If you think no one will find out, you are foolish. God sees all of our sexual sin. We will be held accountable for it on judgment day. It will not go unnoticed. Even if by chance we avoid all of the consequences in this life, we will not avoid judgment. The church has been too focused lately on self-help. So we often merely talk about sexual sin at the level of temporal consequences. Our appeal is to our self-centeredness: "C'mon, you don't want to get pregnant, do you? You don't want to get an STD, do you? You don't want to ruin intimacy for your future marriage, do you? You don't want to lose your money, do you?" We are so afraid to use the word *hell* because we don't want to seem old-fashioned. But we need to use this word because sexual sin will drag us there. Solomon makes this clear throughout Proverbs 5–7. This raises an important question.

## How Do We Fight It?

Solomon gives us two ways to fight this sin: vertical and horizontal. Your vertical relationship with the Lord must be right in order for your horizontal relationship with your spouse to be right. These work in concert.

### *Horizontally, Be Satisfied in Your Spouse (5:15-20)*

The antidote to sexual sin is to be sexually active with your wife. True intimacy is found in exclusivity. You become an expert on one person that you are committed to for a lifetime. You might say, "Well, I'm trapped in a loveless marriage right now." The truth is that if you will remain faithful and exclusive, over time intimacy will develop. That does not mean that you should not seek counsel or that there are not things to work on, but do not give up on God's picture.

Paul utilizes the same strategy as Solomon. In 1 Corinthians 6 he exhorts the Corinthians to flee sexual immorality, and in 1 Corinthians 7 he says to enjoy sex regularly in marriage. He says it is dangerous to withhold sex from one another. If you are not having sex regularly in marriage, that is a danger sign. It can destroy your marriage. Sexual intimacy binds you together with your spouse in a way you are not bound with anyone else. You must develop this part of your marriage. Meet your spouse's needs rather than insisting on your needs being met (Phil 2:3-5). Practically: Do not sleep in separate rooms. Do getaways without the children. Be gracious and kind to one another.

Solomon uses graphic imagery when he says, "Drink water from your own cistern" (v. 15; cf. Song 1:2-3; 4:1-7). He says, "Take pleasure in the wife of your youth" (v. 18; you got married young, and you're still together!). He exhorts his son to be intoxicated with her breasts and her love (5:19). As Tremper Longman said, "The best defense against committing adultery is a strong offense in marriage" (*Proverbs*, 158). Solomon does not even mention procreation here. Experiencing regular sexual pleasure in marriage will guard against unfaithfulness.

If you're not married, this counsel in Proverbs can also refer to your future wife. Marry young. Do not delay marriage.

Do not "just say no" in regard to sex when you talk about it with your children. The "no" alone will not work because sex is too powerful. The church has often neglected our duty to talk about this topic that is all over the Bible. God gave sex as a good gift to be enjoyed in marriage. So instead of "just saying no" with your kids, point them to the beauty of marriage and the goodness of sex in marriage. Yes, of course the culture downplays marriage because it is a picture of the gospel (Eph 5). But we need to tell our kids that their desires and urges teach them they are meant to be married.

### *Vertically, Be in a Saving Relationship with Jesus (7:4)*

The immoral woman is the rival to the father. She is the rival to Woman Wisdom. Whom will the son listen to? Whom will he embrace? This immoral woman is a major character in Proverbs. She stands for a literal person with whom the son can be sexually unfaithful. However, later she will be personified as Woman Folly, the rival to Woman Wisdom (Prov 9). If the son embraces this forbidden woman, it will reveal that he has rejected his father, Woman Wisdom, and Yahweh himself. Sexual sin and spiritual sin are tied together throughout the Bible. Adultery is the distortion of the most intimate human relationship, and it is used as a metaphor to speak of the distortion of our relationship to God. Idolatry is spiritual unfaithfulness. That's the whole point of Proverbs 1–9. If our horizontal relationships are off, it reveals that our vertical relationship with God is off as well. Solomon knows this because the "foreign women" he was intimate with led him into idolatry. Falling for this woman would reveal that the son is not in right relationship with the Lord.

So yes, there is a real adulteress who can tempt the son, but Woman Folly stands behind that adulteress. In the context of the whole Bible, we know that Woman Wisdom points to Jesus, and we will see that Woman Folly stands for Satan. (Longman, *How to Read Proverbs,* lays out this case.) There is a personal being that stands behind the people or things that would tempt you to sexual sin. Satan wants to destroy you and drag you to hell. One of the ways that he most often attacks is sexual sin. If you are not experiencing regular sex with your spouse, there is room for Satan to tempt you (1 Cor 7:5). He and his minions observe the things that entice you and bring you pleasure, and when the time is right they might just offer them to you in order to ruin you.

The whole point of Proverbs 1–9 is the father trying to get the son to be in a relationship with Wisdom instead of Folly. That's the question: "Whom will you choose to follow? Whom will you choose to marry?" You cannot walk in wisdom in terms of sexual ethics if you are not in a right relationship with Jesus. Your vertical relationship will affect your horizontal marriage, and vice versa. So Solomon says, marry Wisdom—Jesus. That may seem like strong language, but that is precisely the antidote to sexual sin. He says to call Wisdom "my sister" (7:4). That may seem weird, but that is exactly what Solomon calls his bride (Song 4:9–5:2). You must be in a one-flesh union with Christ. Through believing the gospel you can become a part of Christ's bride—the church.

Once you are part of Christ's body, the law of the parents is written on the tablet of your heart (Prov 7:1-3) so that you can obey and live a life of safety in terms of sexual ethics. Those who fall for sexual sin lack the heart necessary to obey God (6:32 literally says in the Hebrew, "The one committing adultery with a woman lacks a heart"). You need to meet Jesus and get a new heart with new desires, so that you can live up to the sexual ethic laid out in Proverbs.

## Conclusion

God created his world good and everything worked right, including relationships and sex. But sin broke our relationship with God and with each other, so nothing right now works as it was designed. Instead of intimacy and satisfaction in marriage, there are distrust, barriers, and unfaithfulness. Sex is still a good, God-given gift, but it is not used properly because we are sinners. Fire can be both good and destructive. When it is in a fireplace it can warm a house so you do not freeze in the winter, but when it is outside the fireplace it will destroy the house. Like a fire, sex is very good in the right context (i.e., marriage) but very destructive in the wrong context. Because of our sinful nature, we use sex in destructive ways that God never intended.

Because of human sin, our vertical relationship with the Lord is off; and as a result so are our horizontal relationships like marriage. We need to be brought back into right relationship with God in order for our marriages to work properly. That's the point of Proverbs. Your relationship with the Lord—fear of Yahweh—is directly connected with your relationship with your spouse. Solomon understands this full well, and that is why in Proverbs 1–9 he constantly talks about two relationships. He talks about our spiritual relationships (Wisdom or Folly; Yahweh or idols), and he speaks of our practical relationships (wife or immoral woman). Each relationship has a direct effect on the other. If your spiritual relationship is off, it can destroy the practical, and vice versa! Solomon's heart was pulled toward other women, and his heart was pulled toward idols!

Here's the good news: Jesus Christ—the Wisdom of God—went into Sheol for our sexual sin, and he came back victorious three days later. Through his death and resurrection, we can be reconciled to God. In Christ, there is no condemnation for our sexual sin. And by the power of Christ's Spirit and our new hearts, we can be transformed to live out God's plan for our lives, including sexually. That is good news indeed!

## Reflect and Discuss

1. Solomon models warning and informing his child about sexual sin. How can you more effectively address sexual issues with your children? With those you disciple? With your church?
2. Why does Solomon use the illustration of a seductive woman? Isn't that a backward, misogynistic, and overly negative generalization of women?
3. What does Proverbs present as the first means of sexual temptation? How should that affect the way we view seemingly innocent interactions?
4. Sexually explicit and enticing material is ubiquitous and readily available today. What steps can you take to prevent access for yourself and your family?

5. Proverbs shows that there is a personal being, Woman Folly (Satan), who stands behind the people or things that would tempt you to sexual sin. What does that tell us about our temptations? Are they random? Disconnected?
6. What is the resounding biblical precedent for dealing with sexual temptation (see Prov 5:8; Matt 5:29; 1 Cor 6:18)?
7. What are some temporal consequences Solomon lays out for sexual sin? How have you seen these play out in the lives of others? What about your own life?
8. Even if we escape the temporal consequences of sexual sin, what reason does Solomon give for the assurance of eternal consequences (see 5:21)?
9. What's the first line of defense Solomon gives against sexual sin?
10. The Bible consistently stresses that spiritual sin and sexual sin are tied together. If our horizontal relationships are off (lust, sexual sin, adultery), what does it reveal about our vertical relationship with God?

# Come Thou Wisdom from On High

## PROVERBS 8

**Main Idea:** You must be in a relationship with Wisdom in order to be wise in daily life.

---

**I. Marry Wisdom Because Jesus Tells You the Truth about Reality (8:1-11).**
**II. Marry Wisdom Because Jesus Produces Right Living in His Followers (8:12-16).**
**III. Marry Wisdom Because Jesus Rewards His Followers (8:17-21).**
**IV. Marry Wisdom Because Jesus Brings His Followers into Harmony with God, Others, and the World (8:22-31).**
**V. Marry Wisdom Because Jesus Gives Abundant and Eternal Life (8:32-36).**

---

One of the things I ask couples in premarital counseling is, "Why do you want to marry this person?" Too often the groom-to-be will give me spiritualized answers that they think a pastor will want to hear. "She has a great quiet time and prayer life." "She's just so sweet and godly." After listening to this for several minutes, I will stop the young man and ask, "So, are you attracted to her? Because you haven't mentioned that." This lets the young man know he can let his spiritualized guard down, so he answers, "Well of course, I think she's gorgeous!" This is an important question to answer: Why do you want to marry her, or why did you marry your wife? What qualities attracted you to her?

This is the question that Solomon wants to answer for his son in Proverbs 8. Solomon has told us repeatedly that wisdom is not a set of ideas; Wisdom is a person. Solomon has repeatedly tried to get his son to marry Wisdom. Here in Proverbs 8 he makes another push by telling him why he should marry her. He details all of her amazing qualities (Kidner, *Wisdom of Proverbs*, 22–24).[13]

---

[13] Kidner has a great discussion of Woman Wisdom and how she functions in this way. He also believes that the New Testament reader should see this as Jesus, as I argue in the next paragraph.

We find out in this chapter that Wisdom does not just stand for Solomon's wisdom; it stands for God's Wisdom. In the fullness of time, Paul reveals to us that Jesus is the Wisdom of God (1 Cor 1:24,30). So, through the Spirit, Proverbs 8 is exhorting us to be in a personal relationship with Jesus because of all his amazing attributes. You cannot be wise or have skill at life without this relationship. Choose Jesus over anything or anyone else because he will make you wise now and forever. As you read the entirety of Proverbs 8, ask yourself the question: Who in the world can this be describing?

Now, why should you marry this Wisdom?

## Marry Wisdom Because Jesus Tells You the Truth about Reality

### PROVERBS 8:1-11

Woman Wisdom is a personification of Solomon's wise teaching. She is presented as a female because the Hebrew word for "wisdom" is a feminine noun, and the audience of Solomon's teaching is a young man. But this passage reveals more to us than the previous passages have. Wisdom is not just a personification of Solomon's wisdom; Wisdom is also a personification of God's Wisdom that he used to create the universe. Let's see how this text describes God's Wisdom.

Wisdom cries out in the public places where there are tons of people because she wants everyone to hear. Wisdom is competing against rivals (i.e., the immoral woman of Proverbs 5–7 and the Woman Folly in Proverbs 9) for the people's attention. Her activity is in broad daylight instead of at nightfall (7:9). Wisdom stands at the public crossroads (8:2) where a decision must be made (Fox, *Proverbs 1–9*, 265).[14] Whom will you follow? Folly (cf. 9:13-18)? Wisdom? She wants everyone's attention and allegiance. She calls out to all of humanity, especially the inexperienced and the fools. She will teach them common sense (8:5). She can make them wise—that's why they should listen. You should listen to Wisdom—Jesus—because he can make you wise.

Listen to her because she speaks the truth and tells you the way the world really works (8:6-9). She tells you what is "right"—the difference between good and evil. Not only morality, but she tells you the order of

---

[14] Fox draws out this contrast.

the world, and she does not twist or pervert that order. That is what her teaching in the rest of the book is about. Hard work is better than laziness or get-rich-quick schemes. While it may seem like indulging pleasure will gladden you, it will actually sadden you (cf. 21:17). Wisdom tells it like it really is, whereas Folly twists things. Folly tells you what you *want* to hear but not what you *need* to hear. Take the short cut, indulge pleasure, hoard your possessions, hold a grudge, and more.

Wisdom distinguishes between wickedness and righteousness too. She does not distort the truth like Folly. You see, the fool may sincerely believe what he says is true, but he cannot see how he misrepresents truth and reality because what he says is not true. One example of this is calling "good" something that God says is sin. Proverbs 24:24 talks about the one who says to the guilty, "You are innocent." Justifying sin or saying it is not sin is distortion of reality. Wisdom will not do that. She calls sin what it is. She will help you understand this, and she will produce this kind of truthful speech in you. You can avoid lies, gossip, and slander if you will follow Wisdom (i.e., Jesus).

The perceptive person knows that Wisdom's words are right and that they will help him or her to navigate through this life, so they submit to her (8:9). Following Wisdom's instruction is better than riches because Wisdom is vastly superior to worldly wealth (vv. 10-11). Nothing you desire can compare with Wisdom. Wisdom is the pearl of great price. This is what Proverbs teaches. Money can be a good thing if it is not given first place in your life. After all, Jesus says you cannot serve two masters (Matt 6:24). Wisdom will not tolerate rivals. So seek Wisdom first, and all these things will be added to you! Make a faith decision to get Wisdom—Jesus—and be satisfied in him above all else.

## Marry Wisdom Because Jesus Produces Right Living in His Followers

### PROVERBS 8:12-16

Wisdom has associates that she will share with you: shrewdness, knowledge, and discretion. If you want these qualities, you have to know Wisdom. If you want these qualities, you have to go to Jesus. The ability to make right decisions, the ability to carefully consider a situation without making a snap judgment, and the ability to read people are available through a relationship with Jesus. Wisdom teaches you how to navigate life in a way that avoids your ruining things.

Wisdom here first shows you who to associate with, and then she tells you whom to avoid. The fear of Yahweh, which is the beginning of wisdom, is to hate evil (v. 13). She hates pride, arrogance, the evil way, and perverted speech (we saw that earlier in the text). She despises those who won't humble themselves under authority and counsel. She will keep you off the wicked path if you embrace her. She will produce counsel, sound wisdom, insight, and strength in her followers (v. 14). Strength reveals that wisdom is not simply the ability to discern the right decision, but it's also the wherewithal to carry it out.

Wisdom is the means by which kings reign and decree justice. Wisdom is needed to rule and establish the kingdom. Wisdom is how a king will order his kingdom. Solomon recognized this so he asked for wisdom in 1 Kings 3. Wisdom is the skill to rule. This is promised of the coming Messiah in Isaiah 11. He will reorder the entire creation through wisdom. Jesus is the fulfillment. He is the Messiah who patterns his kingdom after wisdom (see the Sermon on the Mount in Matt 5–7). Those of us who follow Christ will also rule with him, so we need the wisdom of this book. We are in an internship for eternity right now.

## Marry Wisdom Because Jesus Rewards His Followers

### PROVERBS 8:17-21

Wisdom says, "I love those who love me, and those who search for me find me" (v. 17; cf. Matt 7:7). So commit to the wisdom of Proverbs and commit to the Wisdom of Proverbs—the word and the Word (cf. John 1). In order for you to live out the word, you must first be in a personal relationship with Jesus.

Getting Wisdom is most important, but there are blessings that will be added to you if you do. The rewards of wisdom are lasting riches, a good name, and righteousness (v. 18). This is not teaching a prosperity gospel because, as Proverbs has already shown us, the rewards may not come immediately in a fallen world. But there will be eternal blessings for getting Wisdom—Jesus. Wisdom says that what she produces in you—wisdom and righteousness—is better than money. It is better than money because she will lead you down the right path (i.e., obedience to the law), which means a greater reward later. She will reward you with an inheritance if you love her, and she will fill your treasuries (v. 21).

Again, these kinds of physical rewards may come now, especially the rewards of a good reputation and walking in righteousness, but they will surely come in the new creation.

## Marry Wisdom Because Jesus Brings His Followers into Harmony with God, Others, and the World

### PROVERBS 8:22-31

This section is rich and complicated. We see a heightening of Wisdom's description. Wisdom is presented here not just as Solomon's wisdom but rather as Yahweh's Wisdom. Wisdom is the only begotten child of God (v. 22). We see that this description of Wisdom can no longer be seen just as a poetic device. The description is too lofty, and it is too much like Jesus. After all, Revelation 3:14 calls Jesus "the originator of God's creation" (Nestle, *Novum Testamentum Graece*, 788).[15] This doesn't mean that Jesus was created; it means that he is supreme over the creation.

Wisdom existed before the creation and is superior to the creation. Wisdom knows the created order because Wisdom was there, and Wisdom seems to have assisted in creating (vv. 22-30; cf. John 1; Col 1) (Goldsworthy, *Tree of Life*, 79–81). Before humanity was created from the dust, Wisdom was there. The mention of the "first soil" (v. 26) reveals the fragility of humanity. If humanity lives contrary to the wise design of the creation, we will return to our prior state (i.e., from dust to dust) (Garrett, *Proverbs*, 109). Wisdom knows the order of things and can share that order with humanity because Wisdom assisted Yahweh in creating the world. Wisdom builds the creation. Wisdom also built the tabernacle (Exod 31) and the temple (1 Kgs 7), which are patterned after creation. The wise Messiah will rebuild the cosmos (Isa 11). Wisdom builds her house in Proverbs 9, as we will see. Jesus created the world in the beginning, Jesus upholds the world now (Heb 1), and Jesus will make all things new at the end. So one must know him in order to perceive and live according to the pattern of the world. Because he made the world, he knows how it works.

---

[15] The editors of the Nestle-Aland Greek New Testament see Revelation 3:14 as a citation or an allusion to Proverbs 8:22, thus connecting Proverbs 8 with Jesus in Revelation 3.

Wisdom says in effect, "I delighted in God, his world, and humanity." Wisdom is the mediator in the relationships of all three: (1) between man and God, (2) between man and man, and (3) between man and the world. Wisdom orders these three relationships as it was in Eden. So you must know Wisdom—Jesus—in order to live in harmony with God, with other people, and with the world around you.

There is a design in the way that the world works, and this order can be observed by anyone who is looking (e.g., at the ant in Prov 6). If you try to live against the grain of this order, it will injure you. Adultery will cause you to lose much of what you have. The famous golfer Tiger Woods can attest to this. Unchecked greed will lead to much debt. The American government can attest to this. Laziness will lead to inability to hold down a job and failure to provide for your family. There is a way that the world works. You see, it is not just that sin is wrong, although it is. Sin is also destructive.

Our big problem is that even if we can observe how things work, we so often fail to apply the knowledge we gain. We need Jesus. He is the one who can give us harmony with God, which will lead to harmony in our relationships and safe passage through daily life in the world around us. That leads to the final reason to marry Wisdom.

## Marry Wisdom Because Jesus Gives Abundant and Eternal Life

### PROVERBS 8:32-36

Wisdom finishes her sermon by saying, "Listen to me; those who keep my ways are happy" (v. 32). Following Wisdom is the path to blessing; neglecting Wisdom is the path to death (v. 36). Searching for and finding Wisdom is the path to life and a right relationship with God by grace (v. 35). This means that following after Wisdom—Jesus—is the path to a good life now and an eternal life later. And following after Folly will injure you now and cause you to perish later.

Who can speak like this? Who can say, if you find me, you will receive life and the grace of God? And who can say, if you fail to find me, you will die? Only Jesus could say these things. Jesus is saying you must choose. He's saying, choosing me or not choosing me is the difference between life and death. That's a massive claim, but then again Jesus is the Wisdom of God.

## Conclusion

The old Christmas carol "O Come, O Come, Emmanuel" says of Jesus,

> O come Thou Wisdom from on high,
> And order all things, far and nigh;
> To us the path of knowledge show,
> And cause us in her ways to go. (Henry Sloane Coffin)

Christianity has confessed for a long time in song what Proverbs 8 has taught us. The Wisdom of God, who ordered the cosmos and can teach us the right path, took on flesh in Bethlehem (John 1:14). If you want to be wise in daily life—if you want to know how the world works—then you must be in a relationship with him. If you're not walking in wisdom, it reveals an issue with Jesus in your life. Confess that to him, turn from it, and let him reorder your life like he orders the universe.

## Reflect and Discuss

1. Is it surprising that Solomon wants his son and us to be attracted to and to marry Wisdom? What does this point reemphasize about Wisdom's nature?
2. What is the significance of Wisdom crying out at the crossroads? What do both she and Folly challenge us to do?
3. The rest of Proverbs consists of Wisdom's teaching. How does she instruct us? What does she teach us?
4. Being in relationship with Wisdom is a package deal. Who are some of her "associates" she will bring with her?
5. Wisdom also teaches what to avoid. What are some things that Wisdom hates?
6. Solomon teaches that Wisdom rewards those who are in relationship with her. How are these rewards better than riches?
7. How does Proverbs 8:22-31 elevate Wisdom's description beyond just a poetic device? Who does this section reveal Wisdom to be?
8. Because Wisdom assisted Yahweh in creating the world, what does she have to share now with humanity?
9. How is Wisdom the mediator between God, humanity, and the world?
10. Proverbs 8:35-36 says that Wisdom is the path to God, and neglecting Wisdom is the path to death. What New Testament passage does this recall? Who can speak like this?

# The Marriage Supper of Wisdom

## PROVERBS 9

**Main Idea:** If you accept Wisdom's invitation, you will be made wise.

---

I. **Accept the Invitation of Wisdom—Jesus—to Become Wise and Receive Life (9:1-6).**
II. **How You Act Reveals Which Invitation You Have Accepted (9:7-12).**
III. **Reject the Deadly Invitation of Folly—Idols (9:13-18).**

---

Throughout Proverbs, two women have been competing for the son's affections: Lady Wisdom and the immoral woman. As we have seen, Wisdom will make you wise and grant you life, and the immoral woman will kill you. Proverbs 9 is the climax to the introduction of the book. In this chapter, the immoral woman is personified as Folly. This is the lynchpin to the book of Proverbs. This chapter sums up all that came before and sets up all that comes after. It all comes down to this: Whom will you love? Whom will you marry? It's a choice between being wise and being a fool—between life and death. The choice you make will determine whether you walk the path of wisdom or foolishness in life.[16]

There are two competing invitations given in this chapter. There is an invitation from Wisdom (Jesus) to a party, and there is an invitation from Folly (idols or Satan) to a party. Which will you accept? If you accept the invitation of Wisdom (Jesus), you will be made wise and receive true life forever. On the other hand, if you accept the invitation of Folly (idols or Satan), you will be a fool who wrecks his life and then perishes.

This has huge implications for your life right now—for the nitty-gritty details of your life. If you want to live the wise life and receive eternal life, you must accept Jesus's invitation. If you are walking in wisdom in your daily life right now, it shows that you have accepted Jesus's invitation. It reveals that you are walking toward him, walking with him,

---

[16] Longman explains how Wisdom and Folly point to Jesus and idols or Satan, and he shows how this decision affects whether or not one can follow the wisdom of the rest of Proverbs. His insights are extremely helpful here. Longman, *Proverbs*, 58-60, 64-69.

and trusting in him. On the other hand, if you're walking in foolishness, it shows that you are walking toward idols (Satan) and trusting in them. This is revealed in the seemingly mundane details of your life according to Proverbs. If you are lazy, quarrelsome, cannot accept correction, cannot pay the bills on time, or your kids run amok, it is because you are acting like an idolater! But if you work hard, can be trusted with secrets, and can correct your kids, then you are acting like a follower of Jesus.

The bottom line is this: If you do not have a relationship with Jesus, you will not be wise because you cannot be wise. If you are not walking in wisdom right now, it shows a problem with Jesus in your life that you need to repent of. The time is now to make this decision because that choice determines whether or not you can follow the wisdom of Proverbs 10–31.

## Accept the Invitation of Wisdom—Jesus—to Become Wise and Receive Life

### PROVERBS 9:1-6

Wisdom built her house, and it is a temple because it's at the highest point of the city (v. 3). Perhaps Solomon's temple had "seven pillars" (cf. 1 Kgs 7:17) (Murphy and Huwiler, *Proverbs*, 42). As we have seen, Wisdom is a personification of Solomon's wisdom and God's Wisdom; and this poetic device points to Jesus, so it is natural for Wisdom to dwell in a temple. As we have seen, Wisdom built creation (Prov 3; 8), the tabernacle (Exod 31), and the temple (1 Kgs 7). Wisdom here prepares a marriage feast of meat and wine. As in Isaiah 55, this meal is free. As in Isaiah 25, this meal gives life (Prov 9:6). Through her maids, Wisdom invites everyone in the most public places to come to the party (v. 3), especially those who lack a heart and need a new one. The phrase translated "lacks sense" in verse 4 literally says "lacks a heart." The inexperienced are those who have not yet made a decision. Wisdom calls to them to turn in at her house, come to her party, eat her feast, and drink her wine. This is very similar to the parables in Matthew 22 and Luke 14, where the kingdom of God is compared to a wedding feast—a banquet. All are ultimately invited to this feast. The servants are sent out to the highways and hedges to invite all. This meal gives life, and those who refuse it will die.

Wisdom is not just offering food and drink. Like Jesus, she is offering herself as food and drink that brings life (cf. John 6) (Leithart, *Blessed*

*Are the Hungry*, 71–74). Accepting this invitation entails repentance (i.e., turning from your simple ways), receiving life, and walking in the way of understanding (Prov 9:6). In essence, what Wisdom is saying is, "Repent of your foolishness, come to my party, marry me, and I will make you wise and give you an abundant and eternal life. You will live wisely if you know me." So recognize that you are a fool, marry Wisdom, eat her food, and Wisdom—Jesus—will produce wisdom in you now and give you eternal life.

## How You Act Reveals Which Invitation You Have Accepted

**PROVERBS 9:7-12**

There's a big question to ask about Proverbs 9:7-12: How do these verses fit, sandwiched between the two invitations of Wisdom and Folly? The answer is that they are giving examples of Wisdom's teachings so that you know how to read the rest of Proverbs. These verses seem straightforward, but they must be read in this context. After all, these verses contrast the two ways (i.e., the two invitations): wisdom and wickedness. These verses show what these two women teach and produce in their followers progressively. The party you choose to go to determines if you keep these. The party that you choose to go to determines how you act in daily life. Whether you act wickedly or wisely reveals which party you chose. Belief always determines behavior, but behavior reveals what you believe. This is a worship issue.

Here is the wise teaching. Do not correct a mocker (ESV, "scoffer") because you will just get hurt in the process, and the mocker will hate you (vv. 7-8). Correcting a mocker is a waste of time because he will not listen to you. It will have no effect on him. All you will receive are verbal attacks from him in return. You will be humiliated. There are some who will never listen to wise counsel and will never humbly submit to authority. On the other hand, you should correct a wise man. He will love you for it, and he will become wiser (vv. 8-9). A wise man is humble enough to know he needs correction.

So according to these verses, wisdom is the discernment to know whom to correct and whom not to correct. You do this by discerning the outcome. How will your correction be received? This is wisdom. Since Jesus is the Wisdom of God, that means being formed into Christlikeness is not just growing in a reduction of sinfulness, although that is part of it. It is also growth in discernment. Being like Jesus means having the ability to see the situation you are in. It means recognizing when to correct people and when not to correct them because it will only make things worse. It also means knowing when not to play the coward and to speak up and say something in the right situation.

There is also the implication in these verses that if you are the kind of person who cannot accept correction, you are a mocker. If you get angry when someone confronts you, you are a mocker. On the other hand, if you can humbly accept correction because you know you have not arrived, then you are wise, and you will love the person who had the courage to confront you. How do you respond to confrontation? Do you automatically get angry? Or do you listen and try to see the truth in it? Do you have any relationship where someone has the freedom to ask you tough questions? Wisdom is the ability to hear and respond correctly to criticism so that you don't repeat the same mistakes.

The point of Proverbs 9 is that if you cannot accept a rebuke, it is not just because that is your personality type; it reveals idolatry in your life (perhaps worship of self). This is true in all kinds of practical areas that Proverbs touches on. If you are stingy, it reveals an idolatry of money. If you have a porn addiction, it reveals an idol of sex. If you cannot discipline your children, it might reveal that you have made your kids an idol.

The starting point for practical wisdom is a covenant relationship with Yahweh (the fear of the Lord; v. 10). You cannot be wise without this relationship. There is no secular and sacred divide in life. Covenantal faith in Yahweh will lead to balancing your checkbook, cleaning your room at your mom's request, enjoying being with your family more than making money. If you cannot do these things, it is not just a character flaw; it is a spiritual problem.

This is the last time Wisdom talks. She urges you to pick wisdom, but it's your choice. If you pick her, it will lead to life (v. 11). She will produce wisdom in you and reward you with longer life. But you are responsible to make your own decision, and how you live reveals which invitation you accepted.

## Reject the Deadly Invitation of Folly—Idols

### PROVERBS 9:13-18

The forbidden woman is now personified as Folly. Woman Folly is the power behind this forbidden woman. Embracing Woman Folly will lead to the same place as embracing the forbidden woman—the grave (5:5; 9:18). The forbidden woman epitomizes folly (just like the noble wife epitomizes Woman Wisdom; ch. 31). This Woman Folly is a counterfeit who copies but perverts everything Wisdom does. Folly's house is a temple too because it is at the highest point of the city (9:14). This is how we know that Folly stands for idols (Longman, *Proverbs,* 222). Turning away from Wisdom was characterized as unfaithfulness to God (1:32). One is unfaithful to God when one is whoring after idols. That's exactly what's happening here.

Woman Folly is loud, seductive, ignorant, and lazy (9:13-14). She will produce this in her followers. She invites everyone to her party (vv. 15-16). She calls out to the same crowd as Wisdom—those who lack heart. She says to turn in at her house, come to her party. Her meal is illicit. Her water is stolen, and her bread is to be eaten in secret. This may seem "tasty" (v. 17), but the way that seems right will not end well. Picking up on Proverbs 5:15, where water refers to sex, this seems to be an invitation to an affair. She's not just offering food and drink; she's offering herself as food and drink. She's offering an illicit relationship that will lead to apostasy, to walking away from God. Solomon knows that sexual sin leads to abandoning God. We see that she seduces her victims by giving them half-truths. Yes, this affair will bring temporary pleasure, but she does not reveal the death that awaits them (v. 18). That's what foolishness is. Foolishness is not seeing the connection between your actions and their consequences. Like a cow walking into a slaughterhouse, you don't know that you're about to become filet mignon. Her guests do not realize that accepting her invitation is accepting an invitation to their own funeral. They go into the grave (v. 18; "depths of Sheol"). There may be a destruction now like public shame, loss of family, or loss of money; but all of that is simply a foretaste of what's to come—hell.

## Conclusion

Proverbs 9 is the story of Wisdom sending out her servants to invite us to a meal—a party—that brings life instead of death. Proverbs says that those who eat this meal will be made wise. The New Testament says that Jesus is the Wisdom of God, and he invites us to a meal as well. He invites us to feast on him. Those who eat this meal—those who feast on Christ's flesh and blood—will live and be a part of his kingdom. Christ's meal is not for those who think they're wise; it is for those who know they are fools and who want to grow in wisdom. Have you accepted Christ's invitation?

Jesus lived a perfectly wise life, yet he took the punishment our foolishness deserved. He went into Sheol—the grave—and came back in victory three days later. He invites you to accept forgiveness from him. If you do, he will transform you into a wise person. The choice is yours! If you are an unbeliever, recognize the foolishness in your life, repent for the first time, and come to Jesus for salvation. If you are a believer, ask the Lord to reveal your foolishness to you, then confess it to him, repent of it, run to Jesus, and ask to be made like him.

## Reflect and Discuss

1. What does this passage teach us about the nature of wisdom and the way someone can become wise?
2. How does your choice of Jesus or idols affect whether or not you walk in wisdom in your daily life?
3. In what ways do the details of your daily life—like finishing tasks and controlling your tongue—reveal your relationship with Jesus?
4. How do you "marry" Wisdom? What does that look like?
5. What are some indicators that a person who will not listen to your correction might be a mocker? What are some indicators that a person might be wise and instructed by your correction?
6. How do you respond when you are confronted or corrected? What does that reveal about you?
7. What are the consequences of marrying Wisdom? What are the consequences of marrying Folly? How should these consequences affect your pursuit?
8. What does this passage teach you about sin?
9. What does this passage teach you about redemption in Christ?
10. In Christ, how can you obey the commands of this passage? What will that look like in your daily life?

# How to Read Proverbs

## PROVERBS 10:1-32

**Main Idea:** Jesus will produce the wisdom of Proverbs in your life progressively.

---

**I. Jesus Produces Wisdom in the Area of Your Work and Money (10:2-5).**
**II. Jesus Produces Wisdom in the Area of Your Words and Mouth (10:8).**
**III. Jesus Produces Wisdom in the Area of Your Relationships (10:1,12).**
**IV. Jesus Produces Wisdom That Leads to Rewards in Your Life and the Life to Come (10:24-32).**

---

Proverbs 10 starts a new section in Proverbs. This is what we think of today when we think about Proverbs: the one- or two-line sayings of earthy wisdom in Proverbs 10–31. We will look at this chapter to learn how to read Proverbs. We cannot cover all of it, but we want to answer the question, How do you read Proverbs? How do you understand the book?

For those of you who know something about the book of Proverbs or who have read it or have several verses memorized, that may seem like a strange task. That may seem like a weird question: How do I rightly read Proverbs? We might understand that question if it were asked about Romans or Isaiah or Leviticus but not with Proverbs, because it is pretty simple and straightforward for the most part. It gives practical advice. I may not understand sacrificing a goat and what to do with the entrails in Leviticus, but I understand when the Bible tells me to not be lazy or to discipline my children. Those are easy to comprehend. For the most part we would say that the majority of the Proverbs are easy to understand.

Here is the problem—there is a right way and a wrong way to read the book of Proverbs. There is a right way to read Proverbs that leads to joy and life, and there is a wrong way to read Proverbs that leads to misery or pride. Here's the difference—you can read the Proverbs like a Pharisee and say, "I need to do these things in order for God to love me. I need to obey these practical bits of advice because if I do them, God will accept me." That is one way to read the book of Proverbs—and that is the wrong way! We should not read it like a Pharisee. Instead, we need to read the Proverbs like blood-bought Christians who say, "These are not the things that we do in order to get God to love us; these are the things that we do because God already loves us. We do not do these things to become his children; we do these things because in Jesus Christ we have already been adopted into his family, and now here is how we live our lives." There is a huge difference between those two approaches. Reading the Bible like Pharisees will lead you into either misery when you fail or pride when you feel like you succeed. But if you read it like a Christian, it will lead you to become wise and joyful.

The behaviors that we read about here—most of Proverbs 10–31 does talk about conduct—are not things that God tells you to do in order to become his child. They are not things God tells you to do in order for him to love you. These behaviors are what the Lord is producing in those who are already his children—those who are already a part of his family. He is slowly, progressively conforming you to the image of Christ; he is making you more like Jesus Christ, who is the Wisdom of God. Proverbs is very much a book on sanctification.

If you say, "I don't have these things in my life. My life is a wreck," then maybe the reason you do not have them is because you are not a believer in Jesus. I hope Proverbs 10 will reveal to you the areas of your life where you are a fool and sinful, and then will drive you to Jesus Christ as your Savior. Then, through faith in Christ, the wisdom of Proverbs is what God will produce in your life daily. The gospel is not about making yourself righteous; it is not about doing these things to become righteous. The gospel is about how the righteousness of Jesus has been credited to your account by virtue of your faith in him and how, by his Spirit and by his Word, he is molding you and shaping you to become more like him. It's a slow process. It is gradual. You can take two steps forward, one step or three steps back, then a few steps forward again. But it is a process whereby God is molding you and shaping you into the image of his Wisdom, who is Jesus Christ.

The Christian life is lived by faith. You live by faith recognizing your sin and foolishness, and then you daily repent of the areas where you are not believing the gospel or worshiping Jesus rightly. As you do that, the Lord shapes you into the image of Christ so that you can live out the wisdom of Proverbs. We are not saved by faith plus works, but we are saved by a faith that does work. Faith will produce obedience and wisdom in your life.

Proverbs 9 teaches us this truth. Proverbs teaches that when we fail to live up to God's wisdom it is evidence of idols in our hearts that we are worshiping rather than Jesus. It reveals a problem with Jesus in our lives. Proverbs 9 was the key chapter—the hinge chapter—because it summed up everything that came before it (Prov 1–8) and it sets up everything that comes after it (Prov 10–31). The whole point of Proverbs 9 was that you have two beings that vie for your affection, love, and worship (Longman, *Proverbs*, 58–61, 64–68).[17] One is the Wisdom of God (Jesus) and the other is Folly, who represents idols. Solomon tells his son that if you want to be wise, you need to have a personal relationship with Wisdom (Jesus); and if you want to be a fool, you will choose a relationship with idols. And the choice is a matter of life and death. The choice you make determines whether or not you can walk the path of wisdom in your daily life. The choice determines whether or not you can follow the wise advice given here in chapters 10–31. To walk the wise path and obey this practical advice that he gives to his son, one must have a personal relationship with Jesus Christ. You can be smart, you can have a high IQ, and you can be very intellectual; but without a relationship with Jesus you cannot be wise. No matter how smart or wise you may be in the eyes of the world, without a relationship with Jesus you cannot walk in wisdom as it is laid out in the book of Proverbs.

The interpretation of Proverbs 9 is critical for us to understand as we head into this new section in Proverbs 10. The heading "Solomon's proverbs" in 10:1 indicates the start of a new section. It is different from what has come before. The second part of the book—the proverbs proper—is what we typically think of when we think about Proverbs. These are the short, pithy, sometimes random sayings of practical wisdom rather than extended discourses.[18]

Whether or not you are walking in wisdom daily—which means all kinds of things from whether or not you listen to your parents when they tell you to do something, whether you can finish an assignment on time, or whether you can control your tongue—reveals whether you are worshiping Jesus or worshiping idols. Whether you walk in wisdom or

---

[17] Many of these insights on how Proverbs 9 helps us understand how to read Proverbs 10–31 come from Longman's terrific discussion.

[18] For a good discussion of the structure of Proverbs, see Garrett, *Proverbs*, 39–46.

foolishness reveals whether you are in right relationship with Jesus or you are an idolater.

If you see patterns of foolishness in your life with finances or relationships or a hundred other things, it reveals that you are worshiping someone or something other than Jesus. It could be multiple idols, and Proverbs does not necessarily spell out what the specific ones are. In a lot of places the main idol that leads us into foolishness is ourselves! When we exalt ourselves and put ourselves number one in our own lives, that will lead to all kinds of foolishness. Self is the idol at the root of so much foolishness in Proverbs, like not listening to anyone else when they give you advice or try to correct you because you think you know so much more than everyone else. For others, money is the idol at the root of their foolishness, which manifests itself as greed, covetousness, or trying get-rich-quick schemes. For others, comfort is their idol, so they are lazy.

For others, their children are their idols, so they put their children up on a pedestal and refuse to discipline them. They act like their children are little deities they have to appease at all costs so that they will not get mad at them. That is what idolatry looks like. In impoverished countries, people think they have to give food or money to the idol at the temple so the idol will not unleash evil spirits on them. That is the kind of worship we see every time a child pitches a temper tantrum in the toy aisle at Target and their parents give them the toy they want! When we worship something or someone other than Jesus, it leads to all sorts of practical foolishness in our lives.

The practicalities of life laid out in Proverbs 10–31 reveal our worship life. Worship is not just about singing on Sunday. The Bible says that you should do everything, whether you eat or drink or whatever it is, to the glory of God (1 Cor 10:31). That is what Proverbs is about if you want to boil it down—it reveals where your life is idolatrous and where you are not believing the gospel.

Proverbs 10–31 is random and disconnected, but there are major categories that you can look at thematically (as we will in this book). The major categories are things like words, work, finances, relationships, and future rewards. Since these things reveal whether we are in right relationship with Jesus or worshiping idols, what Proverbs shows us is that there is no spiritual and secular divide in life. You do not have your religious life over here and your secular life over there. Proverbs says all of the areas of your daily life are spiritual in nature. It does not matter how morally neutral the advice Solomon gives here may seem to be; it is not neutral. These practical areas of your life either show you are moving toward Jesus or you are moving away from Jesus. That has everything to do with whether or not you can clean your room, whether or not you have right relationships, and whether or not you can balance your checkbook. So we must read chapters 10–31 in this context.

God lays out for us through Solomon how life works best. Life works best when first you have harmony with God (i.e., you have been reconciled to him), which leads to harmony in your relationships with other people and the world around you. God knows this because he is the one who made the world. He knows the way the world works because he made it. He is good, he loves us, and he wants to share that key with us through the Spirit here in Proverbs. Often it seems that when we read God's counsel and advice, we think to ourselves, "I don't like that. That doesn't seem like it's going to make me happy. That seems like it might hurt me in the long run." What the Bible tells us instead is that the reason God tells you these things is not because he does not want you to be happy. He tells you these things so you can have a true happiness that lasts forever. He loves you. He wants you to know the way life works best. He knows that a life filled with idols will destroy you and everyone around you.

We will walk briefly through Proverbs 10 and some cross-reference verses in other parts of Proverbs to see examples of the wisdom of Proverbs so we can know how to read the whole book as a book about Jesus and our wisdom in him. Proverbs 10 mainly contrasts the two ways or paths that we have seen so far. There is a way of wisdom and a way of foolishness. There is a way of righteousness (synonymous with wisdom) and a way of wickedness (synonymous with foolishness) (Waltke, *Proverbs, Chapters 1–15*, 447).[19] Solomon constantly contrasts these two paths in these major categories of life. We will see how that is laid out here and see that Proverbs 10–31 points us to how Jesus will produce this kind of wisdom progressively in his followers.

What we see differently starting in chapter 10 is how random everything is now. Let me talk to you about being a wise son, then let's talk about money, then let's talk about laziness, then let's talk about the blessing of the Lord, then let's talk about how you use your mouth, and then let's talk about how you discipline your children. It is all over

[19] Waltke sees 10:1–15:29 as paralleling the righteous versus the wicked.

the place and scattershot. We should not think this is by accident. The reason it is random is because the book of Proverbs is Solomon obeying the command to parents in Deuteronomy 6 to teach their children the law.[20] God gave very specific commands to the parents about how to teach their children the law. He said you do it when they wake up, when they sit, when they walk along the road, and when they lie down. How much of your day is given to waking up, sitting, walking around, and lying down? The entire day! That is the point. He is saying that your task as a parent is to teach your children the law throughout the day. How does that work? For those of you who are parents, do you sit children down one day and say, "OK. Let me map out our week. Monday, I will teach you everything you need to know about marriage and dating and romance (most of you probably do not have a lot of material here). Tuesday, I will teach you everything you need to know about work. Wednesday, I will teach you everything you need to know about how to communicate." And so on. Is that the way we teach our children? Do you just sit them down and pour every bit of information you have into them? Of course not. Instead, we may talk about a hundred different things as we go through the day. We will talk to them about things from the mundane to the sublime, like how to throw a baseball, how to drive a car, how to do a job interview, how to spend money wisely, how to handle a conflict with a friend, how to handle dating issues, how to improve their prayer life—all kinds of things. We go through our day, and as conversations and topics come up, we have the responsibility to teach our children. That is what's happening in Proverbs. Solomon says that as you go throughout the day, conversations will come up about all kinds of different topics, and you need to be ready to instruct your children and impart wisdom to them.

There are some broad categories that we can use to arrange things in a sermon so that it is easier for us to walk through them. In fact, in the rest of this commentary there will be different thematic series that will tackle all of these in more detail; but in this message we want to get a glimpse of what Proverbs says about these different areas of life so that we can understand how to read the book rightly in its entirety.

---

[20] For a good discussion of how Proverbs functions as Solomon obeying Deuteronomy 6, see the discussion by Hamilton in *God's Glory,* 320.

## Jesus Produces Wisdom in the Area of Your Work and Money

### PROVERBS 10:2-5

Jesus produces wisdom in your life in the way you work and handle money. We see these themes early on in this section in Proverbs 10:2-5 that deal with money and our work ethic. Solomon writes in verse 2, "Ill-gotten gains do not profit anyone, but righteousness rescues from death." If you are a greedy person, if you are a person who cheats the government, or if you are a person who cheats your employer, then that will not profit you like you think it will. You are an idolater. Sometimes idolatry is not worship of bad things. It can be the worship of good things that you have put in the place of God.

Proverbs says many things about money. Proverbs can be very positive. It says that if you are a wise person, you will make more money, generally speaking. But the Proverbs are not always positive about money. They do not say that every time you accumulate money you should take it as a sign of God's blessing in your life.[21] Money—if it is not gotten in the right way or if you trust in it (11:28)—is destructive. I had a friend who in college worked for a company that would sell things to senior adults that senior adults really did not need. After a couple of weeks, the person felt extremely guilty for selling things to people that they did not need and talking them into spending money they did not have. Yet, the employer was pressuring for more and more sales. My friend considered the people on these sales calls and thought, "I'm swindling my grandmother." My friend quit the job. The Bible says that these wrong ways of getting money are destructive and harmful to you. Other examples where we can see this are the Enron debacle and Ponzi schemes.

But the problem that many of us have with this text is the question, Is this really true? The reason we have that problem is because we have observed in our lives people who have cheated the system and gotten away with it. They made tons of money and had financial security even though they went about it the wrong way. So are these proverbs true? Is this really the way the world works? Proverbs 10:3 says that the Lord will not let the righteous go hungry. What about Christians in the Sudan who are starving to death? What about Christians in your church who

---

[21] Longman has a great discussion on wealth and poverty in Proverbs. See Longman, *Proverbs*, 573–76.

lost their jobs and now their families are struggling? Does that mean they are not God's children or that God does not love them?

The key to understanding the Proverbs is that we must view them in light of Christ and eternity. Do not view them in terms of immediacy. *Generally* these things are true immediately, but they will *always* be true ultimately (Dever, *The Message*, 510). The wicked may make more money now and the righteous may starve right now, but in the end those who are outside of Christ will have trouble and those who are in Christ will be trouble free. Those in Christ will be enriched, and those outside of Christ will lose all that they have. How can you come to know this for certain? Look to the life of Jesus.[22] Judas—who gets money in the wrong way—ends up dead; but the righteous one, Jesus, is delivered from death, just like verse 2 promised! Jesus is the only one who is righteous. If you are in him, you will be rescued from death later and freed from love of money in the present.

Proverbs 10:4-5 turns to the issue of work ethic when it says,

> *Idle hands make one poor, but diligent hands bring riches. The son who gathers during summer is prudent; the son who sleeps during harvest is disgraceful.*

Solomon says two things: laziness will lead to poverty and shaming your parents, while diligence and hard work lead to riches where you are able to provide and bring joy to your parents. Again, wisdom is about the effect your actions have on you and the people around you. The problem is that hardly anyone confesses that they are a lazy person. No one has ever walked into my office for counseling and said, "I'm really wrestling with laziness." No one thinks they are lazy because the picture of laziness in their mind is the couch potato who watches soap operas all day long while eating Klondike bars in their bathrobe. In Proverbs, laziness refers to people who cannot see their assignments through to completion (see Moore, "Finding Jesus"). They might start a task and get to the middle of it, but they walk away before it is finished. It's the son who helped plant the crops but is not there during harvest to finish the task. In our day, the laziness of Proverbs looks like distractions that keep you from staying on task. You cannot complete your assignments because Facebook distracts you for thirty minutes. You come back and do five

---

[22] See the excellent discussion by Dennis Johnson (*Him We Proclaim*, 303–13) on how to preach Christ from texts like this. His insights greatly helped me.

minutes of work, but then check Twitter for fifteen minutes. Laziness is seen in the extended adolescence of our culture where kids can't grow up and provide for themselves but keep ending up back at Mom and Dad's house (bringing shame to their parents, even if the parents won't admit it). Laziness keeps you from providing for your family or from the ability to have a family, and the failure to provide for your family is a failure to believe the gospel—it's a Jesus problem (cf. 1 Tim 5:8).

We see these same themes throughout the Proverbs. Proverbs 13:11 says in the ESV, "Wealth gained hastily will dwindle, but whoever gathers little by little will increase it." Murphy and Huwiler prefer that translation as well and writes, "The sense is that when money comes too easily for a person, it will not last" (*Proverbs*, 65). Proverbs consistently condemns get-rich-quick schemes as disastrous. We can sit back and observe that this is truly the case. How many stories have you heard of NFL or NBA stars who made millions and were bankrupt before they hit forty? For many, they gained all that money too quickly, without having formed the kind of wisdom that was necessary for them to know how to handle and steward that money well. That is true for us as well. We have to be shaped and molded with the kind of character it takes to be able to handle money rightly. That kind of wisdom typically comes by gaining money little by little. Jesus works in your life so that he who is faithful with a few things can now be given many things.

## Jesus Produces Wisdom in the Area of Your Words and Mouth

### PROVERBS 10:8

Jesus grows you in wisdom when it comes to the use of your tongue. We see this theme again and again in Proverbs 10. For example, verse 8 says, "A wise heart accepts commands, but foolish lips will be destroyed." The ESV uses the phrase "babbling fool" at the end of the verse, which Waltke seems to prefer when he writes,

> The fool is so full of himself that instead of having the capacity to accept wisdom he dangerously prattles out his own 'clever opinions,' which are devoid of true wisdom. (*Proverbs, Chapters 1–15*, 459)

Here is the point, and this is a major theme in Proverbs: If you are the kind of person who loves to hear the sound of your own voice and who speaks more than you listen, then you're probably a fool. You are probably worshiping the idol of self.

How many of you know people who, when you have a conversation with them, they look like they are not listening to a word you are saying at all but rather are just waiting for you to take a breath so they can speak? They want to tell you their thoughts on things, but they do not want to hear your thoughts at all. Maybe you are that kind of person. If you are the kind of person who loves to talk and cannot receive commands or advice from others, then you are a fool and it will end up hurting you. You will come to ruin. Why? Because if you cannot listen to someone else's instructions, you will never learn from your own mistakes.

All of us think that we are right. Obviously, I think my views are right on everything! Otherwise I would change to a different view. If I thought I was wrong, why would I keep holding on to the wrong view? So I think that all of my views on everything are right, but I know in my heart that my views could not possibly all be right. I just can't figure out which ones are right and which ones are wrong. But if you are the kind of person who loves to talk and never listen to others with the awareness that you may be wrong, then you will never grow as a person and you will continually make the same mistakes. You can't learn where your views, decisions, and choices are off unless you are willing to receive commands and counsel from others. Wisdom is being able to receive advice humbly and follow it. This has everything to do with Jesus, who perfectly accepted the commands of his Father and knew when and how to speak rightly.

We see this theme throughout Proverbs. Proverbs 13:3 says, "The one who guards his mouth protects his life; the one who opens his lips invites his own ruin." Proverbs repeatedly says that those who speak a lot also sin a lot and are destructive to themselves and the people around them. Since we are sinners, the more we talk, sooner or later something stupid will come out of our mouths. How many times have you said something and immediately wished you could take it back? But you can't! Jesus produces the ability to guard your tongue.

## Jesus Produces Wisdom in the Area of Your Relationships

### PROVERBS 10:1,12

Wisdom has to do with relationships. Whether you are the kind of person who loves your neighbor or makes fun of your neighbor reveals whether you are wise or a fool (11:12). Whether you are the kind of person who can keep secrets reveals whether you are wise or a fool (11:13). Are you the kind of person who is told something in confidence, then a few days later you confide in another friend, "Hey, I'm only telling you this and you can't tell anyone else, but did you know that . . ."? If you do that, you are an idolatrous fool. Most likely the inability to keep secrets reveals that you worship yourself because you like to be the person who has and disseminates information. That has everything to do with your relationship with Jesus.

Wisdom has to do with all kinds of relationships. Whether or not you are generous to the poor (11:24), take care of your animals (12:10), listen to your parents (13:1), keep good company (13:20), or date the right people reveals whether or not you are wise and walking with Jesus. Jesus doesn't just reconcile you to God; he reconciles you to others (Eph 2:14).

We see an example of this here at the start of Proverbs 10. Verse 1 states, "A wise son brings joy to his father, but a foolish son, heartache to his mother." Those are parallel lines that complement each other. Do not misread the text so that you think it means that the mom will not be happy if her son is wise, or that the dad will not be heartbroken if his son is a fool. No, it is a parallelism with the father in the first line and the mother in the second line. The basic idea is that if you are a wise child, you will make your parents happy, but if you are foolish, you will break your parents' hearts. The whole principle that Solomon teaches is that your wisdom or foolishness has emotional consequences for the people around you, specifically your parents. You need to observe the response that your behavior elicits from your parents to know whether you are wise and in right relationship with Jesus or whether you are a fool who is walking away from Jesus.[23] Wisdom has everything to do with the emotional results you bring out of your parents. If you bring your parents shame because of foolish decisions, words, or actions, you have a problem with Jesus. If you choose friends who corrupt you, if you choose dating relationships that are harmful for you, or if you get involved with peers in drugs and alcohol and break your parents' hearts, that reveals idolatry in your life. Plenty of parents feel this heartache because of decisions their children have made.

---

[23] The exposition of this verse was greatly helped by Longman's insights in *Proverbs*, 229.

This reality has everything to do with your relationship with Jesus. I (Jon) think that all of us would have to admit that we have made decisions that hurt our parents. I'm not exempt from that. The good news of the gospel is that this convicting reality points us to Jesus. Jesus is the one who perfectly fulfills the wisdom of Proverbs. Jesus was the one who was perfectly wise and perfectly honored his parents. That is why Luke 2:51 points out that Jesus submitted in everything to Mary and Joseph. That is why in John's Gospel when Jesus hangs on the cross suffocating to death, he makes provisions for his mom to be taken care of after he dies (John 19:26-27). Why did Jesus do that? Jesus did that because he perfectly honored his parents. The truth of the gospel is not only that Jesus kept the fifth commandment for us but also that Jesus died the death we deserved to die for shaming our parents. He offers us his perfect record of righteousness and wisdom through faith. He offers to wipe our slate clean of all the times we dishonored our parents. Through the Spirit, Jesus makes us the kind of children who bring joy to our parents.

Relationships are again addressed in Proverbs 10:12, "Hatred stirs up conflicts, but love covers all offenses." Hatred, anger, and a violent temper are not good conflict-resolution techniques. That seems simple, but we all need to hear it. Again, the root of this is idolatry, most likely worship of self that prevents you from letting go of a perceived wrong against you. What is a good conflict-resolution technique? Love! Seeking the best in others, not just seeking the best in yourself. Giving the benefit of the doubt to others, not just giving the benefit of the doubt to yourself. Forgiving other people, not just overlooking your own sin while you fixate on others' sins. If you are constantly angry, if you are the kind of person who loves a good fight, and if you are continually stirring up conflict, you are a fool. The way that you resolve conflict in wisdom is this: "A gentle answer turns away anger" (15:1). You resolve conflicts by loving others and letting go of the offenses (see Eph 4:32). Again we see this fulfilled in Jesus. Jesus—by his love on the cross—covers our offenses against God and reconciles us to God. Not only does he resolve the conflict between us and God, but that vertical reconciliation should also lead to horizontal reconciliation where we love and forgive others around us. Being a blood-bought, wise Christian means that you see the way God dealt with you and your sin and your offense against him, and then you deal that way with others who wrong you: You love them! You forgive them!

## Jesus Produces Wisdom That Leads to Rewards in Your Life and the Life to Come

### PROVERBS 10:24-32

Following Jesus leads to rewards in this life and in the one to come. Proverbs 10–31 really boils down to conduct and the consequences that come out of that conduct. Solomon is a good teacher. Solomon doesn't just tell his son what to do, he tells him why he should do it. Here is what will happen. If you are wise, here is the good that can result. But if you are foolish in your life, here is the bad and the harm that could come out of it. He teaches his son using both the *what* and the *why*.

These themes come up repeatedly in Proverbs 10 as well. Verses 24-32 deal with the rewards and consequences of wisdom and foolishness. It is a matter of life and death. Verse 24 states, "What the wicked dreads will come to him, but what the righteous desire will be given to them." What do you fear? What are your nightmares? Do you fear financial ruin? Marital ruin? Do you fear your children not turning out the way that you want them to? Do you fear not succeeding at your job? Do you fear not having a good reputation? Do you fear death and the judgment of hell? Solomon says that if you are a fool—outside of Christ—those are the things you will receive. What you fear is exactly what will happen to you. But if you are wise and righteous through Christ, which means your desires have now been transformed to be God's desires for you, then you will get what you desire! Whether that desire is eternal life, a strong marriage, a godly family, or whatever God is molding you and shaping you to desire, those are the things you will receive. Those rewards may come now in this life, but they will certainly come in the life to come because verse 25 says the righteous will be established "forever."

Throughout Proverbs 10 and following, these consequences are presented both as present and future. Proverbs 12:21 promises stability in your life and not chaos when you walk in wisdom, whereas 12:28 promises that the righteous will never die. The problem is, none of us are righteous; so this verse means hell for us. But in Christ we are counted righteous; and even though we might die, yet we will live forever. Faith in Jesus leads to life eternal beginning the moment you put your trust in him.

## Conclusion

Often when I (Jon) read Proverbs, it can be very discouraging because when I read these things and take stock of my life, I think about how often I've messed up. I think about how often I did not listen to my parents. I think about how often decisions that I made brought sadness to my parents instead of happiness. I think of how often I've said things to people that were harmful and hurtful. I think of how often I did not listen to some bit of advice that I needed to hear, that someone told me because they loved me. I think of how often I shared secrets that I should've kept. I think of how often I procrastinated on tasks that were assigned to me. I think of how often I didn't forgive somebody who wronged me. In all of these things that Proverbs lays out, I see how I have messed up repeatedly.

But here is how we read these things in Proverbs rightly, and in a way that brings joy and not discouragement. It is summed up in the words of Graeme Goldsworthy on the book of Proverbs:

> Jesus has fulfilled in our place the perfection God demands. He was the truly wise and fully sanctified human on our behalf. Thus, as we struggle to become wise, we know that our failures do not disqualify us from life because Christ himself is our only qualification. He, when all is said and done, is our wisdom, and to possess Christ is to be accounted wise by the only judge who matters. (*Tree of Life*, 98)

## Reflect and Discuss

1. What books of the Bible do you think are most difficult to understand?
2. Why might Proverbs be more difficult to understand than we might think at first glance?
3. How does foolishness in your daily life reveal your top priorities?
4. What are some areas of your life that you previously thought were not really spiritual, but Proverbs shows God's great concern for as well?
5. In what way does the randomness of Proverbs 10–31 instruct us in how to impart wisdom to our children?
6. What are some ways that we are distracted from work?
7. How does gaining money a little at a time help us to better steward it than coming into a lot of money at once?
8. In what ways does thinking you are wise actually reveal you might not be?
9. If you are heartbroken over the heartache that you caused your parents by your foolish decisions, what does the Bible call you to do?
10. What are your greatest fears?

# The Ways of the Fool

## PROVERBS 18:1-9

**Main Idea:** Fools make poor lifestyle decisions that reveal an absence of godly wisdom and lead to humiliating and destructive behavior.

---

**I. A Fool Lacks Wisdom (18:1-3).**
   A. He isolates himself (18:1).
   B. He is opinionated (18:2).
   C. He will be humiliated (18:3).
**II. A Fool Is Loose with His Words (18:4-8).**
   A. He does not see the delight of his words (18:4).
   B. He does not see the disgrace of his words (18:5).
   C. He does not see the danger in his words (18:6).
   D. He does not see the destruction in his words (18:7).
   E. He does not see the disease in his words (18:8).
**III. A Fool Is Lazy concerning Work (18:9).**
   A. He is poor in his performance.
   B. He keeps company with destructive partners.

---

The early twenty-first century is a time of remarkable change and transition. It is mind-boggling to think about how rapidly things change and also how much has changed. It is an awesome time to be alive. It is also an anxious time to be alive.

Yes, the world today is definitely a different world from the one we left behind just a few years back. Go back less than a century and what do you discover? You discover a world where there is no penicillin, polio vaccine, frozen foods, photocopiers, contact lenses, Frisbees, or "the pill."

There are no credit cards, laser beams, ballpoint pens, pantyhose, dishwashers, microwave ovens, clothes dryers, electric blankets, air conditioners, or permanent press clothes.

There are no FM radios (much less satellite radio!), CD players (which will soon be gone), electric typewriters, word processors, computers, iPads, or cell phones. Smartphones?! Imagine the laughter such a phrase would have generated.

- A "chip" means a piece of wood.

- "Hardware" means a hammer and nails.
- "Software" is not even a word!

There really are five-and-dime stores where you can really buy things for a nickel or a dime. For a nickel you can

- buy an ice cream cone with sprinkles;
- buy a soft drink (called a soda pop);
- make a phone call in a telephone booth; or
- buy enough stamps to mail a letter and two postcards.

Gasoline is eleven cents. Grass is something you mow not smoke. Coke is a soft drink not an illegal drug. Pot is something you cook in. AIDS are helpers not a disease. School shootings and metal detectors are not even science fiction.

Yes, the world certainly has changed, and we can expect even greater changes in the very near future. We are smarter and wealthier people, but a nagging question continually haunts us: Are we wiser? Have we really learned anything? Are we ready for what lies ahead? Are we ready to meet our God?

Every generation has the potential for good or evil, to live wisely or play the fool. It is hard to be optimistic when you take an honest look at our world today. Several years ago an outrageous rock star named Marilyn Manson commented just one week after the massacre at Columbine High School, "I try to show people that everything is a lie—pick the lie you like best . . . and I hope mine is the best" (Veith, "Youth Anti-culture").

Perhaps we could adjust the Bible a bit, as we too often want to do, and describe the modern mindset this way: "Father, forgive us, for we know not what we are doing—and please don't tell us. We won't listen!" We too easily buy into lies. We too readily play the fool. We can easily see this foolishness in someone like Marilyn Manson, but we often do not see it in ourselves. We disobey God's Word because we think that our lives, our marriages, our money, or our parenting situations are the exception to God's clear teaching. When we think that, we show we would rather live a lie—like a fool—than live the truth.

Proverbs continually contrasts the way of the wise with the way of the fool. Proverbs 18:1-9 continues that pattern with "a description of the fool's antisocial nature, activity, and consequences" (Waltke, *Proverbs, Chapters 15–31,* 68). Waltke notes the text naturally divides into three sections: verses 1-3, 4-8, and 9. He points out that the fool "is mentioned explicitly in verses 1, 2, 3, 6, 7, and 8 and inferentially in verses 5 and 9. Verse 5 speaks of an ordinary person in contrast to the wise. Moreover, verse 5 is the only one containing antithetical parallels to contrast the two. All the rest are synthetic, devoted entirely to the fool" (ibid.).

As we analyze these verses in three movements, what does King Solomon teach his son about the ways of the fool? In particular, what does he teach him concerning a fool's antisocial behavior (vv. 1-3), his words (vv. 4-8), and his work ethic (v. 9)?

## A Fool Lacks Wisdom

### PROVERBS 18:1-3

A fool in Proverbs is a person who lacks wisdom. He is a person who "does not delight in understanding" (v. 2). He is not able to see life from God's perspective and act accordingly. He is oblivious to the ways of God and refuses the counsel of true friends. Three aspects of his lack of wisdom are noted in verses 1-3.

#### *He Isolates Himself (18:1)*

A fool is a person who isolates himself from others. He is antisocial and a loner who is absorbed with himself. His interests are located in his own desires, his own self-gratification. Further, because he is self-centered, he does not listen to the "sound wisdom" of others. When those who love him try to reason with him, "he breaks out" (ESV), "he starts a quarrel" (NIV), "he rebels" (CSB). The fool is a loudmouth who only causes trouble because he never listens to anyone. He is quick tempered, rages emotionally out of control, and refuses to receive godly wisdom. *The Message* paraphrases verse 1 this way: "Loners who care only for themselves spit on the common good." Proverbs 11:14 reminds us, "Without guidance, a people will fall, but with many counselors there is deliverance." A wise person will surround himself with good and godly friends who love him enough to tell him the truth—even when it hurts. He will not play the Lone Ranger. After all, even the Lone Ranger needed Tonto!

#### *He Is Opinionated (18:2)*

Verse 2 informs us, "A fool does not delight [ESV, "takes no pleasure"] in understanding, but only wants to show off his opinions." The fool has a closed mind but an open mouth, a small mind and a big mouth. He does not listen, but he is quick to tell others what he thinks. Pride is alive and well in his soul. He is convinced that what he thinks is what everyone else ought to think. He is too clever and cute for his own good. God gave us two ears and one mouth; perhaps we would all be wise to listen twice as much as we talk. James 1:19 provides a very wise word of counsel at this point: "Understand this: Everyone should be quick to listen, slow to speak, and slow to anger."

### *He Will Be Humiliated (18:3)*

Because a fool keeps to himself, will not listen, and loves to hear the sound of his own voice, he will eventually humiliate himself. In this instance his foolishness leads him into wickedness. Because his character is flawed, wickedness characterizes his life. He is not a wise person but a foolish person. He is not a good person but "a wicked person." His foolish choices eventually cost him, and they cost him big time. Three words describe the fool's humiliation: contempt, dishonor, and disgrace or derision. Derek Kidner calls these three "sin's traveling companions" (*Proverbs,* 127). Robert Alden notes,

> Sin belongs with shame as dishonor goes with disgrace. The series starts with sin which leads to shame (or contempt). Shame is just a step away from dishonor which leads to disgrace. . . . Sin is a road which progresses downward; the consequences of walking it are progressively more severe. (*Proverbs,* 138)

## A Fool Is Loose with His Words

**PROVERBS 18:4-8**

When you go to the doctor for your check-up he or she always looks at your tongue because it is an indicator of your physical health. God says that you should listen to what flows from your tongue because it is an indicator of your spiritual health. Unfortunately, apart from salvation in Jesus, who redeems the total person, the tongue runs wild and spews all sorts of poison and venom. James 3:8 says, "No one can tame the tongue. It is a restless evil, full of deadly poison." Proverbs repeatedly speaks to the importance and power of the tongue, and it does so again in 18:4-8. Here the focus is specifically on the words that come bubbling out of the mouth of the fool.

### *He Does Not See the Delight of His Words (18:4)*

This verse contrasts the words of the fool with the words of the wise. The idea is that the words of a wise man are a continuous supply of blessing and nourishing counsel (Ross, "Proverbs," 1023). Deep waters are cool, pure, and refreshing. They bless and do not curse. They build up; they do not tear down. They are like a beautiful "flowing river" or a "fountain of wisdom." A contrast is implied: a fool's words are stale, possibly bitter, potentially poisonous. They cater to the wicked (v. 5), stir up strife (v. 6), ruin lives (v. 7), and find a home with those who gossip (v. 8). There is no delight to be seen in the fool's words.

### *He Does Not See the Disgrace of His Words (18:5)*

Verse 5 places us in the context of the courtroom. The fool shows "partiality to the guilty by perverting the justice due the innocent." He takes the side of the wicked (through his testimony?) against the righteous. Perhaps he thinks the evil person can help him out and further his agenda while the innocent person cannot. His actions and words turn truth upside down and betray the innocent. We cannot help but immediately think of Jesus and the false witnesses who sided with the wicked and powerful Sanhedrin against the innocent and sinless Son of God (Mark 14:55-59). The fool forgets or ignores the wisdom of Proverbs 19:5: "A false witness will not go unpunished, and one who utters lies will not escape."

### *He Does Not See the Danger in His Words (18:6)*

"The 10 Commandments of Human Relations" are attributed to Robert G. Lee, pastor of Bellevue Baptist Church in Memphis, Tennessee, 1927–60:

1. Speak to people. There is nothing as nice as a cheerful word of greeting.
2. Smile at people. It takes seventy-two muscles to frown, only four to smile.
3. Call people by name. The sweetest music to anyone's ear is the sound of one's own name.
4. Be friendly and helpful. If you would have friends, be friendly.
5. Be genuinely interested in people. You can like almost everybody, if you try. (If you cannot like them, you can still love them through Jesus.)

6. Be generous with praise—and cautious with criticism.
7. Be considerate with feelings of others. There are usually three sides to a controversy: yours, the other person's, and the right one.
8. Be alert to give service. What counts most in life is what we do for others.
9. Learn to trust people. That trust builds relationships.
10. Have a sense of humor. If you add to the above a good sense of humor, a big dose of patience, and a dash of humility, you will be rewarded manifold.

As you might expect, a fool values none of this wise counsel. Actually a fool, as verse 6 teaches, is really good at talking himself into trouble. "A fool's lips lead to strife, and his mouth provokes a beating." The ESV says, "A fool's lips walk into a fight, and his mouth invites a beating." *The Message* paraphrases it quite colorfully: "The words of a fool start fights; do him a favor and gag him" (cf. 19:29). A fool's words push people over the edge, and he is the one who pays the price with a tail-whipping!

### *He Does Not See the Destruction in His Words (18:7)*

Verse 7 repeats the idea of verse 6, but it advances the argument. The fool receives a beating in verse 6, but he is destroyed in verse 7 (Waltke, *Proverbs, Chapters 1–15*, 73). Solomon tells us, "A fool's mouth is his devastation [ESV, "ruin"; NIV, "undoing"], and his lips are a trap for his life." Words are powerful weapons, and sometimes we use them to our own ruin and destruction. The picture is of a man who lays a deadly trap and he does so for himself! And he does this with his own lips, his own words. The fool is the man who cannot keep his mouth shut even though his words will ruin him; they will wreck his life. There is a self-destructive nature to the words of a fool as he reaps what he has sown (Gal 6:6-7). Proverbs 10:14 reinforces the truth of his verse: "The wise store up knowledge, but the mouth of the fool hastens destruction." Proverbs 12:13 adds, "By rebellious speech an evil person is trapped, but a righteous person escapes from trouble."

A wise man will never forget that a lifetime of building a good reputation can come crashing down and be destroyed with one careless word. He will also remember a very simple axiom: if I don't say it, I won't have to apologize for it. There are far more regrets in life for what we did say (tweet, post on Facebook) than there are for what we did not say. Jesus reminds us in Matthew 12:36-37,

> *I tell you that on the day of judgment people will have to account for every careless word they speak. For by your words you will be acquitted, and by your words you will be condemned.*

### *He Does Not See the Disease in His Words (18:8)*

Proverbs 18:8 and 26:22 are identical. They address the wicked and destructive sin of gossip. People love to gossip. It is virtually a universal human addiction. We just cannot get enough. Like a man strung out on heroin or crack cocaine, we just have to have more. Solomon helps us understand why this sin—and it is sin—is so powerful. He tells us that gossip is like "choice food [ESV, "delicious morsels"] that goes down to one's innermost being." The GNT says, "Gossip is so tasty—how we love to swallow it!" Going into the innermost being, the words become a part of who we are. And they always "stimulate the desire for more" (Ross, "Proverbs," 1025). Waltke says they are "a delectable contagion and so more dangerous" (Waltke, *Proverbs, Chapters 1–15*, 73). Proverbs 16:28 says, "A contrary person spreads conflict, and a gossip separates close friends." Proverbs 26:20 adds, "Without wood, fire goes out; without a gossip, conflict dies down." Ray Ortlund summarizes the matter of gossip well:

> Let's all admit it. We love gossip. We love negative information about other people. We love controversy. We find it delicious. It is a delicacy—to our corrupt hearts. We gulp these words down with relish. But the contagion goes down into us and makes a deep impression and leaves us even sicker than we were before. Truly, God is not mocked.

He then goes on to raise some very good questions and, in the process, he puts every one of us on the spot! Ortlund asks,

> Do you speak up when others are put down? Or do you just stand there and listen in sinful silence as the blast of gossip and slander hits you in the face? God says, "Open your mouth." With every unkind word that goes unconfronted a reputation dies. So much is at stake in our words. They matter not just to us but even more, far more, to God. We are always speaking before the face of God. (*Proverbs*, 134)

## A Fool Is Lazy concerning Work

### PROVERBS 18:9

Verse 9 concludes this section with a quick and simple word about our work ethic. Walt Disney said success is "doing something so well that people will pay to see you do it again." President Theodore Roosevelt said, "Far and away the best prize that life offers is the chance to work hard at work worth doing" ("Address to the New York State Agricultural Association"). Unfortunately the Proverbs fool is completely out of touch with these kinds of perspectives. Shoddy workmanship and a poor work ethic is no problem for the fool. He has no problem being a slacker.

### *He Is Poor in His Performance*

A fool is lazy in doing his job, or "slack in his work" (ESV). He is content to do just enough to get by. A poor job performance review is of no concern as long as he keeps his job. He is not known as a hard worker and he does not care. He is not known as an honest worker and he does not care. He is not known as the guy who gives 110 percent and he does not care. He is not known as the guy who will go the extra mile and he does not care. Colossians 3:23-24 calls the devoted follower of King Jesus to a different and higher mindset when it comes to our work. There Paul writes,

> *Whatever you do, do it from the heart, as something done for the Lord and not for people, knowing that you will receive the reward of an inheritance from the Lord. You serve the Lord Christ.*

### *He Keeps Company with Destructive Partners*

The fool is a slacker and "is brother to a vandal." Laziness and slothfulness are destructive. Laziness and destruction are twins, two peas in a pod, bedfellows. They are related to one another, similar in nature. Ross says, "The one who is slack may look for shortcuts, and may make things that fall apart. His destruction may be indirect and slow in coming, but it is just as problematic" ("Proverbs," 1025). Do you cut corners at work? Then you are a fool. Do you take shortcuts to save time and energy? Then you are a fool. You are selling yourself short, neglecting the gifts and abilities God has given you, cheating others, and potentially putting people at great risk. So I don't tighten the bolt on the car wheel. What's the big deal?! When you realize that you are always working for a King who knows your name and sees everything that you do, it will make a difference in how hard you work and in the quality of your work. He gave his best for you. Does he not deserve the same from you?

## Conclusion

Jesus Christ is the quintessential Proverbs man, the embodiment of the Wisdom of God (1 Cor 1:30). He is also the antithesis of the fool in 18:1-9. The fool lacks wisdom, but Jesus is full of grace and truth (John 1:14). Jesus was not isolated but surrounded himself with friends and companions with whom he shared life. He was not opinionated but spoke words of truth, healing, and grace. As John 7:46 says, "No man ever spoke like this!" It must be admitted that he was humiliated, but his humiliation was for the benefit of others as "he humbled himself by becoming obedient to the point of death—even death on a cross" (Phil 2:8). He was dishonored and disgraced so that we would not have to be. And slack in his work? Not a chance. Not a hint. John 4:34 nails it: "My food is to do the will of him who sent me and to finish his work." Praise God, Jesus did finish the work the Father gave him and declared it to be so in John 19:30 when he said, "It is finished." The Wisdom of God, the Lord Jesus, makes it possible for us to walk in wisdom and to not play the fool. His invitation is to all. How you will respond is up to you.

## Reflect and Discuss

1. Do you often make decisions that focus on yourself and disregard the interests of others?
2. Are you open to, and even desirous of, the counsel of others?
3. Are you a loner? Can you identify a circle of good and faithful friends?
4. Are you more of a listener or a talker?
5. Do you feel like you always have to win an argument? Do you see destructive results from such conversations?
6. Would you characterize your speech as a flowing river of wisdom? If yes, why? If no, why?
7. Do you cozy up to those who can further your agenda whether or not they walk with Christ? If yes, is this really wise?
8. Can you think of times when your mouth has gotten you into trouble?
9. What are your attitude and actions concerning gossip? Try to answer honestly.
10. Evaluate your work ethic. Do you do your work as unto the Lord, knowing that it is Christ you serve?

# Section 2—Riddle Me This: Unlocking the Difficult Proverbs

# The Sovereignty of God

## PROVERBS 16:1-15

**Main Idea:** Submit to the sovereign rule of God and his Messiah.

---

**I. God Is in Complete Control (16:1-3).**
**II. God Will Sovereignly Judge Evil (16:4-5).**
**III. God Sovereignly Saves and Rewards Sinners Who Submit to Him (16:6-9).**
**IV. God Sovereignly Rules the World through the Messiah (16:10-15).**

---

Sometimes the Word of God is difficult to swallow. The Bible is clear that God is supremely sovereign and in control of all things. He knows everything before it happens. He declares the end from the beginning (Isa 46:10). Nothing surprises him. But God's sovereignty means more than that. God does whatever he wants (Ps 115:3). Whatever God wants to happen is what will happen. These things are not difficult to understand, but they can be really difficult to accept. They can really challenge our faith.

The concept of God's sovereignty makes us uncomfortable because "I've got free will, and God can't infringe on my choices, otherwise it's not free will." Well, yes, you do have free will, and no, you really don't. There is no such thing as absolute free will. There are two biblical reasons we understand that our free will is not absolute, that we cannot do anything we want to do. First, your will is constrained by your nature. You can only make choices in accordance with your nature. For example, I'm free to dunk a basketball, but I (Jon) cannot because I lack the ability in my nature. Since you are a sinner by nature, you cannot choose not to sin. It is inevitable that you will sin, regardless of how much you might not want to sin. While we might have the natural ability to make certain choices, our sin nature constricts us morally from actually doing it.

Second, the Bible teaches that God can and does override human free will when he so desires. Proverbs 21:1 says, "A king's heart is like channeled water in the LORD's hand: he directs it wherever he chooses." God looks at a human king and says, I can turn you whichever direction I want to turn you. We see an example of this in Genesis 20 when Abraham goes to Gerar, where King Abimelech reigns. As Abraham was prone to do, he lied about his wife Sarai and said she was his sister. He was fearful that the men of that region would try to kill him and take beautiful Sarai as their wife. King Abimelech likes what he sees, and so he takes Sarai to be part of his harem of wives. But God comes to Abimelech in a dream and says he is a dead man because he is about to commit adultery with another man's wife. Abimelech objects that he did not know that. And God says this: "Yes, I know that you did this with a clear conscience. I have also *kept you from sinning against me.* Therefore *I have not let you touch her*" (Gen 20:6; emphasis mine). Abimelech certainly wanted to touch her, but God would not allow him. God can override the will of a human king, and he certainly can do that with us. God can prevent you from doing certain things. He can keep you from sinning.

God is supremely sovereign: he ordains everything that happens (without being the author of evil; see Jas 1:13). Everything that happens in the world or in your life, he either causes it or permits it. While this concept makes many uncomfortable, it is actually really, really good news. God's sovereignty means that he can use evil acts to accomplish his good purposes. God can turn the suffering in our lives into something really good for his glory and our good (Rom 8:28). For example, Joseph was cruelly mistreated by his brothers and sold into slavery, but God used all of that suffering to save the people of Egypt and the members of Jacob's family. So Joseph told his brothers, "You planned evil against me; God planned it for good to bring about the present result—the survival of many people" (Gen 50:20). God is sovereign because he can take rebellious acts meant for evil and use them to bring about his good plan. Nothing will thwart or frustrate or prevent his will and plan for the world or for your life as a Christian (Eph 1:11). Therefore, the miseries in our lives are never the final word because we serve a sovereign God. This is the greatest news in the world. We see Solomon lay this out clearly in Proverbs 16:1-15.

## God Is in Complete Control

### PROVERBS 16:1-3

Proverbs 16:1-15 is one of those rare texts in Proverbs 10–31 that is a unit, where Solomon is making a sustained argument, rather than a random collection of verses (Waltke, *Proverbs, Chapters 1–15*, 5–6). The passage is a unified whole because thematically it speaks of God's sovereignty, man's responsibility, and God's sovereign rule on earth through the Messiah, symbolized here by a "king." And we know it is a unity because of key catchwords: *detestable* (both in reference to Yahweh and the Messiah; vv. 5,12), *wicked* (those who come against Yahweh and the Messiah; vv. 4,12), and *atone* or *appease* (vv. 6,14). These words link verses 1-9 about Yahweh with verses 10-15 about the Messiah. God exercises his sovereign rule on earth through the Messiah.

God is sovereign over every aspect of our lives, including our free actions and choices. He is sovereign over the areas we think we control. Proverbs 16:1 says, "The reflections [or the plans] of the heart belong to mankind, but the answer of the tongue is from the LORD." That means we make plans, but God's will is what determines if they succeed, not our ingenuity (Murphy and Hurwiler, *Proverbs*, 79). Yes, we are responsible to plan and make wise decisions, but God is the final determiner of whether they succeed or fail. Verse 3 says this reality should cause humble dependence on him: "Commit your activities [ESV, "work"] to the LORD, and your plans will be established." God's sovereignty is meant to diminish our pride, so the right response is to lean on him. These verses do not discourage planning or decision-making at all, but they do make us humbly aware of God's role in the final outcome (Longman, *Proverbs*, 328). The result belongs to God, not to you. So we don't say, "Look what I did," but rather, "Look what God did." God is the one who oversees all of this.

Verse 2 says that God's sovereignty extends to judgment: "All a person's ways seem right to him, but the LORD weighs motives." God is the sovereign judge because he judges rightly. He judges motives, not just actions. We all think we are right. As sinful human beings, we have a tendency to deceive ourselves about our own goodness (Longman, *Proverbs*, 328). If judgment belonged to us, we would certainly find ourselves innocent. But that is because we are judging ourselves against our own standard and because we typically want to see the good in ourselves. We are much harsher judges of other people than we are of ourselves. We are also masters of justifying and rationalizing our sin so that we are at peace with it. We say, "I know I shouldn't have lost my temper, but what they did to me was really awful." Or, "I know I have troubling controlling my tongue, but there's this guy at work who swears like a sailor. At least I'm better than him." We measure ourselves against our own, wrong standard that is far beneath God's standard. That is a big problem for us because God judges us against his righteous standard. And he even knows the secrets of our hearts (1 Cor 4:4-5). We might put on masks with other people, but nothing is hidden from him, not even our motives and thoughts. He even knows the times that you do a good thing but do it for your own selfish gain. That is a scary thought!

Our response should be to commit our work to him (16:3). Submit to him in all things. Waltke connects the first three verses and says,

> Since the Lord assumes ownership of the disciple's initiatives (v. 1) and he alone can evaluate the purity of the motives behind them (v. 2), the disciple should commit his planned deeds to the Lord (v. 3a) to establish them permanently, outlasting the wicked person's temporary triumphs (v. 3b). (*Proverbs, Chapters 15–31*, 11)

Now let's be clear. We are not to be determinists. We are not fatalists. That is a pagan concept. We make real choices. We are free and responsible to make wise decisions. Divine sovereignty and human responsibility go together and somehow work together. The Bible says to embrace both of them.

There are two wrong assumptions that we often make. First, we think for us to be truly free, God cannot be completely sovereign. Second, we conclude for God to be truly sovereign, we have to be robots. Both of those assumptions are dead wrong. The Bible teaches both that God is in complete control and that we make real choices that really matter and for which we are accountable.

These verses mean you should not go about doing your own work and making your own plans and then pray and ask God to make them successful (Longman, *Proverbs*, 328). Rather, you pray beforehand and allow God's Word to be the supreme guide as you make your plans. Then you work hard to do your work, submitting all of it to the Lord. Do not be paralyzed in fear forever. Act. Plan. Work. Trust. Depend. Submit. Recognize that even if your plans do not work out as you had hoped, God can use what happened for a deeper, better plan in your life that you may not see. Live in peace, recognizing that God is in control and you can sleep at night. We really misunderstand the Bible if the doctrine of God's sovereignty makes us scared and uncomfortable. It is meant to be a soft pillow at night. God has got this! You are not in control of your life, so stop fretting like you are. After all, as we sang in VBS, "He's got the whole world in his hands."

## God Will Sovereignly Judge Evil

### PROVERBS 16:4-5

Proverbs 16:4 is one of those verses that grates us. It reads, "The LORD has prepared everything for his purpose—even the wicked for the day of disaster." God brings everything to his desired end and goal, even the wicked for judgment. There are two possible ways to interpret the last line of that verse. Either it means that God has created the wicked for destruction or that even the punishment of the wicked is part of his plan. Whichever option you take, the Bible is clear that God is not the author of evil. It seems to best fit the flow of the passage if we interpret this verse as meaning that God uses human rebellion for his good purposes (as Longman argues, *Proverbs*, 329).

Again, this truth is good news because it means that nothing escapes God, including wickedness. There is no exception. Even though it may look like the wicked are getting away with it, verse 5 assures us that the prideful who do not submit to God will not go unpunished. They will not escape judgment. It is certain that there will be an ultimate reckoning and a final accountability. The wicked will not get away with it in the end. The text is not concerned with the how or the when; it is just concerned with the certainty of it. That is both frightening, since we are sinners, and comforting, since all of us have thought from time to time, "Why doesn't God do something about the evil and injustice in the world?" He will!

Also, these verses teach that people's wickedness does not frustrate or thwart the plan of God. That's also good news! He actually uses their evil to accomplish his plan. No one can stop God's plan from coming to fruition. God can even use the wickedness of evil men crucifying the Son of God to sovereignly accomplish his purpose of saving the world.

God's sovereignty is good news because it means that evil and suffering won't last forever. Evil and suffering won't win in the end; God does. If you ever find yourself uncomfortable or questioning the notion of God's supreme sovereignty, ask yourself the question, "Do I really want to live in a world where God is not supreme and in control?" If God is not in complete control, how can we be sure that what Revelation 21 says about a day with no more tears will actually come about? If he is not sovereign, we cannot be certain that he will conquer evil and stop suffering. Without the sovereignty of God, there is no way to say that there will be no more tears, sickness, pain, sorrow, or death.

## God Sovereignly Saves and Rewards Sinners Who Submit to Him

### PROVERBS 16:6-9

God must pour out his wrath on sin, but he also makes atonement for sin. All evil breaks his heart and must be judged, but he graciously judges human sin at the cross so we can escape hell. Proverbs 16:6 says, "Iniquity is atoned for by loyalty and faithfulness, and one turns from evil by the fear of the LORD." All sin is evil and an affront to God, but God graciously turns his wrath away from our sin by the blood of a substitute in our place. In the Old Testament, atonement was made by the blood of an animal, but all of the animal blood of the old covenant points to the final sacrifice of Christ on the cross for the sins of the world. He is the Lamb of God who takes away the sin of the world (John 1:29). Proverbs 16:6 indicates that atonement reveals God's covenant love—his loyalty and faithfulness—toward us (Murphy and Huwiler, *Proverbs*, 80).

We know that atonement leads to being made more like Jesus because the end of verse 6, after atonement has been made, references the fear of the Lord and turning away from evil. After you are saved by the atonement, you are then made wise and holy through fear of the Lord—dependence on him. Verse 7 says that salvation includes the defeat of your enemies. In the new covenant our enemies are not flesh and blood but rather sin, Satan, and death. Jesus has defeated them all in his death and resurrection, and we get to share in that. God's sovereignty is good news because it means that he saves us from our sin, makes us wise (see Rom 8:28-29), and defeats our enemies.

The cross of Christ clearly reveals the supreme sovereignty of God. The cross is the ultimate example of God using evil to accomplish his good plan. Acts 2:23 states, "Though [Jesus] was delivered up according to God's determined plan and foreknowledge, you used lawless people to nail him to a cross and kill him." The cross was God's plan, but lawless people hung Jesus there because they wanted him dead. Acts 2 holds both man's responsibility and God's sovereign plan together. Acts 4:27-28 says,

> *For, in fact, in this city both Herod and Pontius Pilate, with the Gentiles and the people of Israel, assembled together against your holy Servant Jesus, whom you anointed, to do whatever your hand and your will had predestined to take place.*

God predestined the cross, but men freely and wickedly chose to kill Jesus. These work together. Pontius Pilate, Herod, the Jews, and the Romans were not kicking and screaming with their hands tied behind their backs saying, "We don't want Jesus to die, but we are being forced to do this." God used the wicked choices of man to bring about his glorious, sovereign plan.

God's sovereignty is good news because it means he can take evil and use it for good. His sovereignty means that the suffering and chaos in your life is not meaningless or ultimate. You may not see how in the world what is happening to you could ever be a good thing, and you may never understand it until eternity, but you can trust that a God who did not remain distant from your suffering—but rather entered into your world, suffered even beyond what you are suffering, and died in your place—has a good reason and plan for why he is allowing all these things to happen in your life. Plus, one day he will do away with evil and suffering forever. Revelation 21–22 is on the way!

God makes sure that things work out in the end. Proverbs 16:8 is the only verse in 16:1-9 that does not mention God. We think there is a reason for that. We take Waltke's argument that the absence is intentional because he seems absent in a "morally upside-down world" (*Proverbs, Chapters 15–31*, 16). It says, "Better a little with righteousness than great income with injustice." It is better to be poor and righteous than to be rich having gotten your money in a sinful way. This verse is a qualification. Generally in Proverbs the righteous get rich and the wicked become poor, but Solomon says it doesn't always work out that way. There will be times when the wicked become enriched because of their wickedness, and there are times when the righteous will be poor because of their righteousness. In those times, you will be tempted to think God is absent and not involved, but he is still working all things together for his good purposes. There may be a season where it looks like evil is winning and things are not working out the way they should. But even though it may seem that God is not there, he is working and superintending the process. Evil can succeed temporarily and the righteous can suffer, but in the end God turns the tables.

Proverbs 16:9 ends this section on God's sovereignty by saying, "A person's heart plans his way, but the LORD determines his steps." Verse 9 caps Solomon's argument with a final statement on God's ultimate sovereignty. We make plans, but God orders our steps. He ordains all things.

## God Sovereignly Rules the World through the Messiah

### PROVERBS 16:10-15

Proverbs 16:10-15 gives the picture of the ideal, messianic king who rules as God's vice-regent on earth (see Waltke's great discussion on this in *Proverbs, Chapters 15–31*, 16–22). The word "king" is prominent, appearing in every verse but verse 11 (just as God appeared in every verse in 1-9 except 8). These verses are deliberately paired with the sovereignty of God in verses 1-9 to show that Messiah's reign mirrors the sovereign reign of God.

In the Old Testament, God's sovereignty is mediated to the people through the human king. Let's walk through this description and see God's rule through the Messiah. Verse 10 says that God's verdict is on the king's lips so that he can make infallible judgments. When the king judges, he judges rightly. He does not do anything that is unjust. When he judges, he literally speaks for God. So the Davidic king reigns and judges on earth in God's stead, upholding and executing justice. This is ultimately fulfilled in Jesus (see Acts 2:25-36).

Proverbs 16:11 gives an example of Yahweh's justice, which is mediated through the king, when it talks about honest scales. This advises against an unethical business practice where sellers would cheat the buyer by changing up the weight system, perhaps by having heavy counterweights for buying and lighter ones for selling (Deut 25:13). Solomon says that God oversees that and is concerned about people not being cheated. The way God oversees it on earth is through the human king. The messianic king will make sure there is equity in his kingdom. The church, as an outpost of the kingdom, should model fairness, equity, and righteousness to the world.

Verse 12 shows how and why the king must uphold justice. Similarly to verse 11, it indicates that wicked behavior is detestable to any king. Those who practice wickedness—like the merchants with unfair weights—are abhorrent to the king (just like the wicked of v. 5 are repulsive to Yahweh). It is detestable to the king because his dynasty—his throne—will only last if he reigns in righteousness and justice. This is the point of Proverbs. Solomon attempts to train his son to be the ideal king who sets up the messianic kingdom by righteousness. Solomon wants to be a Deuteronomy 6 parent who trains his son in the law so that his son can become a Deuteronomy 17 king who is a man of the law. The problem is Solomon and all of his descendants fail, and this leads to the hope in Israel for a king who embodies the wisdom of Proverbs

(Isa 11:1-5) and who can finally establish the eternal, Davidic kingdom. This is fulfilled in the Messiah Jesus.[24] Jesus sets up a kingdom where there is no wickedness or injustice. He establishes his eternal kingdom in righteousness by judging the wicked. Goldsworthy notes this as well:

> Jesus comes as the only king of Israel to rule perfectly according to the ideals of kingship set out in Deuteronomy 17:14-20. He is the true son of David, thus fitting that role in a way that sinful Solomon could never do. (*Tree of Life*, 125)

Since the kingdom is established in righteousness, kings are pleased with those who speak rightly (Prov 16:13). The author here encapsulates all of the activities of the kingdom: work, actions, and speech. The king is to govern all of these actions to establish the kingdom. He does this by carrying out judgment, including capital punishment (v. 14). The wise person appeases the king because his favor is like a new creation blessing (v. 15). Thus, the king—fulfilled in Messiah Jesus—is to be judge and punisher. Life and death are in his hands just like they are in Yahweh's hands. The king wields life and death on Yahweh's behalf. Jesus is both Savior and Judge, so we should bow the knee to him.

We see this same picture of Yahweh ruling on earth through his Messiah in Psalm 2. This rule includes wrath against those who stand against the Messiah and Yahweh. The wise person kisses the Son so that he does not become angry (Ps 2:12). As in Proverbs 16:15, blessed are all those who take refuge in the Messiah!

## Conclusion

Our response to the sovereign Lord and his Messiah is to bow the knee. Why? We bow to the King because God's sovereign plan for the world is centered on the Messiah. God's sovereign plan is to exalt the Son and through him to redeem persons from every people group on earth (see Rev 5; 7). God's plan will not be stopped, so do not take a stand against it. Rather, embrace it. It is foolish to attempt to live outside the sovereignty of God. Submit to the King! Anyone who repents of sin and believes in Jesus will be saved and be part of God's plan for the world. For some of you this may be scary, or you might have a hard time agreeing with it, but deep in your heart you believe this and are comforted by

---

[24] This is the thesis of my dissertation. See Jonathan Akin, "Theology of Future Hope."

it. After all, we sing about this all the time: "He's got the whole world in his hands," and "From life's first cry to final breath, Jesus commands my destiny. No pow'r of hell, no scheme of man, can ever pluck me from His hand" (Getty and Townend, "In Christ Alone"). That is good news!

## Reflect and Discuss

1. Why do you think people have such a difficult time accepting the supreme sovereignty of God?
2. What do verses like Proverbs 21:1 and Genesis 20:6 make you feel?
3. How can we see God's sovereignty as good and comforting news?
4. In what ways can you practically commit your plans to the Lord?
5. In what ways do we try to rationalize or justify our sin?
6. Why do we like to play the comparison game rather than evaluate ourselves according to God's standard?
7. How does God's sovereignty help us understand and answer the problem of evil and suffering in the world?
8. How can we as sinners escape the wrath of God?
9. What does it look like in daily life to bow the knee to King Jesus?
10. How do the songs we sing and the prayers we pray reveal that we actually believe in God's sovereignty?

# Is "Train Up a Child" a Promise?

## PROVERBS 22:6

**Main Idea:** Not letting your child always have his or her way is a form of evangelism.

---

**I. This Verse Has Produced a Lot of Guilt in Parents.**
**II. This Verse Is a Warning to Correct Your Children.**
**III. This Verse Tells Us Our Children's Greatest Need Is the Good News about Jesus.**

---

A few years ago a young lady very close to our family "came out" as a lesbian. When that happened her parents, who are faithful Christians, questioned their parenting, saying, "Where did WE go wrong?" They felt responsible for her decision as if it were their fault.

Many Christian parents feel a crushing guilt when their children do not "turn out right." They ask questions like, "What did we do wrong? What else could we have done?" What is more problematic is that the guilt so many Christian parents feel finds its root in the Bible. After all, Proverbs 22:6 states, "Start a youth out on his way; even when he grows old he will not depart from it."

### This Verse Has Produced a Lot of Guilt in Parents

This verse has produced much shame in Christian parents because it seems to promise that if parents will start their children out on the right way when they are young, when they are grown they will continue to live the right way. On the other hand, if you do not raise your children in the right way, they will live the wrong kind of life. The logic seems clear and straightforward from the Scriptures. How your children turn out reveals whether or not you started them out right. Therefore, if you have grown children who are ungodly or did not turn out right, the obvious conclusion is that you did not raise them properly. So added to the heartache of a child not walking with the Lord is the biblical condemnation of your parenting. You blew it. You are the one who messed up.

But is that really what Proverbs 22:6 teaches? Some propose a solution to this apparent dilemma to try to resolve the problem for Christian parents. The solution, they say, is that Proverbs 22:6 is not a promise but rather a general rule of thumb. Longman argues for this solution. He writes,

> It sounds like a promise but a proverb does not give a promise. The book of Proverbs advises its hearers in ways that are most likely to lead them to desired consequences if all things are equal. It is much more likely that a child will be a responsible adult if trained in the right path. . . . The point is that this proverb encourages parents to train their children, but does not guarantee if they do so their children will never stray. (*Proverbs*, 405)

Thus, the argument goes, all things being equal, the usual outcome of life will be that if you raise your children the right way, they will live the right kind of life, but that is not always the case. So can we fix this problem—and ease our consciences—by saying it is not a promise?

I find this approach to Proverbs—and any portion of Scripture—extremely problematic. Nowhere else would we say of a biblical passage that it is mostly true but not always true. Some will object—like Dr. Longman, a wonderful Old Testament scholar—that we have to approach each genre of the Bible in its own unique way, and this is the way wisdom literature works. But is this correct? Do we want to say, for example, that if you trust in the Lord will all your heart, do not lean on your own understanding, and in all your ways acknowledge him, then he will *usually* direct your paths? We believe there is a better way to understand Proverbs. The biblical proverbs are promises that are generally true now, but are always ultimately true in the end (Dever, *The Message*, 510). You can count on them.

So what are we to make of this specific verse then? Does it mean that if I do right by my children now by taking them to church, reading the Bible to them, and leading them in their prayers, I am guaranteed they will turn out right? Does it mean if my children do not turn out right as adults, somehow it is my fault because I did not train them right? What if it is too late, and I did not start them out right, and now they are grown? While this verse is a promise, we think the accepted understanding of it is based on a bad interpretation that showed up in the translation of it. We need to see that Proverbs 22:6 is actually the reverse side of a promise. Here is what we mean.

## This Verse Is a Warning to Correct Your Children

There is a different way to understand Proverbs 22:6 that we have found extremely helpful. Instead of being a promise that if you do right, your children will turn out right, it is a reverse promise—a warning—that if you do not correct your children when they are young, they will run amok wanting their own way as an adult.

Almost every English translation of this verse adds a word to the text that is not in the Hebrew. The English says something along the lines of "train a child in the right way" or the "way he should go." The word "right" or "should" is not in the Hebrew. Literally the verse should be rendered, "Train a child in his way, and when he is old he will not depart from it" (Murphy and Huwiler, *Proverbs*, 109). In the Hebrew, there is no descriptor or qualifier on "way," so English translations add one like "right" or "should." They do this to aid in the translation by making an interpretation of the verse, but we think it is better to take the text as is. After all, the translation that puts the blame on the parents does not fit with the rest of Proverbs, where a son makes his own wise or foolish choices and is held accountable for them. The young man is responsible for how he interacts with the gang of his peers or whether he receives the advances of the immoral woman (2:1-22) (Waltke, *Proverbs, Chapters 15–31*, 206).

The question would be then, if we take the literal translation, what does it mean to "Start a youth out on his way"? There are two options (Garrett, *Proverbs*, 288). First, train a youth according to his nature or bent. Each of your children is different, thus you must become an expert on each one and figure out the best way to communicate and teach each one. This is a perfectly acceptable interpretation, but it is not the one that best fits the flow of Proverbs because Proverbs says our nature is broken. Proverbs teaches that foolishness is in our hearts, and it needs to be corrected (20:9; 22:15). Waltke points out that the other six references to the "youth" in Proverbs characterize his way as foolish (1:4; 7:7; 22:15; 23:13; 29:15) (*Proverbs, Chapters 15–31*, 205).

The clear warning of the Proverbs—despite the messaging we receive from Disney movies—is that following your own heart or your own "way" is the epitome of foolishness. Doing what is right in your own eyes leads to death (14:12). Proverbs teaches that God gives young people to parents who are supposed to correct this condition. You see, the best interpretation of Proverbs 22:6 is sort of sarcastic: Let a child have his way when he is young, and when he is old, he will continue to insist on having his way (Clifford, *Proverbs*, 197). In other words, if you start by letting a young person have his own way, he will continue on that dead-end road when he grows up. Thus, this verse is the flip side of a promise; it is a warning that parents must correct their children's foolish character before it is set. Children left to their own devices will destroy themselves.

Two other verses help us to see why this is the right interpretation in the flow of Proverbs. Proverbs 22:15 says, "Foolishness is bound to the heart of a youth; a rod of discipline will separate it from him." And 29:15 states, "A rod of correction imparts wisdom, but a youth left to himself is a disgrace to his mother." Children do not have to be taught to do wrong because it is already in their hearts, but they do need to be corrected and shown what is right. One day my (Jon's) young son wanted a toy his sister was playing with, and when she didn't give it to him, he reached up and yanked her hair. I can assure you that he had never seen any one of us do that before. He had never seen me pull my wife's hair because I wanted the TV remote. Where did he get that behavior? He got it from his sin nature! All people need discipline and correction to do right, and you harm your children if you do not correct them.

Proverbs 29:15 implies that directing and correcting your children will take different forms over time: spanking ("a rod") and reproof (not leaving a youth to himself). Spanking can be the only way to get through to a young child sometimes because all the reasoning in the world will not help. An ancient Egyptian proverb said of young boys that they have ears on their backsides (Waltke, *Proverbs, Chapters 1–15*, 574). A study at Calvin College actually shows that kids spanked between the ages of two and six earned better grades in school and had a sunnier outlook on life (Black, "Spanking Makes Kids Better"). There is no room for physical abuse of children, but the Bible is also clear that a lack of discipline is a way to abuse your children. However, a verbal reprimand almost always works better as children age, and they should be able to heed a verbal rebuke as they grow in maturity.

The main point is clear. Proverbs says that left to themselves, children will choose the wrong and destructive path. Human beings are not innocent, basically good, or wise. The parental task is to intervene before folly is set and our kids walk off toward hell. Leaving your young child to make his or her own decisions without correction from you is foolish. Leaving teens of the opposite sex alone together is foolish. Letting a four-year-old have his way all the time is foolish. We are to heed the warning of Proverbs 22:6—don't leave your children to their own way or you might watch them march straight into hell!

Proverbs 22:6 moves against the buddy-parent philosophy of so many. If you allow your child to be self-centered now, they will be later (and no one will like them!). You have to say no sometimes. Many times! Do not turn your child into a brat like Veruca Salt from *Willy Wonka and the Chocolate Factory*, who always gets her way but is a miserable person. If you let your children have their way without correction, it will be hurtful to them and to you.

You have to discipline. You have to hold them accountable. You cannot say yes all the time. They don't need to always get their way. I know the world says that repressing things is harmful, but the world's wisdom is foolish. There is an insightful article in *The Atlantic* by Lori Gottlieb where a teacher indicted the inability of parents to just say no.

> Another teacher I spoke with, a 58-year-old mother of grown children who has been teaching kindergarten for 17 years, told me she feels that parents are increasingly getting in the way of their children's development. "I see the way their parents treat them," she said, "and there's a big adjustment when they get into my class. It's good for them to realize that they aren't the center of the world, that sometimes other people's feelings matter more than theirs at a particular moment—but it only helps if they're getting the same limit-setting at home. If not, they become impulsive, because they're not thinking about anybody else." This same teacher—who asked not to be identified, for fear of losing her job—says she sees many parents who think they're setting limits, when actually, they're just being wishy-washy. "A kid will say, 'Can we get ice cream on the way home?' And the parent will say, 'No, it's not our day. Ice-cream day is Friday.' Then the child will push and negotiate, and the parent, who probably thinks negotiating is 'honoring her child's opinion,' will say, 'Fine, we'll get ice cream today, but don't ask me tomorrow, because the answer is no!'" The teacher laughed. "Every year, parents come to me and say, 'Why won't my child listen to me? Why won't she take no for an answer?' And I say, 'Your child won't take no for an answer, because the answer is never no!'" (Gottlieb, "How to Land Your Kid in Therapy")

The main point of Proverbs 22:6 is that the parental task is to intervene and correct your children's foolishness before it becomes set later in life. If we do not, the results will be disastrous in all kinds of ways. It will lead to selfishness, relational issues, impulse-control problems, an inability to submit to a boss's authority, and unwillingness to accept the consequences of actions. This verse reminds us of "Twelve Rules for Raising Delinquent Children," attributed to the Houston Police Department:[25]

1. Begin with infancy to give the child everything he wants. In this way he will grow to believe the world owes him a living.
2. When he picks up bad words, laugh at him. This will make him think he's cute. It will also encourage him to pick up "cuter phrases" that will blow off the top of your head later.
3. Never give him any spiritual training. Wait until he is 21, and then let him "decide for himself."
4. Avoid the use of the word "wrong." It may develop a guilt complex. This will condition him to believe later, when he is arrested for stealing a car, that society is against him and he is being persecuted.
5. Pick up everything he leaves lying around—books, shoes, clothes. Do everything for him so that he will be experienced in throwing all responsibility on others.
6. Let him read any printed matter he can get his hands on. Be careful that the silverware and drinking glasses are sterilized, but don't worry about his mind feasting on garbage.
7. Quarrel frequently in the presence of your children. In this way they will not be too shocked when the home is broken up later.
8. Give the child all the spending money he wants. Never let him earn his. Why should he have things as tough as you did?
9. Satisfy his every craving for food, drink, and comfort. See that every sensual desire is gratified. Denial may lead to harmful frustration.
10. Take his part against neighbors, teachers, policemen. They are all prejudiced against your child.

[25] "Twelve Rules for Raising Delinquent Children," accessed October 13, 2015. There are many variations of this anonymous and often-quoted list, but it is historically attributed to the Juvenile Division of the Houston Police Department. For more information, see http://www.snopes.com/glurge/12rules.asp.

11. When he gets into real trouble, apologize to yourself by saying, "I never could do anything with him!"
12. Prepare yourself for a life of grief. You'll surely have it.

## This Verse Tells Us Our Children's Greatest Need Is the Good News about Jesus

Proverbs 22:6 ultimately demonstrates that our children's greatest need is the good news about Jesus. Our role is not simply behavior modification that will turn our children into Pharisees, or into rebels when the bribes for good behavior and threats toward bad behavior go away. No, our goal for our children is life transformation through Jesus. Proverbs is clear that discipline is evangelism: "Don't withhold discipline from a youth; if you punish him with a rod, he will not die. Punish him with a rod, and you will rescue his life from Sheol" (23:13-14).

Discipline is a rescue mission. We are to step in to rescue our kids from hell and the path that leads there. If we do not correct our children, they will not recognize their sin or that they will be held accountable. Some Christian parents misunderstand grace as calling for a laissez-faire attitude toward discipline, but that is deadly. Loving discipline shows our children that there are consequences and accountability for sinful actions, and it demonstrates that there is a standard of right and wrong—one that they have fallen short of, and thus they need a Savior.

Discipline is not simply meting out punishment; it is an opportunity for a gospel conversation. We want to avoid moralism in favor of gospel-driven discipline where you talk to your child in the discipline moment, confessing that your love for them is unconditional—as is God's love for them—and you are a sinner in need of God's grace as much as they are. I try when I discipline my children to identify with them that I know what it is like to be selfish, frustrated, or angry, and that is why I am so thankful for Jesus, who offers forgiveness for my sins. And if you have grown children and think it's too late to get through to them because of how you royally messed up, perhaps a confession of your sins in parenting, your appeal to them for forgiveness, and your confidence in the mercy of God might go a long way in bringing healing and transformation.

## Conclusion

Proverbs 22:6 should not cause guilt in parents as much as it should cause vigilance. We are not to be buddy-buddy with our kids in the way the world says. We are on a rescue mission where we must lovingly correct our children because there is foolishness in their hearts. So let us heed the warning of Proverbs 22:6 and graciously correct our children, so that in glory we can say with our Lord Jesus, "Here I am with the children God gave me" (Heb 2:13).

## Reflect and Discuss

1. Why do so many Christians parents feel guilt when their children don't turn out right? What part of that guilt is well founded? What is unfounded?
2. Are the Proverbs promises? Why or why not?
3. Though this study doesn't take it as the main interpretation, in what ways do we need to parent each child differently? What should remain the same?
4. How should the "sarcastic" interpretation of Proverbs 22:6 affect our parenting? What does it mean we should do practically?
5. Are we responsible to God for how our children turn out, or are they responsible for their own choices? Explain.
6. What are some unusual or wrong things you have seen your children do that they did not learn from you? What does that say about their nature?
7. How should your discipline of your children change over time?
8. What stands out to you in the Houston Police Department's list?
9. Discipline can seem like such a negative thing. Why does Proverbs say it is loving and evangelistic?
10. What does it mean to have a gospel conversation with your children when you discipline them?

# Does Proverbs Contradict Itself?

## PROVERBS 26:4-5

**Main Idea:** Wisdom is the discernment to know when to correct someone and when to let it go.

---

**I. Don't Stoop to the Fool's Level by Playing His Game.**
**II. Correct a Fool So He Doesn't Think He Is Wise.**
**III. Wisdom Is the Discernment to Know When to Correct.**
**IV. The Power to Grow in Discernment Is in Christ, Not in You.**

---

Life is full of contradictions, and many of them are hilarious! Dolly Parton says, "It costs a fortune to look this cheap." Yogi Berra said, "No wonder no one comes to this restaurant anymore, you can't ever get a table." My (Jon's) daughter Maddy wants to be fiercely independent. She wants to cook her own eggs, take out the trash, and clean the windows of our house; she also wants me to carry her up the stairs when it's bedtime.

We are fallen creatures, so we all have our own contradictions and inconsistencies. But it's one thing for us to have contradictions; it's another thing to charge God with them! You can Google "contradictions in the Bible" and find tons of lists where people try to point out that the Bible says one thing in one place and the opposite thing in another place. It is popular to charge Christianity with contradictions. People want to show the Bible is inconsistent so they can prove it is not God's Word but rather a human book, and therefore they do not have to take its claims—like Jesus being the only way to heaven (John 14:6)—seriously. These so-called contradictions are an attempt to turn people away from the faith. To be honest, most of them are easily addressed. However, there are some instances where it seems like the Bible does say one thing and then another.

We will look at a frequently cited one here in Proverbs 26:4-5. Even in ancient times, the Talmud noted an "apparent" contradiction in this text (see discussion in Longman, *Proverbs*, 464). The passage reads,

> *Don't answer a fool according to his foolishness*
> *or you'll be like him yourself.*

*Answer a fool according to his foolishness*
*or he'll become wise in his own eyes.*

Don't answer a fool . . . answer a fool. Is the Bible contradictory, and therefore untrue? Absolutely not! So what do these verses mean, because they do seem to contradict? Some try to solve the dilemma by saying Proverbs are not timeless or absolutes (see discussion in Waltke, *Proverbs, Chapters 15–31*, 348–50). They are just general rules that are relevant to a given situation. We disagree. Proverbs are absolute truths! They may seem to contradict, but this is only an apparent contradiction, not a real one. When we look at these verses for what they really mean, we will see they do not contradict each other at all.

The sages who collected Solomon's proverbs were not stupid men; they were wise men. Why would they put these two verses right next to each other? If they were trying to get away with something—like putting a contradiction in the Bible—they would separate these verses and hope people did not notice it. The reason the sages put Solomon's proverbs together like this is because they want us to read them together! Together—not separately—they give the true picture of reality on how to discern a situation and to know when to correct a fool.

## Don't Stoop to the Fool's Level by Playing His Game

There are some types of fools and situations where you should not rebuke, correct, confront, or answer. Wisdom is the discernment to read the person or the situation and know if that is the case. How do you know if you should not correct or answer someone? If your answer to them will require stooping to their level, avoid answering them.[26] If your answer or attempt at correction will do no good, if it will drain your energy and not get anyone anywhere, it's best to remain quiet (Longman, *Proverbs*, 212). Proverbs 9:7-9 says something similar:

*The one who corrects a mocker will bring abuse on himself;*
*the one who rebukes the wicked will get hurt.*
*Don't rebuke a mocker, or he will hate you;*
*rebuke the wise, and he will love you.*
*Instruct the wise, and he will be wiser still;*
*teach the righteous, and he will learn more.*

---

[26] Garrett calls this dealing "with a fool on his own terms" in *Proverbs*, 212.

If, despite your best efforts, the person will not be corrected, then stay quiet. If you only hurt yourself by playing his game, stay quiet. There are people who will ask you questions but do not really want to hear your answers because they think they know it all. Do not waste your valuable time thinking through and answering their questions, e-mails, text messages, or Facebook posts.

Proverbs 26:4 also teaches us not to answer a fool in a foolish way.[27] Do not lie, mock, or speak unkindly just to get your point across or to bust them. Even though you think you just have to win the argument and shut them up, it would still be wrong to exaggerate to make your point. Don't fight fire with fire; otherwise you are on the same level with the fool and guilty before God. And no honor is given to the fool (v. 1) (Murphy and Huwiler, *Proverbs*, 129) because he is under judgment.

There are some people you should not answer, correct, or engage in conversation. Do not play her game or play by his rules. If you are going to answer them, change up the rules! For example, when doing evangelism, you need to recognize comments or questions that will sidetrack the conversation and do your best to bypass them. Someone says, "Well, a thousand years ago Christians killed people in the Crusades; why would I want to be a Christian?" I could spend a lot of time answering that and get off track. Or I could kindly say, "Why don't we discuss that another day and right now keep the focus on what Jesus did?" Keep the focus on Jesus, not objections about obscure manuscripts, battles that took place a millennia ago, or why there are so many different denominations. Do not let people deflect their own conviction or their need to deal with Jesus by getting off into tangential and unprofitable arguments.

But this is true in any type of conversation, dialogue, or relational interaction. In any family interaction, church relationship, office dynamic, blog post, or any kind of situation where advice is being given to solve people's problems, you can be dragged into playing a game that you don't need to play. Refuse to play the fool's game with anyone! You need to be aware of whether or not you should engage the person. It is so easy for us to get sucked into responding on Facebook or Twitter or at the water cooler because we want to be seen as right. That leads to a long, drawn-out argument and then stalemate. Sometimes you just need

---

[27] Waltke argues that this is how one stoops to the fool's level by answering insult with insult (*Proverbs, Chapters 15–31*, 349).

to let it go. As sportswriter and commentator Skip Bayless says, "Don't press 'send.'"

One time a man whose son was dating a Hindu tried to convince me that Jesus would have dated non-Christians. He was not trying to have an actual discussion; he was just justifying his son's behavior. That is not even worth responding to. Do not let someone get a rise out of you. Don't get into never-ending arguments where you have to have the last word in your marriage or in a friendship.

However, do not use Proverbs 26:4 as an excuse to chicken out because there is also a time to answer. It is certainly easier to step back and not engage in many situations. Most people don't like to ruffle feathers. But you can't use verse 4 as an excuse to chicken out. Sometimes we are called to correct a fool so that he does not think he is wise (v. 5).

## Correct a Fool So He Doesn't Think He Is Wise

Proverbs 26:5 says that there are some fools and situations that should be confronted, answered, or corrected. Don't stay quiet or be passive in those cases because if you don't answer them, they'll be wise in their own eyes, and verse 12 says that's destructive: "Do you see a person who is wise in his own eyes? There is more hope for a fool than for him." Letting people think they are wise when they are not is deadly. Proverbs repeatedly warns those who think they are wise that they are headed toward judgment. Letting your children indiscriminately run through parking lots without correcting them is foolish and dangerous. You would say something because you do not want them to get hit by a car. In the same way, there are people around you who have patterns of sin and foolishness in their lives that will ruin them, and God has put you in their lives to lovingly say something!

For some, it will do good to correct them because they might listen! Some might listen immediately. Others might get mad initially, storm off, and not talk to you for a while. But then, after having some time to mull it over, they will come to the realization that you were right and only said something because you cared for them.

Also, there are times when there are others around who will be hurt by the person's foolishness, so you cannot stay silent because others might be led astray. Do not tolerate foolishness in such a way that others watching and listening think the person is right. So lovingly correct them—show their folly—without lowering yourself, if it will do that person or others good. If you remain passive, it will look like you are giving your approval of their "wisdom."

The motivation of verse 5 is not you telling someone the way it is. Some people like to brag, "I'm not unkind; I just tell it like it is." No, you are a jerk. There is a big difference between being a truth-teller and acting like a jerk. The proper motivation is for their good. If we remain passive, they might think they are smart because no one is correcting them. This is true in matters like evangelism where people might be saying false things about God, in marital issues where a coworker is giving ungodly advice to someone like "get out of the marriage," or in personal struggles where people just do not see things clearly. Speak up in those situations! But it's also true in "little" matters like spending, laziness, or bad thinking on a specific subject. You will regret not speaking up when you had the chance, especially if they keep hurting themselves.

### Wisdom Is the Discernment to Know When to Correct

Solomon's point is this: Wisdom is the discernment to read people and situations and know when to respond and when to stay silent. Wisdom is growing in the knowledge of when to correct someone and when not to correct them. You grow in discerning the outcome. You come to know when answering will help him or when you are just playing his game. Daily life is filled with both situations, and wisdom is the ability to assess them and decide what to do. Goldsworthy writes,

> Thus, one situation is best handled by refusing to play the fool's game with him, while another demands some rejoinder to his folly. Life is full of both kinds of situations. . . . One must assess each situation carefully and decide whether to engage the fool or disengage from his company. (*Tree of Life*, 165)

Wisdom means growing in that kind of decision-making.

Proverbs has taught us that Wisdom is not a thing; Wisdom is a person—Jesus of Nazareth. So growth in him does not just mean growth in not sinning as much, although it does include that (Moore, *Walking the Line*). It also means growth in discernment! You begin to know whether answering will get you nowhere or will help the person or others around them. This is what growing in Christlikeness looks like. You are able to perceive motivations and outcomes. You are able to let things go and remain silent when you should. You are able to be bold and speak up when you should.

## The Power to Grow in Discernment Is in Christ, Not in You

If you do not grow in this kind of discernment, it reveals you have a problem with Jesus. You are not walking with him as you should because of some idol in your life. If you are too cowardly to confront, your idol may be self-approval or pride. If you are a jerk who loves to tell people off, your idol might be self-justification. But if you are not able to read a situation and know when to speak up or let it lie, you are not growing in Christlikeness.

After all, Jesus amazed people with this ability. He knew when to stay silent because a reply would do no good. And he knew when to correct. He could read people and situations and know exactly how to respond or not respond.

For example, in Matthew 15:1-9 the Pharisees challenged Jesus because his disciples did not follow the rules for hand washing. Jesus turned around and swatted them for using their rules to justify not honoring their moms and dads. He revealed their hypocrisy so that they would not be wise in their own eyes or the eyes of the crowd. In Matthew 16 Peter foolishly rebuked Jesus concerning the cross, and Jesus answered him rather directly to correct his folly, "Get behind me, Satan!" (v. 23). What Peter was saying was satanic, so Jesus corrected him.

Jesus also knew when to not play people's games. The chief priests tried to challenge Jesus's authority in the temple by asking by what authority he did what he did. Jesus knew their game, so he asked a follow-up question about John's baptism that the priests refused to answer. He refused to answer fools according to their folly. Matthew 21:27 says, "So they answered Jesus, 'We don't know.' And he said to them, 'Neither will I tell you by what authority I do these things.'" He refused to play their game.

Jesus knew when people were testing him. In Matthew 22:15-17 the Pharisees sought to entrap Jesus in his words by asking about taxes. But Matthew 22:18 tells us, "Perceiving their malicious intent, Jesus said, 'Why are you testing me, hypocrites?'" Jesus discerned the situation and knew how to answer about taxes, the resurrection of the dead, the greatest commandment, and David's Son so that Matthew 22:46 says, "No one was able to answer him at all, and from that day no one dared to question him anymore."

Jesus knows how to read people and situations. He knows when to answer, how to answer, and when to stay silent. After all, he did not answer the Jewish leaders' questions at his trial (Matt 26:63), he refused to speak to Herod (Luke 23:9), and he amazed Pilate by not answering him just before he was crucified (Mark 15:5).

## Conclusion

Jesus grew in wisdom (Luke 2:52), which means he grew in the ability to read people and situations. Growth in Christlikeness will mean growth in the area of discernment. Jesus produces this in his followers. We see this with the deacon Stephen at his trial; the opponents could not resist Stephen's wisdom (Acts 6:10). So if you are not growing in this ability, confess that to God, repent of it, and go to Jesus. Cry out to him, "Lord, show me where I lack discernment. Judge me in this and give me wisdom" (Moore, *Walking the Line*). Lack of discernment might be because you are not a believer and need to trust Jesus for the first time. It might be because you are a believer but not walking with Christ in this area of your life. But the answer is the same for all—repent and believe!

## Reflect and Discuss

1. What are some apparent contradictions that people point out about the Bible?
2. How would you answer those contradictions?
3. Why do people like to try to point out biblical contradictions?
4. How is Proverbs 26:4-5 not an actual contradiction?
5. In what kinds of situations and ways do we feel the temptation to stoop to the fool's level and play his game?
6. What are some clues that will help you read a situation and decide whether or not to respond?
7. Why do we usually tend toward passivity in these interactions rather than engagement?
8. Have you ever answered someone and regretted it? Describe what happened and what you learned from it.
9. Have you ever answered someone and it went well? Describe what happened and what you learned from it.
10. What are some things that you should do if you aren't growing in discernment?

# The Proverbs Code: What Do All These Numbers Mean?

## PROVERBS 30:1-33

**Main Idea:** Wisdom is the way the world works, and that can only be perceived through God's Son.

---

**I. Look to Christ for Wisdom (30:1-9).**
**II. Look to Christ for Salvation from Sin (30:10-14).**
**III. Look at the World through the Lens of Christ (30:15-33).**
   A. Warnings about uncontrolled appetites
   B. Instruction in wisdom

---

My (Jon's) dad taught me and instilled many things in me, but how to fix things was definitely not one of them. He is mechanically challenged. Not having that skill in my own life did not prove to be a problem until Ashley and I started having children. So Ashley's dad, Jimmy, who is really good at fixing things, began to try to teach me how to do certain things. He and I put together all kinds of things like cribs, rockers, and swing sets. Inevitably what would happen is that, even though Jimmy is good at putting things together, we would rush into the project, put it together, and then notice that we had made a mistake somewhere along the way. For example, we put a sofa table together, and when we finished we noticed the legs of the table were facing outward rather than inward like they were supposed to. At that point, we had to go back and actually look at the instructions for the first time, see where we went wrong, and start again the right way. We had to go the manufacturer's manual to see how it really worked so we could do the job in accordance with the furniture's design.

Proverbs 30 gets at this kind of thing in the grand scheme of life when it comes to wisdom and your way in the world. There is a pattern to the world. There is a certain way that it works, and you need to live according to the pattern because that's wise. Wisdom is the skill to live according to that pattern. To understand what that skill is, you have to go the Maker—the one who created the world—to see how the world works. That is what Proverbs 30 is all about, and it shows us three important truths.

## Look to Christ for Wisdom

### PROVERBS 30:1-9

The author of this passage is Agur the son of Jakeh (v. 1). We do not know who Agur is because this is the only place he is mentioned in the Bible. Some do not take this as a proper name but rather interpret the meaning of the names as "I am a sojourner (Agur) and son of Yahweh the Holy (Jakeh)" since Jakeh is shorthand for "Yahweh the Holy" (see Skehan, *Studies*, 27–45). That is a possible interpretation. Regardless, the author is a follower of the one true God. Not only do we not know exactly who Agur is, but we also do not know the recipients to whom he is writing: Ithiel and Ucal.[28] What we do know is that the Holy Spirit of God breathed out these words for us.

Agur starts the passage in verses 2-3 by claiming to be ignorant:

> *I am more stupid than any other person, and I lack a human's ability to understand. I have not gained wisdom, and I have no knowledge of the Holy One.*

He confesses that he is limited when it comes to wisdom. But Proverbs repeatedly indicates that humility is the first step to wisdom. To become wise, you need to recognize that you are not and look to God for it.

Just as Solomon recognized that wisdom begins with fear of the Lord, Agur recognizes that wisdom begins with God—with knowledge of the Holy One. Not only does wisdom reside with God, but it also resides with God's Son. Agur asks a series of rhetorical questions in verse 4 to indicate humanity's finitude and to point out that wisdom belongs to the Almighty Creator and his Son. No human has gone up to heaven and come back down. No human can gather the wind in his hands. No human created the world. We read this from a different vantage point than Agur. Agur asks the name of the son, but he does not know it. We do know it—Jesus Christ! We know that Jesus is the God-Man who came down from heaven as wisdom for us. Goldsworthy points out,

> Agur's question in verse 4 is answered directly in Jesus's reply to Nicodemus in John 3:13, "No one has ever gone into

---

[28] There are many thorny issues in the superscript. For a good discussion see Waltke, *Proverbs, Chapters 15–31*, 454–67.

heaven except the one who came from heaven—the Son of man." (*Tree of Life*, 186)

The point is that God's Son is the one who has access to God's wisdom because he came from heaven, so look to God and his Son for wisdom.

How do you do that? I think verses 5-6 give us the answer:

*Every word of God is pure; he is a shield to those who take refuge in him. Don't add to his words, or he will rebuke you, and you will be proved a liar.*

God reveals this unknowable wisdom to us in his Word, so we must submit to it. For us to know wisdom, God must reveal it to us, and he has in his Word. His Word is true, a shield to those who trust in him, and sufficient. Don't add to it. There is a warning to those who do. Don't sit in judgment on God's Word as if it's lacking something. That was the problem for humanity in Genesis 3. They did not see God's word as sufficient for their lives. We do the same thing. We know what the Bible says, but we think our ideas in certain situations are better. We often come to Scripture and act like God forgot to put the exception clause in there for our case. People will say, "Well, I know what God says about divorce, but you don't know my husband," or, "Well, I know what God says about parenting, but you don't know my children," or, "Well, I know what the Bible says about submission to authority, but you don't know my boss." We think our case is the exception that somehow just got left out of the Bible. Proverbs warns that God will rebuke you and prove you to be a liar if you act like the Word is not enough for you. In fact, Revelation threatens a curse to those who do this (Rev 22:18-19).

Agur then turns around and does for himself what he has recommended for others. He looks to the Lord for wisdom. He humbly depends upon God for wisdom by asking for it in prayer (Longman, *Proverbs*, 524–25). James 1:5 says that if we lack wisdom, we should ask God for it in prayer and he will give it to us generously. Agur prays for wisdom in Proverbs 30:7-9. Agur asks two things for his life that he knows he can't produce in his own power. He is saying that in his own power he can't be an honest or content person. He says he will depend on God to grant those things because his own human effort can't save him from deception and greed (Waltke, *Proverbs, Chapters 15–31*, 478). We learn from this that the power does not lie with us.

The two things that he asks God for are honesty and contentment. The main emphasis is on finances, and it seems that the subject of deception introduces the subject of money because money can lie to you. Garrett argues that the two requests are actually (1) do not give me poverty and (2) do not give me wealth, and the reference to deception refers to poverty and wealth (Garrett, *Proverbs*, 238). Poverty lies to you: "God can't help you. God won't provide for you. You need to help yourself." And riches lie to you: "You don't need God because everything is good in your life. You are doing a great job by yourself. Depend on you not him."

Agur pleads with the Lord to feed him with the food that he needs. Give me my daily bread. Let me have just enough for my needs to be met. Help me to be content with that and not greedy for more. Why? He gives the reasons for his supplication. First, if he has too much, he will deny the Lord (v. 9). After all, the reason God gave Israel daily manna from heaven in the wilderness was to teach them to depend on him and not on financial provision. He wanted them to learn that man lives by the word of God, not by bread. In Deuteronomy 8 God says that the purpose of the manna in the wilderness was that Israel was about to enter a land flowing with milk and honey, and when they got to that abundance they were going to forget God and think they did this on their own. That is what Proverbs 30 is warning us about. If you have too much, you won't depend on God. It's not saying that all rich people are greedy or profaners, but it is saying that wealth is so deceptive that it is hard for the rich to recognize their need of God.

Second, if he has too little, he will be tempted to steal (v. 9). If he is poor, he will be tempted to cheat on his tax return, misuse petty cash, be stingy toward the poor, or take money off his mom's dresser. He makes the strangest of requests to American ears because he wants the middle ground—not too much and not too little.

The point is that both riches and poverty can lead to a lack of dependence on God. If you are rich, you think you do not need God because you can do this yourself. And if you are poor, you think obviously God isn't helping you so you need to do this yourself. Agur asks God to give him the kind of life where he can learn to depend on and praise God's name the best—the way of contentment. The motivation for his prayer is not his own needs; the motivation for his prayer is the name of God! God, glorify yourself by teaching me to lean wholly on you.

## Look to Christ for Salvation from Sin

### PROVERBS 30:10-14

Proverbs 30:15-33 gives a list of numerical sayings. The verses between the numerical sayings help us understand the meaning of the numerical sayings (Waltke, *Proverbs, Chapters 15–31*, 481–82). He starts by talking about immorality in verses 10-14 to set up the numerical sayings. He says not to slander a servant to his master or he'll curse you and you will become guilty (v. 10). Don't ruin an employee's reputation by slandering them to the boss, making fun of them, telling lies, stabbing them in the back, or being overly critical. That person will respond by verbally cursing you, and God will uphold the curse. Yikes! You are being foolish and wicked when you slander and gossip against someone, and by doing that you are incurring judgment on yourself. When the person retaliates verbally, it indicts you before God for your own wickedness (Waltke, *Proverbs, Chapters 15–31*, 483).

In fact, judgment of sin governs this whole section. Agur describes in this section behavior that deserves condemnation. So verse 10 sets up the listing of verses 11-14 and gives us a key for how to interpret them. In verses 11-14 he gives four "generations" or types of sinners who will be condemned by God (Murphy and Huwiler, *Proverbs*, 146).

First, there is a generation that curses instead of blessing its parents (v. 11). The Bart Simpsons of the world who are smart-alecks to their parents; the angst-ridden teens who yell at their parents, "I hate you!"; the bratty three-year-old who shouts "No!" to his parents' directions; or even the grown child who refuses to provide care for aging parents. I (Jon) remember when I pastored in Louisville, we were hit with a huge ice storm one winter that left thousands without power. We received a call from the grown daughter of one of our elderly members who was worried about her parents and wanted the church to take bread and milk to them and make sure that they were OK. We were happy to do so. The problem was that this grown—and fully healthy—daughter lived in the same town as her parents and she did not lift a finger to help them herself. Proverbs says this sort of behavior is condemned before God. The behavior that honors God is what Christ displayed—obeying his parents in childhood (Luke 2:51) and caring for his aging mother as he died (John 19:26-27).

Second, there is a generation that is pure in its own eyes but is not washed from its filth (30:12). This verse presents a disgusting image of self-righteousness and hypocrisy. The word for "filth" in the Hebrew is literally the word for dung.[29] The picture is of someone who is unaware that they stepped in dog mess, and now it's smeared on their clothes. They think everything is fine with their lives morally, yet they are nasty. This is what self-righteousness looks like to God. Those who think they are not sinners and look down on others as if they are better than them look disgusting in God's eyes! When we try to categorize sins by calling the sins of the culture worse than the sins of the church, that is gross to God. The word *pure* refers to those who are able to approach the presence of God in the temple. These folks think they can when they can't. Proverbs is clear—like the rest of the Bible—that you cannot come to God unless you first know that you are filthy. The first step to salvation is recognizing you are not clean and coming to God through Jesus for cleansing. After all, Jesus is the one who lived out the wisdom of Proverbs (Luke 2:52). We are always in danger of thinking more highly of ourselves than we ought. It keeps us from Christ. He must cleanse us because we are not clean and we cannot clean ourselves.

Third, there is a prideful generation (v. 13). You can see it in their eyes! Again, the temptation to think more highly of yourself than you ought is a strong one. Pride is almost the essence of foolishness in Proverbs. Proverbs repeatedly condemns it as the path to death.

Fourth, there is a generation whose teeth are like knives that devour the poor (v. 14). There are people who are stingy toward the needy. There are those who take advantage of the poor. They slice and dice without a second thought. There are those who are simply indifferent to the oppressed. Proverbs repeatedly brings up the poor. It condemns those who mistreat them, and it honors those who are generous to them.

Proverbs 30:17 gives us the outcome for these generations, specifically those who curse parents, but it applies to all: "As for the eye that ridicules a father and despises obedience to a mother, may ravens of the valley pluck it out and young vultures eat it."[30] This outcome is the end for those who roll their eyes at their parents. Judgment will fall on these generations, and it is described in the grossest of ways. The language of being eaten by vultures outside the camp is the sign of someone who is accursed. God's judgment is described sometimes as being eaten by birds (Rev 19:17-18).

---

[29] See Longman's explanation of excrement and ritual uncleanness in *Proverbs*, 527.
[30] Waltke argues that verse 17 covers all four actions. See *Proverbs, Chapters 15–31*, 489.

The good news is that Jesus took this curse for us (Gal 3). The entire curse that we deserve for not honoring our parents, for our self-righteousness, for our arrogance, and for our indifference to the poor crushed Jesus on the cross in our place. He was taken outside the camp, executed under the judgment of God, and then raised from the dead in vindication so all who believe in him will be declared right before God! So look to Jesus for salvation from your sins.

## Look at the World through the Lens of Christ

### PROVERBS 30:15-33

We must observe the way the world works; that will help us navigate skillfully through life. Only through Christ can we perceive and follow this pattern of the world. That is what is happening with these numbered sayings. Agur—like Solomon (1 Kgs 4:33-34)—observes nature and gives wise principles about how the world works based on his observations. Wisdom is living in accordance with the pattern of the world. His observations will do two things: warn us about uncontrolled appetites and instruct us in wisdom.

### *Warnings about Uncontrolled Appetites*

First, Agur observes that the way the world works warns us about uncontrolled appetites for money, sex, and status. For example, verses 15-16 deal with an uncontrolled appetite for money. A leech is a literal bloodsucker that attaches to a host to drain resources and energy. Agur uses this metaphorically to talk about an uncontrolled appetite for stuff. We even use the term "leech" metaphorically for someone who consumes and consumes but does not produce. He says the leech has two daughters, referring to the suckers on the leech by which it attaches itself and drains the host (see Waltke, *Proverbs, Chapters 15–31*, 486–87). These two want more and more and more. The dad can never get his girls enough stuff! They cannot ever be satisfied. They always want a little more. They can be just like Rockefeller, who was asked how much money would be enough, and he replied, "Just a little bit more." Agur's point is to warn you to avoid people who are like this and to warn you not to become like them because this is the path to destruction. Don't let a leech drain you of your time, money, and energy; and don't be a greedy person who constantly craves more and more. He observes four things in nature that are never satisfied to warn you that if you are not a content person then you will never be satisfied. Sheol is never satisfied because the grave always wants one more dead body. The childless womb always craves a child—like Rachel who said, "Give me sons, or I will die!" (Gen 30:1). The land never gets enough water because after the rain the water soaks away. Fire always wants to rage out of control. This is a warning to you if you are the kind of person who can't live within your means because your appetite is out of control and you constantly want more. The warning is that you will never be satisfied. Instead, be content with the gifts God has given you.

Next, he warns about uncontrolled appetites for sex in verses 18-20. What Agur observes here are things that move on or in something else, but what moves does not leave any trace of itself behind.[31] They do not leave any tracks. An eagle does not leave a path in the sky, a serpent leaves no trail on a rock, and the waves behind the ship settle so no one ever knows it was there. The other three observations about things that move on or in something without leaving a trace serve the final, human observation: the way of a man "with" (though the best translation like the other three is "in") a virgin or a young woman. This is talking of the proper context of sexual relations between a man and a woman in marriage. Unlike, say, a plow or a sword, these four things involve graceful movement and leave no damage or scar.

This fourth and final observation sets up the horrific nature of the next verse, which is the point. All four "ways" in verse 19 set up the "way" of verse 20. The way of a man with his wife provides the contrast for the impropriety of the "way" of an adulteress—sexual relations outside of marriage. The adulteress eats, wipes her mouth, and says, "I've done nothing wrong." She acts as though she too leaves no damage or scar, but in fact she has done something wrong; her behavior is vulgar, and she has caused grievous damage. Eating is a metaphor for sexual sin. She wipes her mouth, which means she removes the trace or evidence of her actions, and that is the connection with the four observations of nature. She goes on and forgets all about it. She treats sex like the common act of eating a meal, just like so many treat sex today. They say it's just a natural urge that you need to satisfy, just like you eat when you're hungry. They say if you repress it, you will harm yourself; this is what we are made to do, how we evolved. It is just a bodily function. But

---

[31] This section was greatly aided by Waltke, *Proverbs, Chapters 15–31*, 490–92.

1 Corinthians 6 points out that is not the case at all—it is a very spiritual act with huge consequences. Paul points out that it's not just like eating a meal.

This woman in Proverbs feels as little compunction about her illicit act with another woman's husband as she does about eating breakfast. She wipes away the trace and goes on with no guilt, saying she's done nothing wrong. While she doesn't feel guilty, she does try to get rid of the evidence. So many people do the exact same thing. They clear an Internet history, erase an e-mail, or pay in cash at the motel so that no one finds out. Your conscience can become so seared that you no longer feel bad sneaking around in the shadows and betraying your spouse. But in fact you need to have a controlled appetite when it comes to sex, where you enjoy it rightly in marriage, otherwise you will wreck your life and face the judgment of God. While these four things behaving properly in nature leave no trace, an immoral person's ways are before the eyes of the Lord (5:21).

Finally, Agur turns to uncontrolled appetites for status and pride in Proverbs 30:21-23. These verses talk about judgment against uncontrolled appetites for status that overturn the social order and threaten the cosmic order. It is inappropriate for a servant to become a king because he is not ready to rule (Longman, *Proverbs*, 531). The former slave had so many things withheld from him that when he suddenly has no constraints he will want to consume as much as possible. We observe this in history with rebellions that overthrow tyrannical governments. Often, a tyranny that is on par or worse than the previous tyranny arises in its place. (This is the point of the book *Animal Farm* in its indictment of the communists who overthrew the tsar but set up a system just as oppressive.) A perfect example of this is when Scar becomes the king of Pride Rock in *The Lion King*. His appetite is out of control, so that he consumes without producing and Pride Rock becomes a wilderness. He wants to be king, but he is not the kind of person who can be king. Pride Rock—like us—needs a king who can control his appetites so that the world works the way it should (this is a large point in Judges). Mufasa—like Solomon with his son in Proverbs—tries to instill this in Simba by telling him that he can't just do anything he wants. There is a circle of life—a way the world works—that you must rule by and by which Simba restores order.

Next, it's inappropriate when a fool is filled with food because a fool doesn't know how to have a moderate lifestyle. He will become a drunk and a glutton. Third, it's inappropriate when an unloved woman gets a husband. She becomes a torment (Garrett, *Proverbs*, 242). A woman who goes throughout life unloved starts to crave affection and attention and seek it in the wrong ways. Once she becomes married, she will crave her husband's attention in a way that damages the relationship (this is a warning to dads to love their daughters well so that they are not unloved). She craved the status of marriage, but now that she has it, it is not enough. Finally, and similar to the first observation in this set, it's inappropriate when a servant girl becomes queen.

### *Instruction in Wisdom*

Not only does Agur observe the world and warn about uncontrolled appetites, but second, he moves on to observations that instruct us in skillful living. He observes four small but wise animals in verses 24-28 and then more stately animals in verses 29-31. You learn wisdom by observing these animals. Again, wisdom is not IQ; it's skill for life. None of these animals could take an IQ test, but they instruct us in wisdom because they have the ability to navigate through life despite the limitations they have (Longman, *Proverbs*, 532). So observe these animals and do likewise.

He begins with four small animals.[32] First, the ant survives because it provides (v. 25). The ant is wise to store up during the good times so it can be prepared during the bad times. This reality provides a nice contrast with the uncontrolled appetite for money and stuff we have seen previously in the chapter. Agur's point in making this observation is that you should do likewise. You should work hard, you should save, you should not overspend, and you should have a plan for lean times. Second, the hyrax or rock badger is a very small animal that makes its home in the cliffs so it's safe from predators against which it would be no match (v. 26). The point is that you need to learn how to live a life that is secure from things that might destroy you. You need to learn to resist peer pressure that might cause you to make a stupid decision that gets you in trouble. You need to learn how to resist the temptation toward adultery that would destroy your family. Third, he observes the locusts, who have no king but march in ranks (v. 27). This observation shows our need for community and cooperation. You need to be in a group that

---

[32] Garrett's discussion helped this section tremendously. See Garrett, *Proverbs*, 242.

takes care of each other. Finally, the vulnerable little lizard that manages to live in the palace transitions to the next set of observations about stately things (v. 28).

He observes things that are stately in their stride—in contrast with the small things above. He observes the lion, the rooster, and the he-goat, which leads to the final observation of the king (vv. 29-31). Here is the whole point. You observe the tiny ants and lizards because they are humble, limited creatures that despite their limitations, even because of their limitations, develop wisdom and competency. Go and do likewise.[33] You learn your weaknesses, your limits, your drawbacks, and then you humble yourself before God and you will be made wise. Proverbs is often set up as a king instructing the prince so that he can rule, and you see some of that at play here. After all, the lion is a messianic animal (Gen 49:9-10), and Solomon wants to train the line of David to be wise so that the messianic kingdom might be established. But that will only happen through humility, so learn from small creatures. And like our Messiah who humbled himself, we also must humble ourselves in dependence on God so we can make our way wisely through the world.

These observations bear a striking resemblance to the Joseph story. Joseph—like the ant—stored food in good season in preparation for the famine. This leads to him being exalted as a ruler in Egypt who saves the world. This is fulfilled in Jesus because he is the humble King who saves the world, who can rule his own appetites, and who orders his kingdom after wisdom.

Agur ends this chapter on the same note that began it. Reject foolish self-exaltation (vv. 32-33). If you have been promoting yourself, then shut up, turn off Twitter, ignore Facebook, and repent, or it will lead to a bloody conflict.

## Conclusion

What we have seen in Proverbs is how it's all centered on Christ. If you have a problem with uncontrolled appetites for money, sex, or status; if you are not honoring your parents; if you are mistreating the poor; or if you can't see how the world really works it's because you have a problem with Jesus! So humble yourself and seek forgiveness and transformation in Jesus Christ.

---

[33] Waltke makes these connections, including the royal connection, in *Proverbs, Chapters 15–31,* 495–500.

There is an order to the world. The Maker made it to work a certain way. That order is Christ-centered. Christ is the one who made the world, upholds the world, and will make the world new again (Col 1:15-20). The pattern of the seasons was woven into creation with the death of winter that gives way to the resurrection of spring in order to point us to Christ. The pattern of the seven-day week was woven into creation to point us to passion week where the new Adam—the gardener—steps out of the grave into a new world on the eighth day. After all, in *The Lion King*, when the rightful king overthrows the usurper and assumes the throne, even the creation itself is healed. That's the gospel (cf. Isa 11). King Jesus sets the world right, and you can only navigate through that world—you can only be wise—through him.

## Reflect and Discuss

1. We recognize that a designer gets to decide how his or her project works. In what ways does that apply to God and what he tells us about the world?
2. In what ways does recognizing our limitations help us to become wise? How does thinking you are wise actually make you foolish?
3. If wisdom truly resides with God, his Son, and his Word, then how do we go about learning and growing in that wisdom practically?
4. How do we effectively add to and subtract from the Bible?
5. How do you relate to God in lean times? Times of plenty?
6. How should children honor their parents practically?
7. Why do you think we are strongly drawn toward self-righteousness?
8. In what ways do we justify our sin as if it's not wrong, like the adulteress?
9. What are some practical ways you can practice making wise provision like the ant?
10. How does having a church community help you grow in wisdom?

# Section 3—Family Relationships

# Manhood

## PROVERBS 13:22 ET AL.

**Main Idea:** A real man loves Jesus, his wife, his kids, and discipline.

---

**I. A Real Man Loves Jesus.**
**II. A Real Man Loves (and Leads) His Wife.**
**III. A Real Man Loves (and Leads) His Children.**
**IV. A Real Man Loves Discipline.**

---

When it comes to the topic of what it really means to be a man, we are fighting against cultural errors, even in the Christian subculture. Some people erroneously think manhood means machismo. They think a real man loves UFC, beer guzzling, conquests, and bravado. Others think manhood does not really matter. They would rather talk about personhood. A real man can be a kind of genderless androgyne because the sexes are equal not only in essence but also in function.

Added to that confusion is the extended adolescence of our culture. Instead of young men moving out of their parents' house, finishing their education, getting a job to pay bills, marrying a woman, and beginning to have children in their twenties, they are now staying at home longer and starting these adult activities much later in their twenties, or even in their thirties. There are a bunch of middle-aged boys living in their parents' basement playing video games all day.

These contrasting pictures of manhood have been around since the fall in Eden (Gen 3). Since sin entered the world, men are prone to be domineering or passive. Adam stood by passively while his wife was taken advantage of, and then passed the buck to her when God called him to give an account. Part of the curse of sin is that now husbands will want to rule their wives in a harsh and domineering way (Gen 3:16). That sin nature has been passed down to us, and now it is celebrated in our culture!

We have no real shot at being real men. After all, what does that even mean? You might even ask, "Shouldn't we want to be godly men instead of real men?" Those two are the same thing. Being a real man means being the man God intended you to be both by creation and by redemption. Obviously we have all fallen miserably short of God's design. But, thank God, one man did not—Jesus. We must look to him to see what it means to be a real man. Jesus is what it means to be the man God intended us to be, and that is the picture of manhood presented in Proverbs. Proverbs is a man (a dad) telling another man (a son) how to be a mature man. And Jesus is the one who lived this out. Jesus is the one who grew in wisdom, stature, and favor with God and with people (Luke 2:52). Therefore, only through Jesus can we see what real manhood is and live it out.

This message is not just for men. Children need to hear it because boys need to aspire to be this kind of man and girls need to learn what to look for in a man. Single women need this message because they need to know the kind of man they should want to marry. Wives need this message because this is who they need to pray for and help their men to become. And yes, husbands and fathers need this message because they need to know what to be and what to model for their girls (how godly men treat women) and for their boys (how they should treat women).

It is vital that we get this because the consequences of not being a real man are catastrophic, as we see all around us in our broken culture. If you do not learn to become this kind of man, you can destroy your marriage, your family, your career, and your reputation. You will miss out on the joy God has planned for you. God tells you how the world works because he loves you and wants the best for you. So what is a real man according to Proverbs?

## A Real Man Loves Jesus

This first point runs the risk of alienating men. What guy wants to hear that he needs to love another guy? In some ways, this is a problem in Christianity. Lots of churches have a mushy or sappy sentimentality that turns guys off. Many men think the church has been feminized or that it is only suited for women and children. We can even play into this with praise songs that almost sound like we are singing to Jesus like a girl would sing to her boyfriend. Lyrics like "I want to touch you" do not resonate with most men. Even hymns like "In the Garden" by C. Austin Miles play into this. What guy would normally sing about going to a garden alone with their buddy? Put your friend's name in the lyrics:

> I come to the garden alone,
> while the dew is still on the roses,

and the voice I hear falling on my ear,
my buddy David discloses.
And David walks with me, and David talks with me,
and David tells me I am his own;
and the joy David and I share as we tarry there,
none other has ever known.
David speaks, and the sound of his voice
is so sweet the birds hush their singing. . . .

It is kind of creepy!

On the other hand, we do need to recover masculine love where men have deep relationships with one another. When I say that real men "love" Jesus, I mean that Jesus was a real man who laid his life down for you, and you need to honor him and follow him.

What does this look like in Proverbs? It looks like loving the word of God. Proverbs 13:13 says, "Whoever despises the word brings destruction on himself, but he who reveres the commandment will be rewarded" (ESV). Do you revere the Word of God? Do you read it on your own—not just in church? Do you study it, listen attentively in the corporate gathering, and engage in Bible study? Loving Jesus also looks like confession of sin. Proverbs 28:13 says, "The one who conceals his sins will not prosper, but whoever confesses and renounces them will find mercy."[34] You love Jesus by confessing your sin, repenting of it, and trusting in the gospel. Love of Jesus also looks like trusting the Lord (3:5-6). Wisdom is a person—Jesus Christ—so you need to be in a personal relationship with him by faith. He will make you wise in daily life. You cannot be a real man without loving Jesus!

## A Real Man Loves (and Leads) His Wife

According to Ephesians 5, a man is called to play the role of Christ in the life of his wife. We are called to sacrificially love and lead our wives. One of the main ways that Proverbs lays this out is in the area of keeping your covenant commitment to your spouse. Your vows are promises, and real men keep their word.

Solomon repeatedly warns his son about the danger of unfaithfulness (chs. 2; 5; 6; 7). Truly being faithful to your covenant commitment

---

[34] Goldsworthy argues we will have disorder in our lives until we have a right relationship with God (*Tree of Life,* 174).

means you are faithful both outwardly and inwardly. Jesus tells us that even lust is a betrayal (Matt 5:27-30). This leads men to be traitors against their wives (Prov 23:26-28).

As we see elsewhere in Proverbs, there are two main ways that you can be pulled away: communication and attraction. Real men are not the flirty guy because that is dangerous. Real men do not have things like a "work wife" that they flirt with in the office. That is stupid and ridiculous. Real men do not wonder about their old high school girlfriend and message her on Facebook. Real men guard their communication with the opposite sex.

Also, real men do not watch shows, movies, or things on the Internet that will cause their hearts to lust for a woman who is not their wife. Real men also do not give unfettered access to a smartphone to their pubescent sons, which basically trains them in being turned on by porn. Stay in your teenager's business and do not give them privacy when it comes to "their" phone because it is not theirs! Even if your son says, "I will pay for the phone," you should reply, "Until you pay for the house you are using it in, you don't get privacy!" Porn destroys marriages because it warps our minds. It makes a man view sex in a selfish way and the opposite sex as an object. This is true both before and during marriage. Be vigilant to view the opposite sex the way God wants you to view them, and fight for purity of mind.

Guard your heart from unfaithfulness by watching out for communication and attraction that might pull your heart away. Heed the warning. Also, employ the positive strategy laid out by Proverbs. Have a strong relationship with God's Wisdom—Jesus Christ. And have a strong "offense" in your marriage relationship (5:15-20) (Longman, *Proverbs*, 161). Romance your wife. Be intimate with her. Be her best friend because real men love their wives.

### A Real Man Loves (and Leads) His Children

Real men love their children and show that love by teaching them. Teach them the Bible, teach them right from wrong, and teach them everyday wisdom. Teach them to throw a baseball, drive a car, do a job interview, tie a tie, and a hundred other things.

Real men love their children by disciplining them and attempting to rescue them from hell. Proverbs 13:24 says, "The one who will not use the rod hates his son, but the one who loves him disciplines him diligently." A real man does not abdicate his role here and become passive like Adam. Too many men do. You need to lovingly correct your children so they know the right path.

Real men love their children by working hard to provide for their family. Real men are not lazy! When I (Jon) was growing up, my pastor told me that he would drive his daughters down to the poorest areas of town and say, "If you marry a lazy bum with no work ethic, you will live here." That may seem like a strange strategy, but Paul says that men who do not provide for their families are worse than unbelievers (1 Tim 5:8)! Proverbs 12:11 says, "The one who works his land will have plenty of food, but whoever chases fantasies lacks sense." If you work hard, you will be able to provide enough for your family. And through a good work ethic and the wise handling of money, a real man can leave an inheritance for his children (Prov 13:22).

## A Real Man Loves Discipline

One of the main teachings of Proverbs is that real men know how to control their appetites for sex, money, power, status, food, and alcohol. A real man is self-controlled! Proverbs 25:28 says, "A person who does not control his temper is like a city whose wall is broken down." A city like that is vulnerable to any kind of attack (Garrett, *Proverbs*, 211). The devil loves to prey on men who are weak like this. He has destroyed many men through their appetites. In contrast, the Spirit of Jesus produces self-control in your life (Gal 5:22-23).

Real men are disciplined when it comes to pride. They know how to be humble because God gives grace to the humble (Prov 3:34). Men have an appetite, according to Proverbs, to always be right in their own eyes. Men are often headstrong. The prideful fool is right in his own eyes and will not listen to what other people have to say (12:15). The antidote is to trust the Lord and receive wise counsel from him and others!

Real men discipline their mouths because a babbling fool will come to ruin (10:8). Proverbs 21:23 says, "The one who guards his mouth and tongue keeps himself out of trouble." What does this look like in Proverbs? Do not be a bragger (27:2), dishonest (26:28), or someone who breaks confidence (20:19).

Real men control their desire for money. They are content (30:8-9). They are honest workers who earn their money the right way (11:1; 16:11; 20:10,23; 22:16). They are generous to the poor (14:21). And they have an eternal perspective, knowing that money and things are temporary and do not last forever (23:4-5).

Real men control their tempers. They are not harsh or quarrelsome. Certainly manliness is not cowardice, but it is not harshness either. Biblical manhood is tough enough to be patient and forgiving. Proverbs 16:32 highly commends men who control their tempers: "Patience is better than power, and controlling one's emotions, than capturing a city." A real man is slow to anger with his wife, his children, his neighbors, his coworkers, and in traffic! A real man is also not quarrelsome. He does not love to argue and stir things up (20:3; 26:21). He is gentle with his words, especially toward his wife and children (15:1). Men need to be paradoxical here in some ways. Do not be a sissy—be able to rebuke men. But also be able to lead your wife and children gently. Real men can rebuke when they need to, stand their ground, not be tossed around by others' opinions, and not be easily led astray. They can also cool tension, lower the temperature in a heated situation, and be kind. Jesus could drive out the money changers with a whip as well as put children who just had to see him on his lap!

Finally, real men are not controlled by what others think about them. Proverbs 29:25 says, "The fear of mankind is a snare, but the one who trusts in the LORD is protected." Real men care more about what God thinks about them than what others do. Peer pressure causes stupid men to do stupid things, but real men are not controlled by it. They do not follow the crowd! They follow Jesus!

## Conclusion

To sum up what a real man does, I want to show you a little blog article I ran across titled "A Daughter Needs a Dad" as a good way to capture this message in a list. A daughter needs a dad for many reasons:

1. To show her that true love is unconditional [like Jesus's love for us]
2. To teach her that her value as a person is more than the way she looks
3. To teach her that family is more important than work
4. To show her that a man can be trustworthy
5. To be the safe spot she can always turn to
6. To teach her that a man's strength is not the force of his hands or his voice, but the kindness of his heart
7. To be the standard against which she will judge all men
8. To help her take risks that will build her confidence

9. To hold her when she cries
10. To teach her she is important by stopping what he is doing to watch her

So men, run to Jesus, submit to him, and this is the kind of man he will help you become! And women, do not beat up your men over this. Pray for them and play your role because only Jesus can change your man!

## Reflect and Discuss

1. How does the world view what a real man is?
2. Why do you think men are prolonging adolescence?
3. How has the church feminized Christianity in many ways? What effect do you think this has on men?
4. What are some things you can actively do to love Jesus?
5. What are some ways that you can proactively and practically guard your marriage?
6. What are some practical things that men need to teach their children?
7. What are some things on the list of what daughters need that dads typically struggle with?
8. How can men fight against the temptation to be controlled by what other men think of them?
9. In what ways can men teach their children a strong work ethic?
10. What are some ways that men can battle against having a quick temper?

# God's Portrait of a Wonderful Wife and Marvelous Mother

## PROVERBS 31:10-31

**Main Idea:** Women who live faithfully before God in the power of the gospel bless their families and honor their Lord.

---

I. **She Is Trusted by Her Husband (31:10-12).**
   A. She is virtuous (31:10).
   B. She is valuable (31:11-12).
II. **She Is a Hard Worker (31:13-19).**
   A. She uses her hands (31:13-15).
   B. She uses her head (31:16-19).
III. **She Is Compassionate (31:20).**
IV. **She Is Ready for Tough Times (31:21-22).**
   A. First she takes care of others (31:21).
   B. Then she takes care of herself (31:22).
V. **She Is a Blessing to Her Husband (31:23).**
   A. She enhances his reputation.
   B. She extends his responsibilities.
VI. **She Is Endowed with Godly Wisdom (31:24-27).**
VII. **She Is Admired by Her Family (31:28-29).**
   A. Her children bless her (31:28).
   B. Her husband praises her (31:28-29).
VIII. **She Is Honored by the Lord (31:30-31).**
   A. She has a godly perspective (31:30).
   B. She receives godly praise (31:30-31).

---

She has haunted and terrified women all over the world for three thousand years. Her massive shadow and imposing stature towers so high that she is held in awe by all who dare to look at her magnificent and unrivaled portrait. Who is this wonder of a woman? Who is this larger-than-life lady? She is the virtuous woman of Proverbs 31. Ray Ortlund says, "She is the role model . . . the ideal woman" (*Proverbs*, 149). Allen Ross refers to her as "the woman of valor." He further notes, "The woman of Proverbs 31 is a symbol of wisdom. . . . The Lady Wisdom in this chapter is the strongest contrast to the adulterous woman in the earlier chapters" ("Proverbs," 245). The ancient Hebrews knew her as the alphabet wife and mother of excellence. Derek Kidner calls her "an Alphabet of wifely excellence" (*Proverbs*, 183).

In Hebrew this poem is a skillfully crafted acrostic. Each verse begins with a successive letter in the Hebrew alphabet. In English, the first few verses might look something like this:

> An **awesome** wife, who can find her?
> A **blessed** lady, her husband trusts her.
> A **caring** woman, she does him good all her life.
> A **diligent** worker, she is skillful with her hands.

Through this elaborate and artful structure, this poem describes in elegant detail a woman who is "everything from A to Z," a woman who, through her trust in the Lord, distinguishes herself as an exemplary wife and mother (Waltke, *Proverbs, Chapters 15–31,* 514).

Interestingly, motherhood is often discussed in contemporary news and commentary outlets. In 2005 *Newsweek* actually had the courage to say "Mother matters" and pointed out that according to Salary.com, "Stay-at-home moms, if compensated for all the hours they work, would net $131,471 a year" (Newsweek Staff, "Survey: Mother Matters"). The article went on to say,

- 71 percent of wives say their husbands get on their nerves more than do their children.
- 50 percent of women say their mom is their best friend.
- 94 percent of dads say moms are as sexy as ever!

Additionally, many working women are reevaluating who they are and what they want out of life. While there remains a great deal of confusion, a significant debate seems to be taking place. Consider, for example, the 2004 *Time* story, "The Case for Staying Home: Why More Moms Are Opting Out of the Rat Race." The article points out,

> Most women who step out of their careers find expected delights on the home front, not to mention the enormous relief of no longer worrying about shortchanging their kids. (Wallis, "The Case for Staying Home")

Motherhood, they find, provides both joy and fulfillment if it is not drowned out by other responsibilities.

Alternatively, the February 21, 2005, cover story from *Newsweek* chose to highlight the stressful side of motherhood. In "The Myth of the Perfect Mother: Why It Drives Real Women Crazy," Judith Warner addresses the tendency of many moms to take responsibility for everything in their house and home on themselves. This burden ultimately robs moms of the joys that come with being a wife and mother.

Contrary to *Newsweek's* title, though, "the perfect mother" is no myth. There is a magnificent portrait of her in Proverbs 31:10-31. Embodying all the wisdom of the book (this woman is a Jesus lady!) that she appropriately concludes, she places before every woman a standard, a bar, an ideal. *Perfection*, however, should not be a mother's goal. That would only frustrate and discourage each and every one of us. However, growth in the *direction* and likeness of this lovely lady who walks in the wisdom of Christ is certainly attainable. Eight exemplary truths present themselves for our careful consideration.

## She Is Trusted by Her Husband

### PROVERBS 31:10-12

The opening words of this poem, "Who can find," do not imply "a capable wife" does not exist. They rather affirm that she does exist and that she is of inestimable worth, she is a treasure, especially to her husband. Two reasons are noted.

### *She Is Virtuous (31:10)*

"Noble" is translated elsewhere as strong, wealthy, able, and valiant. This lady is "capable" (GNT) and a woman of "excellence" (NASB). She is "precious," and the man who finds such a woman is blessed. Indeed, she is a treasure worth far more than jewels (cf. 3:15; 8:11).

### *She Is Valuable (31:11-12)*

Her husband's heart—who he really is on the inside—safely "trusts in her." He harbors no doubts or suspicions, questions or concerns. He has full confidence in her because of her competence and character. Proverbs specifies her adeptness at managing family finances and necessities. She knows what her man and her family need, and she will see that they have it. "He [and they] will not lack anything good."

Verse 12 is remarkable. She will be a blessing to her husband all the days of *her* life. If he should precede her in death, he does not fear what she will say when he is gone. In life and in death, he is confident she will do him good.

Several other proverbs speak to the blessing of having a good wife. Proverbs 12:4 says, "A wife of noble character is her husband's crown, but a wife who causes shame is like rottenness in his bones." Proverbs 18:22 says, "A man who finds a wife finds a good thing and obtains favor from the LORD." And Proverbs 19:14 says, "A house and wealth are inherited from fathers, but a prudent wife is from the LORD." The man who finds such a wife will reap the blessings of her precious character as long as she is living to bless him. "Her commitment to her husband's well-being is true, not false; constant, not temperamental; reliable, not fickle; and discerning" (Waltke, *Proverbs, Chapters 15–31*, 522).

## She Is a Hard Worker

### PROVERBS 31:13-19

This lady is a fountain of energy. Her husband, as the spiritual leader of the home, may be the coach. She, however, is clearly the quarterback. She calls the plays, sets the players in the proper place, and executes the game plan to perfection. She may even call an audible from time to time!

#### *She Uses Her Hands (31:13-15)*

In verse 13 she takes care of the family's clothing. In verse 14 she takes care of the family's food, sailing out and returning daily "like the merchant ships," bringing what they need. And in verse 15 she takes care of the family's schedule, rising before sunrise if necessary to provide food for her whole household.

#### *She Uses Her Head (31:16-19)*

Using her home as a base of operation, she is business savvy (v. 16). "There is no foolish purchasing or indebtedness here" (Ross, "Proverbs," 248). Further, she is strong not weak, vigorous not anemic (v. 17). She has an air of confidence as well as fairness, and she is devoted to excellence (v. 18). She wisely conducts her business, heeding the warning of the Russian proverb that says, "There are two fools in the market. One asks too much and one asks too little." If necessary she will work late into the night to make sure the job gets done. She does what she can with what she has without complaint or self-pity (v. 19).

## She Is Compassionate

### PROVERBS 31:20

This lady is tender in heart and conscience toward those less fortunate than she. A generous and gracious spirit characterizes her life. "She uses her industry in charitable ways" (Ross, "Proverbs," 249). In this one verse we see two aspects of her compassion. First, **she helps the poor**. The Proverbs lady does not become so busy with her home that she cannot see the hurt of others. In this she is very much like Jesus, the embodiment of wisdom. She gladly "opens her arms to the poor" (NIV). She meets them where they are and reaches out to hug and help, to aid and assist.

Second, **she helps the needy**. This lady is sensitive to their needs and works to aid them. She embraces the truth of Proverbs 11:25, which teaches, "The generous man will be prosperous" (NASB). This woman treats her advantages not as an occasion for self-indulgence but as an opportunity to be a blessing to others.

## She Is Ready for Tough Times

### PROVERBS 31:21-22

Life has its ups and downs, its good times and its bad times. The virtuous woman is well aware of this, and she is prepared to face both. When the difficult days confront her, she goes into action. But rather than flailing about erratically, she moves in a very definite manner.

*First She Takes Care of Others (31:21)*

When cold weather comes, she sees that her family is ready, clothed with the finest quality garments she can provide (scarlet according to the Masoretic Text, or double according to the Septuagint). When tough times come, she does not lower the bar. She does her best and begins by looking out for the interest of others (cf. Phil 2:4).

*Then She Takes Care of Herself (31:22)*

The text would indicate this woman was a woman of means. Because of her character and commitments, God could entrust her with material blessings, knowing she will not hoard them but will share them. Working with her own hands, she uses the finest fabrics and highest quality materials available to her. She is strong and elegant, gracious and attractive.

Her outward apparel only enhances the radiant beauty that shines forth from her heart and soul.

## She Is a Blessing to Her Husband

### PROVERBS 31:23

The husband who finds and wins such a wife is a fortunate man. This woman is the kind of wife a man needs in order to make it, and make it well, in this world. She will not tear him down but will build him up. This takes place inside and also outside the home.

*She Enhances His Reputation*

This man's wife is his greatest asset, his best advertisement. Her husband, her man, is known and well thought of in the places of importance. That she is his and he is hers is known by all, and this is a plus for his reputation. That this man could win this lady speaks well of him, and all take notice.

*She Extends His Responsibilities*

As a great woman, she makes her man better not worse. She is not the "not-so-great woman" who takes a great man and drags him down to mediocrity. No, she is a great lady that may take a mediocre man and lift him to greatness. She makes him better than he could be without her. Largely because of the blessing she brings to him, this man takes his seat among the elders, the leaders of the city. He is an esteemed and respected member of the governing body of the town.

## She Is Endowed with Godly Wisdom

### PROVERBS 31:24-27

In her book *Mom, You're Incredible!*, Linda Weber asks, "What in the World Do I Do All Day?" She writes,

> Being a mom is a job with a capital J. We work our fingers to the bone, push our nerves to the edge and use every skill we have to accomplish the day's demands. Just what does a mother do all day? Today's college student can't imagine. Numbers of women are baffled by what they'd do with "all that

time" if they *had* to be home. Sometimes Mom herself can't remember.

Linda then notes (1) what a mother is and (2) what a mother does. Her lists flesh out with remarkable similarity verses 24-27:

What am I? Well, I'm the following:

- baby feeder, changer, bather, rocker, burper, hugger
- listener to crying and fussing and thousands of questions
- picker-upper of food and debris cast on the floor . . .
- comforter, encourager, counselor . . .
- linguistic expert for two-year-old dialects . . .
- listener—to the husband as well as the children—about their day, their needs, their concerns, their aspirations
- teacher of everything from how to chew food to how to drive a car
- assistant on school projects . . .
- censor of TV, movies, and books . . .
- reader of thousands of children's books
- planner and hostess of children's birthday parties
- planner and hostess of adult dinner parties . . .
- central control for getting the appliance fixed or the carpet shampooed
- executioner of ants, roaches, wasps, and other pests
- resident historian in charge of photo albums, baby books, and school record books . . .
- resident encyclopedia source for all those hard questions that seem to arise . . .
- food preservation expert . . .
- keeper and locator of birth certificates and other valuable documents
- ironer of wrinkles . . .
- appointment desk for the family's visits to the doctor, the dentist, the orthodontist, the barber, and the mechanic
- seeker of God, one who prays . . .
- cleaner of the oven, the drawers, the closets, the garage, the curtains, the windows, and even the walls . . .
- refinisher of furniture
- hubby's romantic, attentive spouse . . .
- emergency medical technician and 'ambulance' driver

And what else do I do? Well, among many other things, I do the following:

- clip ten fingernails and ten toenails for each young child regularly
- return library books . . .
- choose gifts, purchase gifts, wrap gifts for birthdays, Christmas, Father's Day, Mother's Day, wedding showers, baby showers, anniversaries, and any other event that might even remotely require a gift . . .
- mail packages, buy stamps
- drop off the dry cleaning; pick up the dry cleaning . . .
- haul everything that needs repair
- attend recitals
- attend every school sporting event imaginable
- chauffeur everyone everywhere . . .
- comb little girl's hairdos . . .
- help in the classroom . . .
- attend school PTA meetings and conferences
- act as a room mother, making things and organizing *more* parties
- chaperon field trips and special events
- coordinate car pools . . .
- serve as a Scout leader, a Blue Bird leader, an AWANA leader, a Sunday school teacher . . .
- deliver forgotten lunches, forgotten homework and forgotten athletic gear . . .
- make bank deposits and withdrawals

(Weber, *Mom, You're Incredible!,* 165–69)

Well, what Linda describes we find right here in our text. What is this marvelous mother like? What does this wonderful wife do? First, **she is active with her hands** (v. 24). She makes clothing and furnishings for herself and her family, making enough to sell the excess for profit. Second, **she is adorned by her character** (v. 25). What she wears is always in style: *strength* and *honor,* as well as a *sense of humor* and a *positive outlook.* Third, **she is appropriate in her speech** (v. 26). Words of wisdom and cascades of kindness flow from her mouth and fall from her tongue. She knows the nuclear power of words, and she uses them well. Wise and gracious, she is blessed with common sense and a carefully guarded gate on that untamable beast called the tongue (cf. Jas 3). Fourth, **she is attentive to her home** (v. 27). This lady is active and not idle, for there is always much to do. She keeps her eyes wide open, watching each member of the family, sensitive to their personalities, conscious of their needs, quick to spot danger.

## She Is Admired by Her Family

### PROVERBS 31:28-29

Iris Krasnow, a former United Press International reporter, candidly confesses,

> I remember when I was a college student home on holiday breaks, the sight of my own stay-at-home mother wearing her red-checked dish towel over one shoulder and doing crossword puzzles . . . used to rile me over the oppression of wives stuck in their kitchens. Today, I am exhilarated by the wife-mother role I once believed to be the death of dreams. . . . Nothing ever felt so powerful, so free, so spiritually right, than being a mother who organizes a home and fights for her children on every front. ("Surrendering to Motherhood")

Such a lady will no doubt win the love, affection, and admiration of her family. Husband and children alike will sing her praises.

#### *Her Children Bless Her (31:28)*

The children of this mother stand to their feet and bless her. They testify to her impact on their lives and her influence that still shapes and guides them. One of the all-time greats as a mother was Susannah Wesley, mother of Charles and John. Mother to seventeen children, she prayed one hour each day just for them, and she spent one hour each week discussing spiritual matters with each one individually. Her children, no doubt, called her blessed. Why? Here are a few of the rules she used in raising her children. At the time, they may have seemed harsh. Later, her children saw the wisdom of them and blessed her for loving them in such clear and tangible ways.

1. Eating between meals not allowed.
2. All children they are to be in bed by 8 p.m.

3. They are required to take medicine without complaining.
4. Subdue self-will in a child, and those working together with God to save the child's soul.
5. Teach a child to pray as soon as he can speak.
6. Require all to be still during Family Worship.
7. Give them nothing that they cry for, and only that when asked for politely.
8. Prevent lying; punish no fault which is first confessed and repented of.
9. Never allow a sinful act to go unpunished.
10. Never punish a child twice for a single offense.
11. Comment and reward good behavior.
12. Any attempt to please, even if poorly performed, should be commended.
13. Preserve property rights, even in smallest matters.
14. Strictly observe all promises.
15. Require no daughter to work before she can read well.
16. Teach children to fear the rod.
    ("16 House Rules")

Any child would be blessed to be loved by a mother in such an intentional manner. As they grow to become parents themselves, they will bless her for how she raised them and what she taught them.

### *Her Husband Praises Her (31:28-29)*

Ross wisely notes, "The wisdom of the noble woman inspires praise from her family—from those who know her the best" ("Proverbs," 251). Joining the chorus of his children, her husband complements their chant—"We have the greatest mother in the world"—with one of his own: "I have the greatest wife in the world." I strongly suspect the children learned to praise Mom by watching Dad. They had learned it from him. I (Danny) have often said to my sons that I made one mistake in marrying their mother when I was twenty-one and she was nineteen. I should have married her when I was twenty and she was eighteen! That would have added an extra year of my being married to the greatest wife in the world as I see it! Now that my sons are grown, they joyfully join me in praising and admiring the godly wife and mother the Lord has given us.

## She Is Honored by the Lord

**PROVERBS 31:30-31**

The tribute to this incredible woman ends as it should: with an eternal perspective and praise from the Lord. It seems best to me to see God as the speaker through the sage in verses 30-31.

### *She Has Godly Perspective (31:30)*

Charm and beauty are not bad; they simply are not what makes a great woman. "Inner spiritual beauty does not deceive" (Waltke, *Proverbs, Chapters 15–31*, 535).

Physical appearance is fleeting; it does not endure. To trust in and focus on these temporary advantages is foolish and self-deceiving. The virtuous woman knows what matters, she knows what lasts, she knows what is eternal. These are the things she values. As one who belongs to Jesus, she seeks the things above. She also sets her mind on things above because her "life is hidden with Christ in God" (Col 3:1-3). Having entered into a relationship with Wisdom himself, Jesus Christ, she fears the Lord, which "is the beginning of knowledge" (Prov 1:7).

### *She Receives Godly Praise (31:30-31)*

What matters is that this lady knows the Lord, loves the Lord, and fears the Lord. Her passion in life is to please him, know him, obey him, and honor him. Such a woman will receive praise (in v. 30 it is implied the praise come from the Lord), and the life she lives day in and day out will be fruitful and worthy of praise (v. 31). At the end of life, looking back over the many years of service for God and service to others, she will quietly and confidently say, "No regrets. No regrets."

## Conclusion

Proverbs begins with a dad telling his son to make Woman Wisdom his wife, and it ends with a husband praising a wise wife. Woman Wisdom points to Jesus, who is the embodiment of God's Wisdom. The wise wife is, therefore, a type of Woman Wisdom, and one can only be that kind of wife if she is in a relationship with the Wisdom of God who is Jesus Christ. The only way to be a positive mom and a Proverbs lady is to be a saved mom, a born again woman of God. The woman of Proverbs 31 is not just any woman. She is a saved woman, a godly woman, a Bible woman, a Jesus woman. The applause and praise of the world mean nothing. The applause and praise of the Lord Jesus means everything. She walks in wisdom as the personification of Lady Wisdom because she knows that the ultimate incarnation of wisdom is the Wisdom of God, Jesus Christ (see 1 Cor 1:30). What an appropriate way to end this chapter. What a Christ-honoring way to end this book!

## Reflect and Discuss

1. Why do you think motherhood is such a disputed topic in Western culture?
2. What does God's design for the family say about the role and importance of mothers?
3. How do wives and mothers reflect the glory of God?
4. How can wives and mothers guard against being crushed by the ideal woman?
5. If you are a wife and/or mother, which characteristics from this passage are most challenging to you?
6. If you are a wife and/or mother, where do you see the grace of God forming you into the character of this excellent woman?
7. If you are a husband, how can you honor the women (wife and daughters) in your life as they strive to be faithful to the role to which God has called them?
8. What aspects of the wife and mother of Proverbs 31 are abused or ignored by those who reject the distinction between man and woman as designed by God?
9. What aspects of the wife and mother of Proverbs 31 are abused or ignored by those who demean women and relegate them to secondary status?
10. How does the gospel of Jesus Christ empower us to live faithfully in the roles to which God has called us?

# Having a Happy Home

## PROVERBS 24:3-4

**Main Idea:** The wisdom of Proverbs is the path to a happy home.

---

**I. Give Your Children Yourself More Than Your Money (24:3-4; 15:1-17; 17:1).**

**II. Give Your Children Parents Who Are Following Jesus (24:3-4; 19:13).**

**III. Give Your Children Training in Wisdom.**

A. Example (14:26)

B. Instruction (24:3-4)

C. Correction (13:24; 23:13-14; 29:15)

---

Stan Toussaint was a much-loved professor at Dallas Theological Seminary for forty-seven years. He loves the Bible. He also loves the family. In an article titled, "Building a Happy Home," Toussaint addresses the importance of priorities in family life. He highlights six:

1. Persons before things
2. Home before occupation
3. Partner before children
4. Children before friends
5. Partner before self
6. Spiritual before material

He concludes his article by saying, "Priorities are indeed peculiar. But they are essential. And they'll go a long way toward producing a strong, biblical, and happy home" (*Kindred Spirit,* date unknown). Unfortunately, what Stan describes is absent in many homes today.

That deficiency is multiplied throughout our country. There are lots of homes today that are dominated by tension and unhappiness. Even though the inhabitants have a lot in worldly terms, they walk on eggshells around each other and are not enjoying life. It could be that the parents are workaholics who are never around, the wife constantly nags the husband, the husband and wife constantly bicker in front of the children, or the husband loses his temper easily.

There are so many broken and unhappy homes, which raises an important question: "If the American Dream does not produce a happy home, how do you get a happy home?" Where are you going to find it? Are you going to look to the world? The world says that we should let children basically raise themselves, give them what they want, be their buddy, forgo rules, let them make their own choices, avoid spanking them, and leave their raising to daycares and schools. How has that worked out?

We need to look to the Word of God. It says that wisdom is the path to a happy home. Repeatedly, Proverbs says that God actively blesses wise families with happiness (10:1; 17:21; 23:15-16,24; 28:7; 29:3). And God actively curses the foolish family with sorrow by handing them over to what they want. So let's look to the wisdom of Proverbs and see the path to a happy home. Proverbs 24:3-4 says, "A house is built by wisdom, and it is established by understanding; by knowledge the rooms are filled with every precious and beautiful treasure."

## Give Your Children Yourself More Than Your Money

**PROVERBS 24:3-4; 15:1-17; 17:1**

Proverbs 24:3-4 says that the means to building, establishing, and enriching a household is wisdom. Many think this is not about literal money but rather a wealth of stable family relationships! (Garrett, *Proverbs*, 198). This truth is huge because one of children's major needs is family security.

Both options could be true—wisdom is the path to a loving family and legitimate wealth. After all, Proverbs gives a balanced view of money. It does not give an unqualified endorsement of money; rather, it says both positive and negative things about money. Money gained through wisdom is good. According to Proverbs, it is good to be content, to be generous, to provide for your family, to save, and to leave an inheritance. On the other hand, money can become an idol that costs you your family. Money is only good in the proper context of contentedly enjoying it in a happy family! Proverbs says that if the choice you have is between a happy home and a wealthy home, choose a happy home every day of the week (Longman, *Proverbs*, 318). A happy, loving home rooted in biblical wisdom is much better than a wealthy home with tension!

Proverbs says this repeatedly. Proverbs 15:16-17 says, "Better a little with the fear of the LORD than great treasure with turmoil. Better a meal of vegetables where there is love than a fattened ox with hatred." And Proverbs 17:1 says, "Better a dry crust with peace than a house full of feasting with strife." The so-called Better Than sayings modify conventional wisdom (Van Leeuwen, "Wealth and Poverty," 29; Waltke, *Proverbs, Chapters 1–15*, 108). Yes, Proverbs says that money can be a good thing, but not at any price! The fear of the Lord is better than money, and so is a harmonious home.

Solomon paints a vivid picture. Greens and crusty bread with no olive oil to dip it in is better than filet mignon in a home with tension where you walk on eggshells! How can veggies be better than steak? If you eat them in a happy and loving home!

The application seems clear: spend more energy loving your children and spending time with them than making money for them. I (Jon) remember counseling with a young husband and father who was about to lose his family because he worked all the time. His statement to me was, "Well, I make the money and she raises the kids." I think many men have that mindset. Yes, you are called to provide (1 Tim 5:8) but not at the expense of the parenting task. Your children need you. They need two parents. I have never counseled with anyone who says, "I was miserable as a child because my parents spent way too much time with me." But I have counseled the opposite many times. So make quality time for your children. Go to their games and recitals, help bathe them, read the Bible and say prayers before bed, talk with them throughout the day, and be an active part of their lives. I am so thankful for a father who modeled this for me and made sure to put our ball games on his calendar so he would not miss them. He built a happy home!

There is a greater possession than money, and it is a godly life that fears the Lord and builds a loving home. Through wisdom, you build a happy home rather than a rich one by the world's standards. The picture painted in Proverbs 17:1 is of a family who is outwardly religious—putting on a show for the public when celebrating the festivals—but on the inside things are awful (Waltke, *Proverbs, Chapters 15–31,* 39). Their so-called spirituality has not affected their daily life in the home. It's a fake spirituality. If your Christianity does not shape the way you parent your children and order your home, it is not real Christianity. That leads to the next wisdom principle for building a happy home. How do you wisely build a happy home?

## Give Your Children Parents Who Are Following Jesus

**PROVERBS 24:3-4; 19:13**

Again, Proverbs 24:3 says that the means to building and establishing a home is wisdom. That makes perfect sense in light of the full context of Proverbs. God created and ordered the world through wisdom (Prov 3; 8).[35] But Proverbs has also told us that wisdom is not a thing; Wisdom is a person—the co-Creator Jesus! Since God created the world and it works in a certain divine way, we need to pattern our homes after the order by which God created the world. Going against the grain is foolishness. Follow the pattern of creation to establish your home, but remember that pattern centers on a person—Jesus of Nazareth. Wisdom is a person to know, and once you begin a relationship with him, he makes you wise for daily life. God built the world through Wisdom, and we are to build our homes through him as well!

God created the world through Wisdom, which means order and harmony with God, each other, and the world around us. Tragically, that harmony was broken through sin and foolishness, so now there is disharmony. You can look at the first family in Eden to see that tension (Gen 3–4)! Proverbs tells us that Wisdom is the path to reestablishing that order and harmony in our families, living life the way it was meant to be lived—as God intended—because the world works a certain way. Admittedly, it does not always work out immediately in a fallen world, but it will work out ultimately. According to Proverbs, this pattern is a person to embrace through the fear of the Lord. Proverbs 8 presents Wisdom (Jesus, according to 1 Cor 1:30) as the mediator that reconciles humankind to God and to each other. So a right relationship with God through Christ will lead to right relationships with others, including your family. If there is a lack of harmony in your home, it's because there is a problem with Jesus. We need to be conformed to the image of Christ, who brings many sons to glory (Heb 2).

Proverbs 19:13 reveals how foolishness can lead to parental or marital relationships that are out of whack. "A foolish son is his father's ruin, and a wife's nagging is an endless dripping." This foolishness exposes the fact that your relationship with Christ is lacking in some way. You can spend three hours in prayer daily and go to four Bible studies weekly;

---

[35] Longman also connects this to home building in *Proverbs*, 436.

but if your home is filled with tension, it shows a problem with Jesus. Many seemingly pious people who are very involved in the church have family lives that are a wreck. It should not be this way. Repentance, confession, and pursuing Christ are the ways to get things back on track. Even confessing to your children that you are a sinner in need of Christ can go a long way!

If you want to have harmony in the home, it starts with embracing Jesus. Your children need parents who have vibrant relationships with Jesus and his body, the church. They need to see that this relationship is authentic by the way it changes your life and parenting. If you are in harmony with Jesus, he will then lead you to harmony in your relationships.

## Give Your Children Training in Wisdom

How do we build a home by wisdom? How can we train our children in wisdom?

### *Example (14:26)*

It starts with your example. Your children need to see a saved parent who walks in wisdom. Psalms 127 and 128 echo these important themes we see in Proverbs. Your children need to see you pray, read Scripture, attend church, sing the songs with a good attitude, listen to the sermons, and serve in the church. In the home, they need to see that you have a hard work ethic, but they also need to see you prioritize time with them and your spouse. They need to see you love well your spouse.

Proverbs 14:26 says, "In the fear of the Lord one has strong confidence and his children have a refuge." Those who trust the Lord live securely because they are under God's protection from the storms of life. The same is true for our children! Your wisdom shields your children because they get to experience the benefits and blessings of it—their lives are affected by your actions. But also, the wise parents, by virtue of their example and teaching, pass wisdom on to their children. Proverbs 20:7 teaches something very similar: "A righteous person acts with integrity; his children who come after him will be happy." Therefore, the ones who model wisdom will pass it and its benefits on to their children.

Why is this so? This is true because children usually turn out to be like their parents. That is both a challenging and a frightening reality. And children are excellent hypocrisy detectors. My (Jon's) kids used to call me out all the time for my hypocrisy in using the "S" word, when

I told them not to use it. They would say, "Dad, you just said 'stupid'!" Children watch you closely, and you have tremendous influence on their lives. Granted, you cannot conclude that every foolish child is unwise because his or her parents messed up, but generally that is the way it works. So what example are you setting for your children? If they turned out like you, would that be a good thing? Chances are that they will!

### *Instruction (24:3-4)*

The second way to train your children in wisdom is to instruct them. You must use your words to teach your children. There should be none of this "preach the gospel at all times and when necessary use words." No! Your wise example must also include wise words of instruction. This truth is one of the major concerns of Proverbs. It is all over the book. It is a dad following the commands of Deuteronomy 6 to teach his son, and pleading with him, "Listen to me!"

Teach your children the wisdom of Proverbs. That means teaching them right from wrong. That means teaching them spiritual realities as well as practical realities like a work ethic, saving money, and controlling their tongues, because there is no sacred/secular divide. God is concerned with every detail of your life. Teach your children the way that life works best.

Do not just teach your children what to do; teach them why they must do it. The "why" is the motivation for the behavior. Solomon constantly tells his son the consequences or benefits of walking in wisdom or walking in folly. He says if you do not do this or you do not listen to that, there are disastrous results. Teach your children why they should do their chores, handle money correctly, control their tongues, and develop conflict resolution and wise planning skills. Lay out both the benefits and the consequences. Teach them why it is a bad idea to buck authority, be too lazy to do their homework, be cocky, gossip, or have sex before marriage.

For example, my (Jon's) parents would not allow me to quit track in the eighth grade because they wanted me to learn to finish what I started. That was the reason. And there are so many things I would not have gotten through if they had not taught me that lesson—like my PhD!

You must be the teacher and authority in their lives on these matters. You must not have just "the talk," but ongoing talks about dating, romance, and sexuality. If you are not the authority, their peers or the

TV will be, and that is a bad idea. This is your role; you can't farm it out to daycares, schools, or youth pastors. You are responsible to get them on the right path because they cannot choose it by themselves.

This also includes teaching them the Bible. Do not hide behind excuses like "That's just not my thing." Make it your thing! Read the Bible to them, share your testimony with them, talk to them in the car on the way home from church about the Lord's Supper, and help them memorize Scripture. You can do it. You memorize meaningless sports facts and movie quotes, so determine to memorize God's Word. It has never been easier. My daughters and I listen to the AWANA CD with memory verses on the way to school. There are free audio Bible apps for your smartphone. Take advantage of the resources!

Finally, this also means being alert for conversations. When your children ask questions, even questions that might make you uncomfortable (How can I get to heaven? Is it wrong to be gay? What is sex?), don't shut them down or put them off. That will just teach them not to come to you with things that concern or interest them. Answer their questions kindly and directly in an age appropriate way. If you are not sure how to do that, just say, "That's a great question. Can I have some time to think about it and talk with you soon about it?" Don't be afraid to seek counsel from older, godly parents. But when your children want to talk, make every effort to make the most of the opportunity.

### *Correction (13:24; 23:13-14; 29:15)*

The third way to train your children in wisdom is to correct them. You do not punish your children simply for the sake of punishing them. Discipline is about correction—putting them on the right path (29:15). That means instruction must accompany discipline.

Some people falsely think, "I just love my children too much to discipline them." However, if you do not discipline your children, it is because you do not really love them. In fact, Proverbs says that you hate them (13:24). When my dad (Danny) was in high school, he was hanging out at a restaurant with some buddies when the subject of curfew came up. All the teenage guys reluctantly told when their curfew was, but one of the guys said, "I don't have a curfew." His friends were incredulous. "How can that be? You are so lucky!" But my dad said his countenance changed, and he said, "My old man doesn't care if I ever come home." The lack of boundaries did not show love; rather, it sadly showed indifference.

We must correct our kids because discipline is an evangelism mission to rescue our kids from hell. Proverbs 23:13-14 says, "Don't withhold discipline from a youth; if you punish him with a rod, he will not die. Punish him with a rod, and you will rescue his life from Sheol." Kids are sinful at heart, and left to themselves they will walk to destruction. It is not loving to be their buddy and let them make their own choices as they march off toward hell. You must start young with discipline. There is a temptation to give in during the early years for the sake of peace, but you must fight against that temptation.

Correction is a gospel issue. You teach them what sin is, that it has consequences, that they will be held accountable, and that it needs to be repented of. If you do not correct them, they will start to think that evil is good.

How do you correct them? Well, Proverbs clearly calls for spanking. If that upsets you, send your e-mails to Solomon not us because it is all over Proverbs, no matter how out of step with the culture it might seem. We all understand this principle when it comes to working out. You discipline your body—introducing a little pain—in order to make it healthier. The same is true with spanking. It is not detrimental if done properly. In fact there are studies that show adults who were spanked as children have a sunnier outlook on life and are more successful (Baklinski, "Young Children"). You should never spank out of anger or because the child simply is not doing what you want them to do—that's called abuse. You should not spank for childish accidents like spilling milk. But you should spank for outright defiance, dishonesty, or rebellion. Do it in private so as not to embarrass your child and so you can talk—have a teachable moment.

This is an important moment for a gospel conversation. Tell them what they did or did not do. Secure an acknowledgement that they know why they are getting a spanking. That can teach them confession. Tell them you love them no matter what, and that your love for them is not determined by their behavior. Hug them afterward and tell them that you are a sinner too who understands the need for forgiveness. That is why you are thankful for Jesus because you have done similar things to what they just did, and you are glad Jesus has forgiven you. Spanking should wait until the child is old enough to understand expectations and can start responding to directions.

Proverbs also seems to call for an adjustment of correction as the child gets older. Proverb 29:15 states, "The rod and reproof give wisdom, but a child left to himself brings shame to his mother" (ESV). As the child gets older, a rebuke (or restriction) should be enough to correct the behavior. Words are always part of the correction process.

Finally, here is some practical advice: Make sure that you and your spouse are on the same page when it comes to correction so that your children cannot play one against another. Give a big playing field and don't be too legalistic, otherwise you won't be consistent in your discipline, and you have to be!

## Conclusion

The "Big Key" to having a happy home is to introduce your children to a Parent whose love is truly unconditional and unchanging—God the Father. And you need his unconditional love as well because you will fail as a parent. You will not do everything perfectly. But you serve a God who can make all things new! It's not too late! Start building a happy home today through the Wisdom of God!

## Reflect and Discuss

1. Why do you think there are so many unhappy homes in one of the wealthiest countries in the history of the world?
2. Where do we often look for tips on how to order our families?
3. How can you prioritize your children over work? Name some very concrete ways.
4. In what ways can going through the motions religiously have a negative impact on your family?
5. What are some practical ways you can introduce your children to Jesus?
6. In what ways have you noticed your children observing and critiquing your example?
7. How do you usually respond when your kids ask you uncomfortable questions?
8. How can you keep your antenna up for important conversations with your children?
9. In what ways can you lovingly correct your children through discipline?
10. Why do you think we are tempted to not discipline our children? Why is that dangerous?

# Section 4—Sticks and Stones: The Power of Words

# Shut Up!

## PROVERBS 26:18-28

**Main Idea:** Harmful words damage relationships and reveal a heart out of tune with Jesus.

---

**I. Don't Use Harmful Words (26:18-28).**
   A. Contentious speech (26:21)
   B. Perverse speech (2:12; 4:24; 15:4; 24:24; 30:20)
   C. Flattery (26:28)
   D. Deception (26:18-19)
   E. Gossip and slander (11:13)
   F. Bragging (27:2)
**II. Harmful Words Hurt Relationships (26:18-19).**
**III. Forgiveness and Change Are Possible in Jesus.**

---

We've all heard the old saying, "Sticks and stones may break my bones, but words will never hurt me." That statement is not true, and we all know it. Physical wounds often heal long before emotional ones. There are words that still haunt you. When you hear them, your stomach turns. Or there are words that you really regret saying and wish you could have back.

Words are powerful. Words like "I hate you" or "I love you" or "You will never amount to anything" or "I'm so proud of you" change lives! Words change history. Words like "I have a dream" or "Mr. Gorbachev, tear down this wall" shape the course of history. Words can shape the course of eternity: "For God loved the world in this way: He gave his one and only Son, so that everyone who believes in him will not perish but have eternal life" (John 3:16); "If you confess with your mouth, 'Jesus is Lord,' and believe in your heart that God raised him from the dead, you will be saved" (Rom 10:9).

The tongue holds the power of life and death (Prov 18:21). The problem is that while our tongues contain this power, we often cannot control them. We try to, but we just cannot. A lack of self-control when it comes to our tongues destroys marriages, families, and friendships.

You blow up on your kids, you continually interrupt your wife, you constantly nitpick your husband, you repeatedly bring up past mistakes, you flirt with a coworker, or you betray a confidence, and the results are ruinous.

As James the brother of Jesus incredulously observes, with our tongues we bless God and curse men made in his image (Jas 3:9). Solomon understands the harmful power of our words, and he warns us about them repeatedly. We know this, and we do not really need to be convinced. Who among us has not thought at one time, "I really wish I had not said that"? We all struggle with using harmful words that hurt us, our relationships with others, and our relationship with God. Let's look at what Proverbs says about harmful words and see if change is possible.

## Don't Use Harmful Words

### PROVERBS 26:18-28

Proverbs describes numerous kinds of harmful words, and it includes a lot more than just cursing. There are ways to talk and use our words that are very destructive. Let's examine what Proverbs says.

### *Contentious Speech (26:21)*

Proverbs talks about contentious or quarrelsome speech. Proverbs 26:21 says, "As charcoal for embers and wood for fire, so is a quarrelsome person for kindling strife." Contentious speech is speech that loves to stir up conflict. It loves to argue and disagree. It thinks that it is cool to constantly criticize things. The argument can be on any topic under the sun. The contentious person loves to argue about sports, sitcoms, the Bible, or politics. They usually start their end of a conversation with, "Well, actually that is not the case . . ." You can find this guy commenting on Facebook a lot!

Unfortunately, you also frequently see this in churches: folks who like to complain about what other people wear or grumble if they do not get their way. Nothing seems to be to their liking. They love to spread dissension and stir trouble in an attempt to get what they want. They even make ultimatums and threats like, "If things do not change around here, I will just have to leave the church."

### *Perverse Speech (2:12; 4:24; 15:4; 24:24; 30:20)*

Wisdom is meant to deliver us from perverse or devious speech (2:12; 4:24; 15:4). Perverse speech is speech that distorts truth and reality.[36] Proverbs talks extensively about this. Perverse speech is not the same thing as deception (see below). Perverse speech distorts truth itself. The person using it may—and probably does—think that what they are saying is true.

Perverse speech would include false religions and false ideas. False religions tell you distortions like, if you kill infidels, you will get numerous virgins in paradise. Or if you just believe in Jesus, he will make you healthy and wealthy.

The category of perverse speech would also include speech that calls sin a good thing. That claim leads people astray. Proverbs 24:24 says, "Whoever says to the guilty, 'You are innocent'—peoples will curse him, and nations will denounce him." Calling a sin something other than sin is perverse. Many in our culture want to do this with things like homosexuality, and even in the church people are waffling on whether or not it is a sin. But we do the same thing when we minimize divorce, gluttony, gossiping, or self-righteousness. It is perverse to call sin anything other than what it is.

Perverse speech also includes the justification of sin. Proverbs 30:20 says, "This is the way of an adulteress: she eats and wipes her mouth and says, 'I've done nothing wrong.'" We can act like our sin is not sin, or we can justify it like it is not that big a deal. Perverse speech justifies our way of life (Garrett, *Proverbs,* 76). This might manifest itself as a lady justifying living with her boyfriend or a man justifying his divorce. With our mouths we can rationalize and minimize and excuse our sin.

Why do we talk like this? We do it because we want to live how we want to live. We want to avoid repentance. We want to live life on our terms and still be able to say, "I am a good person." Instead of trusting Jesus to justify us, we want to prove ourselves right!

### *Flattery (26:28)*

Proverbs 26:28 says, "A lying tongue hates those it crushes, and a flattering mouth causes ruin." Flattery is smooth talk (Goldsworthy, *Tree of Life,*

---

[36] Longman argues similarly. He writes that perverse speech "offends righteousness and goes against the dictates . . . of God himself" (*Proverbs,* 123).

168). Proverbs condemns flirting with or praising others to manipulate the circumstances for your advantage.

Flattery can be deception (Goldsworthy, *Tree of Life*, 168). Flattery can be exaggerating the truth to elicit a reaction from someone who will gratify you. Yes, this includes flirting, but it can also be any situation where you praise another so that they like you or respond the way you want. Flattery is a form of manipulation to advance yourself. It's not a genuine compliment.

Proverbs 7:21 says, "She seduces him with her persistent pleading; she lures with her flattering talk." So flattery can be flirting or flirting back with someone at work, at your children's ballgame, in chat rooms, or by text messages. According to Proverbs, flattery is the number-one factor in cheating. Flattery and listening to flattery pulls your heart away from your spouse. I read the testimony of a pastor who fell morally, and he said it started with flattery. It was fun to him at first, and then he let it linger too long. He began to rationalize what he was doing because he was frustrated and thought there was not really any harm in it. He thought it was not a big deal and that he would not really do anything anyway. Then, all of a sudden, he ended up cheating on his wife! It all started with flattery. Be warned.

Flattery also happens outside of romantic relationships. People are obsequious to others who they think can advance them. People tell others what they want to hear. Why? They want admiration, self-advancement, or some other desired outcome. Proverbs condemns this kind of speech.

### *Deception (26:18-19)*

Proverbs 26:18-19 says, "Like a madman who throws flaming darts and deadly arrows, so is the person who deceives his neighbor and says, 'I was only joking!'" Deception can be embellishment, exaggeration, half-truths, omission, intentional misrepresentation, truth in jest, or perjury. Verse 19 mentions the truth in jesting. You hurt someone's feelings, so you say, "I was just joking," in order to minimize their pain, but really you meant it.

We can use our words to construct false realities. Pro athletes caught using performance-enhancing drugs try to convince people, "I would never do something like that." I (Jon) remember a new kid coming to our high school, and his dad tried to convince our basketball coach that the University of Kentucky was recruiting him because he was such a stud athlete. The kid could barely make the junior varsity team, but his dad tried to convince people he was an all-star.

All of us do this kind of thing. Who has not exaggerated or left details out to come off looking better? We are born deceivers. Children do it to avoid trouble or to get out of trouble. Even when we tell our children, "If you tell me the truth, you won't get in trouble," our children still struggle to come clean. Teenagers are deceivers. They cheat in school to get good grades, and they lie to their parents about where they are going. Adults are deceivers. They lie to their boss about being sick so they can stay home. They hide things from their spouse or omit things to keep the serenity in marriage. In conversations, adults will put the blame on someone else, even when it is their fault, so that their spouse is mad at someone else rather than at them. Adults can exaggerate the truth to avoid doing something they do not want to do. Or adults will tell part of the truth so that they can say to themselves, "Well, technically I didn't lie." They are still trying to manipulate the outcome.

Why do we deceive? We do it because we want something, and we think manipulating the truth will help us get it. This reveals idolatry because it shows we are seeking satisfaction and joy in something other than God. We try to find satisfaction in people's approval, and we value it more than God's approval.

### *Gossip and Slander (11:13)*

Proverbs condemns gossip and slander. Gossip is revealing a secret, while slander is defaming people's reputation or mocking them. When it comes to gossip, some folks just love to be in the know. Some just cannot keep secrets. Proverbs 11:13 says, "A gossip goes around revealing a secret, but a trustworthy person keeps a confidence." Ask yourself: can you keep a confidence, or do you regularly start sentences with "Don't tell anyone else this, but . . ."? Some even try to disguise their gossip and slander as a prayer request: "He's really gone off the deep end. We need to pray for him." Why do we gossip and slander? We do it for revenge, out of jealousy, or out of the pride of wanting to be in the know.

### *Bragging (27:2)*

Proverbs condemns bragging. It says, "Let another praise you, and not your own mouth—a stranger, and not your own lips" (27:2). Do not praise yourself or embellish your accomplishments. A modern paraphrase of this might be something like, "Let another tweet about you and not your own tweet—a stranger and not your own account!" So often self-exaltation is seen as good and necessary to get ahead in our culture. Or you know people who always turn the conversation back to themselves no matter what you say. Toby Keith sings about this when he wants to "talk about me." Why do we do this? We do it because either we are insecure or we want to exalt ourselves. The gospel can cure both of those things because God's approval in Christ is incompatible with insecurity, and the humility of Christ in laying down his life for others is antithetical to self-exaltation.

## Harmful Words Hurt Relationships

**PROVERBS 26:18-19**

Walking in foolishness with your words has all kinds of negative consequences, including destroying your relationships. This is pretty obvious. Proverbs 17:9 says, "Whoever conceals an offense promotes love, but whoever gossips about it separates friends." Gossip spoils friendships (Waltke, *Proverbs, Chapters 15–31,* 50). Those who constantly stir up arguments are annoying to be around. Those who deceive hurt their neighbors (26:18-19). Harmful speech ruins relationships.

But it's more than that. It's not just that being a contentious person will cause conflict and divide groups, although it does. It's not just that flattery ruins marriages and families, although it does. It's not just that deception ruins friendships or careers, although it does. It's not just that gossip divides friends and hurts people's feelings, although it does. It's not just that bragging makes people nauseated to be around you, although it does. The biggest problem is that harmful speech separates you from a relationship with God and invites judgment. All of the temporal consequences of broken relationships are just a foretaste of hell. Jesus says we will be held accountable for every careless word we utter (Matt 12:36). Verses like Proverbs 10:31 teach us, "The mouth of the righteous produces wisdom, but a perverse tongue will be cut out." And 19:9 adds, "A false witness will not go unpunished, and one who utters lies perishes."

## Forgiveness and Change Are Possible in Jesus

Jesus never sinned with his mouth. He never harmed anyone with his words. He never let deceit slip from his lips (1 Pet 2:22). He fully lived out Proverbs. And yet he took the final judgment for our harmful speech to provide us forgiveness in full. The one with no deceit in his mouth died for deceivers like us. The humble died for the bragger. The reconciler died for the contentious.

To the degree that the truth of the gospel grips you, you will no longer need to lie, gossip, slander, or flirt. You will no longer need to exalt yourself with your words because Jesus gives grace to the humble. You will not need to justify yourself because in Christ you have already been justified. You will not need to be slanderous and unforgiving because Jesus has forgiven you. You will not need to lie to get others' approval because you have the approval of Jesus.

## Conclusion

Words are powerful indeed. The tongue is difficult to tame. But there are words that overcome our sinful and uncontrolled tongues. They are words like, "Therefore, there is now no condemnation for those in Christ Jesus" (Rom 8:1), and words like "The fruit of the Spirit is . . . self-control" (Gal 5:22-23). Praise God for those words!

## Reflect and Discuss

1. How is the sticks and stones rhyme so inaccurate?
2. How can you avoid being an argumentative person?
3. Why do we justify our sin but critique the sin of others?
4. Why is flattery so dangerous?
5. In what ways do we deceive people?
6. Why is gossip such a big temptation?
7. How does the social media culture seem to encourage bragging?
8. How has harmful speech hurt your relationships?
9. In what ways can you do a better job of thinking before you speak?
10. How does the gospel help free you from using your tongue in a sinful way?

## Listen Up!

### PROVERBS 15:31-33

**Main Idea:** Wisdom is the ability to listen before you speak.

---

How Can I Be a Fool?

**I. Don't Listen to Anyone but Yourself (12:15; 15:5,22,31,33).**
**II. Speak Before You Listen and Speak More Than You Listen (10:19; 17:27-28).**
**III. Listen to Unwise Counsel (12:5).**

---

There is a hilarious video on YouTube where a man sings southern gospel music in a church auditorium. The man sings a song called "Looking for a City," trying to copy a really talented singer named Brian Free who can raise his voice to a really high pitch. The man claims in this video that he is a better singer than Brian Free as he begins to sing the song and tries to raise his pitch to higher and higher levels. The song is a cacophonous mess that clearly does not come close to what one might call "good singing." It's hilarious!

People are self-deceived. The man on this video is convinced that he is a good singer, but any objective evaluation clearly reveals that he is not. That's not just a problem for him or for singers trying to make it on *American Idol*. It's a problem for all of us. We all can convince ourselves that we are good parents, great spouses, or wonderful employees without actually putting in the work to be skilled at any of these (Ten Elshof, *I Told Me So*, 1–5). This self-deception will catch up to us eventually and can cause more than embarrassment. We know folks who have lost their teaching positions because they were convinced that they were great teachers and did not need to heed their evaluations that they were too abrasive in their interactions with students. We know husbands who have lost their marriages because they do not adequately care for their wives, but they are convinced that their wives are the ones who are deceived!

Proverbs says a lot about self-deception and how it ruins us. It calls us not to lean on our own understanding or follow the way that seems right to us. Because left to ourselves we are self-deceived and go the wrong way, we need a wisdom that sees the world as it really is and can guide us to safety. The answer to our problem is wise instruction from the outside instead of "following our hearts." We need wisdom from outside of ourselves so that we do not deceive ourselves, destroy our relationships, and stumble our way through the world. Solomon began Proverbs by saying that wisdom includes listening and obtaining guidance, but fools reject wisdom (1:5,7). We read the same thing in Proverbs 15:31-33,

> *One who listens to life-giving rebukes*
> *will be at home among the wise.*
> *Anyone who ignores discipline despises himself,*
> *but whoever listens to correction acquires good sense.*
> *The fear of the* LORD *is what wisdom teaches,*
> *and humility comes before honor.*

We are not naturally wise or good at heart, but we think we are, and we head off toward destruction. Therefore, whether or not we can listen to and submit to wise counsel is a life or death matter. So if you want to be a fool and wreck your life, it starts with not listening.

## How Can I Be a Fool? Don't Listen to Anyone but Yourself

### PROVERBS 12:15; 15:5,22,31,33

Proverbs 15:31 indicates that wisdom is listening to wise rebuke, and thus foolishness is the opposite: not listening to a wise rebuke! Wisdom will not come unless we listen to wise counsel from outside of us because it is not in us. As Longman points out, "Only the wise are willing to admit mistakes, change behavior and improve their lives," which requires listening to correction (*Proverbs*, 323).

Proverbs 15:22 says, "Plans fail when there is no counsel, but with many advisers they succeed." We need many advisers to avoid getting just one perspective. We need counsel so we can make good decisions and successful plans. We need this kind of counsel because we so easily deceive ourselves!

Proverbs 12:15 adds, "A fool's way is right in his own eyes, but whoever listens to counsel is wise." The way that seems right leads to death, but if you listen to outside counsel you will be wise. Left to ourselves we do not choose the right path. We see this with our children. They do not naturally share; they have to be made to share. They do not naturally pick up their rooms; they have to be instructed to clean their rooms.

The problem is that very few people admit to not being wise. We all think our assessment of the situation is the correct one—if we did not, we would change our assessment! Young pastors often think they are wiser than older pastors. Teens think they are wiser than their much more experienced parents. Young people who are dating and think they are "in love" persist in their perspective despite everyone who cares about them telling them it's a bad idea. They will not listen to anyone, and they act like everyone sees the situation wrongly except them! This warped reality is true for all of us, yet we obliviously persist in the notion "I see things rightly" because our hearts are broken by sin and we are not naturally wise. Thus, we need to listen to outside counsel and advice to correct our path. We need to listen to God's Word and consider the counsel of trusted friends.

This is true in so many areas of our lives. The need for children to listen to parents is repeated over and over in Proverbs. Proverbs 15:5 states, "A fool despises his father's discipline, but a person who accepts correction is sensible." This verse means that children should listen to what their parents say and obey them while they live under their roof. It also means that they should seek counsel from their parents when they no longer live in the same house! The Bible indicates that church members should hear and obey their leaders who speak God's word to them (Heb 13:7,17). The Bible exhorts younger people to listen to the counsel of the elderly (Titus 2:4). Consequently, younger parents should seek counsel from older parents who are further along in the parenting task. Younger husbands should seek counsel from older husbands on how to handle money, interview for a job, or lead their families.

Proverbs 15:33 explains that listening requires a posture of humility. Instead of "I did it my way," recognize that you do not have everything figured out. Why does it require humility? We are prideful and do not naturally submit ourselves to other people's advice if it does not match up with what we think. Our sinful reaction is immediately to think, "I know better than you!" In our culture people are rarely corrected, and even if we are corrected in love, our first reaction is usually not to thank people for their concern. Rather, we bristle, get mad, and think of reasons why they are not fit to talk to us about this situation. Wisdom is the humility to recognize you do not know everything and to ask for counsel.

In concert with the humility to listen, Solomon teaches that wisdom is ultimately trust and dependence on Yahweh. Whether or not you depend on the Lord is revealed in whether or not you listen to counsel. Whether or not you submit to truth and authority in all the areas of your life reveals what your relationship is like with the Lord. It is hard to humble ourselves and submit to the Lord's authority, and that is shown in the fact that it is hard for us to submit to our earthly authorities like parents, government officials, bosses, or even pastors. It is hard because we think that our way is right. Wisdom requires the ability to recognize that you can deceive yourself, you are not always right, and you need to submit humbly to wise instruction as you submit to the Lord!

So do you want to be a fool? Then do not listen to anyone but yourself. Only take your own ideas. Be convinced that you are the only one who is right and that you are smarter than everyone else. No one else is looking out for you and wants your best interest like you do. So listen to yourself, not others!

## Speak Before You Listen and Speak More Than You Listen

**PROVERBS 10:19; 17:27-28**

Proverbs talks a lot about the use of our tongues, and one key exhortation is, "Don't talk so much!" Some people really struggle with talking too much. I (Jon) confess that I am one of them. I often try to finish my wife's thoughts or jump into the conversation in the middle of her sentence. If you are the kind of person who always wants to give your opinion first, or if you are not really listening to the other person in conversation, or when you are in a conversation you just wait for your turn to talk, then that is a sign of foolishness. Proverbs teaches that we need to learn to restrain our mouths. Proverbs 10:19 states, "When there are many words, sin is unavoidable, but the one who controls his lips is prudent." Proverbs 17:27-28 adds,

> *The one who has knowledge restrains his words, and one who keeps a cool head is a person of understanding. Even a fool is considered wise when he keeps silent—discerning, when he seals his lips.*

These verses sound similar to the more modern proverb attributed to Abraham Lincoln: "Better to remain silent and be thought a fool than to speak out and remove all doubt." Proverbs is clear that speaking a lot leads to sin, whereas a restrained mouth is a sign of wisdom. At the very least, one might be considered wise—even if he is not—with a little less talking. As Goldsworthy points out, "Ironically, the fool who has the wit to keep silent shows at least some potential for wisdom" (*Tree of Life*, 131).

There are at least two key reasons for restraining your mouth. First, control of the tongue protects you from impulsive speech. If you are rash with your words, you can do much damage. Once the words are out there, you cannot get them back. How many of us have come to understand this truth the hard way? How has talking before you listen or talking before you think affected your marriage, your children, your friendships, or your job? Murphy and Huwiler helpfully point out, "Human nature being what it is, garrulousness leads to all kinds of blunders" (*Proverbs*, 51).[37] Do you want to be a fool who ruins his relationships? Then talk too much!

The second reason to restrain your tongue is because it will prevent you from self-confident speech. Proverbs evaluates self-confident speech as foolishness. Self-confident speech is defined as loving to hear yourself talk or always having to give your own opinion on a matter. Proverbs 18:2 says, "A fool does not delight in understanding, but only wants to show off his opinions." Longman explains,

> The verse suggests that fools are again only interested in their own desires and ideas . . . [they do not] want to listen to people with competence. They only want to blurt out what is on their minds. (*Proverbs*, 354)

Do you have a hard time listening to other people? Are you always confident in your evaluations of the matter? Do you think everyone else should listen to you? Do you have a hard time engaging in actual conversations because you are waiting for the other person to take a breath so you can start talking? Then you might be a fool!

If you want to be a fool, speak before you listen. Also, speak more than you listen. But if you want to be wise, be slow to speak and quick to listen.

## Listen to Unwise Counsel

### PROVERBS 12:5

Not only does the fool usually listen only to himself, and not only does the fool speak more than he listens; but when the fool finally decides to listen to someone else, he listens to another fool! When you finally listen to someone else, it is only to unwise, ungodly counsel. For many people this means surrounding themselves with "yes men" who will simply tell them what they want to hear. So ask yourself these questions: Do you surround yourself with people who tell you what you want to hear, but not what you need to hear? Is there anyone in your life who has the freedom to lovingly criticize you or tell you no?

---

[37] A garrulous person is excessively talkative, especially about trivial matters.

Proverbs 12:5 states, "The thoughts of the righteous are just, but guidance from the wicked is deceitful." Unwise counsel will be deceitful because it will not tell you the way things really are. It will not lead you on the best course. It will get you off track. Unfortunately, Solomon pleaded with his son over and over to listen to wise counsel so that he could be a good king; but his son, Rehoboam, did not heed the advice of his father. Instead, Rehoboam listened to his peers—who told him what he wanted to hear—rather than listen to the elders who gave him good counsel, and it ruined his kingdom (1 Kgs 12). Today, people get bad counsel all the time from coworkers or friends. When they have struggles in their marriage because of something their husbands have done, sometimes their coworkers will say things like, "Just dump the loser!" That is hardly the godly advice that one needs to hear to make a marriage work. Proverbs 14:7 warns, "Stay away from a foolish person; you will gain no knowledge from his speech." Wisdom is not just the ability to listen, but it is also the ability to discern whom or what to listen to and what to receive or reject! The criteria for this discernment will be the answer to this question: Is this counsel consistent with God's Word?

Let's make a disclaimer at this point. There is a potential problem in even bringing this discernment up because when we say discernment is required, all of a sudden we "discern" that anyone who disagrees with our opinion on the matter is unwise and should not be heeded. Again, that is because we deceive ourselves and close our minds to counsel. If the person is willing to tell us what we need to hear, even if it is uncomfortable, and if their counsel runs consistent with the Bible, then you can be fairly confident that you need to listen to it. And even if you are not sure, you can always ask the question and ponder, "Is there something I need to hear here?"

Unfortunately, we are amazed by how often ungodly, unbiblical counsel can come from other Christians. I (Jon) once knew an elderly lady who began a relationship with an unbeliever who had multiple failed marriages. They wanted to get married, but their pastor was reluctant because the groom was not a Christian and because of his past failures. They liked each other and were lonely living by themselves, so they wanted to move in together while they waited for a pastor who would marry them. All of her Christian friends told her to go ahead and move in with the guy. They said at her age it was not that big a deal. That is an obvious example of unbiblical counsel, but we all can be guilty of the same thing. Whenever you are listening to counsel, if your situation is seen as an exception clause to the biblical testimony, then you can bet that it is not godly advice. People love to follow God's Word when it suits them, but we always think our situation is the exception. It's not! Do not let anyone tell you otherwise!

## Conclusion

There are two things we need in order to be wise in this area of life. We need Jesus, and we need his body, the church. We need a relationship with Christ and to listen to his Word. Plus, we need brothers and sisters in our lives who can call us out and tell us the truth in love (Eph 4:15).

Proverbs has revealed to us that wisdom is personal. If you recognize a pattern of foolishness in your life in the area of not listening enough or talking too much, it reveals a problem with Jesus. Not listening to counsel and talking too much is a spiritual, gospel issue. It reveals some issue—most likely that you do not recognize just how great a sinner you are! You do not really believe that you are prone to self-deception. Instead, you have set yourself up as god of your own life.

If you have a proper spiritual life, you become progressively holy—more like Christ—as you walk with and submit to him. One of the ways you can tell if you are becoming more holy is if you can successfully receive a rebuke and make a correction in your life. After all, Jesus could remain silent when he needed to be quiet. And Jesus knew how to grow in wisdom by listening to the teachers in the temple (Luke 2:46,52). If you are not growing in your ability to listen to wise counsel and measure your words, something is wrong in your relationship with Jesus Christ.

Not growing in Christlikeness in this area of your life will have nasty consequences. It might ruin your reputation because you just will not listen to correction and you will continue to make the same mistakes. You might wreck your family because you think they are all wrong and you could not possibly be. You could get fired from your job because you think your supervisor's evaluation is crazy. Do you want to be a fool and ruin your life? Then listen only to yourself, talk more than you listen, surround yourself with people who will only tell you what you want to hear, and have the attitude, "This is who I am, and I'm not gonna change!" That is deadly.

The antidote is Jesus. Recognize your foolishness here, confess it to the Lord, and ask him for the wisdom that he gives generously. Ask Jesus to enable you to listen and measure words in the power of the Holy Spirit. Jesus is the Wisdom of God who has become wisdom for you and can make you wise. Read and listen to God's Word to gain wisdom. You will recognize that you are not always right and you need to submit to God's truth.

You also need Christ's body; you need a community of faith. In the church, you live life together and depend on each other. Proverbs is clear that associating with fools will make you foolish, but uniting with the wise will make you wise. Therefore, you need to be in relationships with other Christians who are seeking to walk with Jesus. You need to give these brothers and sisters freedom to speak into your life, just as you have freedom to speak into theirs.

When you are faced with a tough decision, you do not want to seek counsel from those who will simply tell you what you want to hear. You need to be able to ask, "Who are the godliest people I know, and what do they think about this?" Do not adopt a "me and Jesus" approach to decision making. That is foolish because it's usually more "me" than Jesus.

Recognize how easily you deceive yourself, and thus restrain your mouth and listen to godly counsel in your local church. You may have a long prayer by yourself each morning, and you may be involved in three mid-week Bible studies, and you might even serve on a deacon body, but whether or not you can listen to the counsel of others and control your tongue tells you a lot about your relationship with Christ.

## Reflect and Discuss

1. Why can we so easily deceive ourselves and see ourselves in a different light than everyone else?
2. Why does listening to someone else require humility?
3. Why do people persist in unwise romantic relationships even when the people who love them the most say it's a bad idea?
4. Who are the authorities that God has placed in your life right now that you need to listen to?
5. Who are some wise people or wise categories of people that you need to seek counsel from right now?
6. In what ways does speaking rashly or impulsively hurt our relationships? Give specific examples.
7. In what ways should your desire to always air your opinion on social media or around the water cooler warn you about whether you are wise or foolish?
8. Why do we have such a hard time receiving a rebuke?
9. How does the inability to listen to counsel reveal a lack of faith in the gospel?
10. How does the inability to control your tongue reveal a lack of faith in the gospel?

## Speak Up!

### PROVERBS 27:5-6

**Main Idea:** Loving confrontation is the right word from the right person in the right way at the right time to the right person.

---

**I. The Right Word**
**II. From the Right Person**
**III. In the Right Way**
**IV. At the Right Time**
**V. To the Right Person**

---

*American Idol* brought on Ellen DeGeneres to fill the big void left by Simon Cowell's departure, but Ellen did not stay with the music talent show very long. She said she quit because she realized she was not a good fit and added, "I also realized this season that while I love discovering, supporting and nurturing young talent, it was hard for me to judge and sometimes hurt their feelings" ("Ellen DeGeneres Bows Out"). Have you ever watched *Idol*, particularly the early rounds? If there is anywhere on the planet that people need to be told the harsh truth, it is on *American Idol*. People come on the show thinking they should be the next big superstars in America, yet they cannot carry a tune at all. The only reason they are convinced they are good is because the people in their lives have lied to them or pacified them. Their friends and family members have never told them that they need to do something else, instead giving them a false sense of competency with their platitudes like, "You can be anything you want to be!" Because no one has ever told them the hard truth, they do not see reality rightly.

What we observe on *Idol*, we also see in the culture at large. We now live in a society that values personal freedom over the truth and a culture that values "tolerance," which means you cannot ever tell someone he is wrong. We live in a culture that says, "Let people live their lives the way they want to live their lives," or, "It's not your place to tell them how to live their lives," or, "You don't have the right to tell someone that what she believes, thinks, or does is wrong. You worry about yourself, let others live their own lives, and stay out of their business."

We have created the same culture within the church. We hear things like, "Don't judge," "Show grace," or "Mind your own business." I (Jon) heard the story of a time when a pastor's daughter tweeted crass things on social media. When a church member lovingly brought it up to the pastor, the pastor's response was, "Let him who is without sin cast the first stone." The Bible commands us to live in loving and accountable community; yet we reject accountability at every turn, even in the church. There is rarely loving confrontation in the church. We rarely speak up when we see a brother or sister moving into foolish sin. We have been so influenced by a culture that says you cannot impose your standard on someone else that we no longer live out the picture of the New Testament. We isolate ourselves from others and do not really invite people into our lives despite the biblical exhortations that say we need each other. There are over thirty "one another" commands in the Bible! They reveal that we cannot live the Christian life in isolation.

We must learn how to speak up because people need to hear the truth spoken in love (Eph 4:15). We need people who will lovingly tell us the truth! If your friend has something stuck in her teeth or tissue paper on her shoe or his fly is open, it is not loving to simply stay quiet out of fear that he or she might be embarrassed. And if someone is on a fool's path, it is not loving to refuse to confront him simply because the world might say it is harsh. The world is wrong in many cases, and this is one of them!

As followers of Christ, we are commanded to speak up. Despite everyone's favorite phrase to quote out of context—"Do not judge" (Matt 7:1)—we are also commanded to judge Christians corporately in the church (1 Cor 5:12). Why do we speak up? We speak up because we do not want the people we love to destroy their lives. We speak up and correct our children because we want them to learn how to live life. The most loving thing we can do is tell them the truth before they hurt themselves or others. We speak up because the person in sin may be a false professor who has convinced himself he is a believer when he might not be. If he remains in continual, unrepentant sin, he may not be genuinely saved, and we are commanded to confront him before it's too late so that we might gain a brother. We speak up and tell the truth in love to lost people when we witness to them.

Church discipline on the big scale rarely works in our day and age. One of the key reasons is that we are not doing continual church discipline on the small scale. Church discipline should be taking place all the time. Jesus said, "If your brother sins against you, go and rebuke him in private. If he listens to you, you have won your brother" (Matt 18:15). These kinds of private conversations should happen all the time. The problem is that we do not have a culture of open confession of sin in the church because we think we will not be seen as "good Christians" if we admit our struggles. And we do not have a culture of accountability and loving confrontation, so by the time it progresses to excommunication, people are rarely willing to listen. If we could create a culture of loving accountability and regular confrontation—giving and receiving it rightly—then maybe we might have a body that walks in holiness. Proverbs repeats this need many times.

Proverbs 27:5-6 says, "Better an open reprimand than concealed love. The wounds of a friend are trustworthy, but the kisses of an enemy are excessive." We must confront because we love people and want their good. If we do not confront, we do not really love them—we have concealed our love from them. Murphy and Huwiler argue that a rebuke is a "true sign of love" (*Proverbs*, 133). True friends—true brothers—tell you what you *need* to hear, while false friends tell you what you *want* to hear. False friends "kiss" you in a way that makes you think they care, but actually they do not. Do you have a true friend who can get in your face and ask you what in the world you are doing? Are you that kind of friend to others? We need to learn to confront occasionally and rightly for the good of those we love. We need to learn to receive confrontation for our own good.

We all intuitively know there are times we need to speak up. For example, when our friend is in a foolish relationship that is no good for him, we have to say something. When our friend is making dumb decisions with her money that constantly put her in bad situations, we need to speak up. When our brother in Christ is involved in something that jeopardizes his marriage, we have to lovingly confront. Unfortunately, we often bite our tongues and say to ourselves things like, "Oh, I could not possibly say anything." "Oh, they won't listen to me anyway." People make foolish decisions that destroy their reputations, marriages, families, and their eternities. So while it is tough and awkward to speak up, we must do it!

The question we want to examine from Proverbs is, How do I do it? How do I lovingly confront someone I care about? The answer is a math problem of sorts, and most if not everything in the formula needs to be present in confrontation. If most of these things are present, do not let fear keep you from speaking up:

|   |   |
|---|---|
|   | The Right Word |
| + | FROM the Right Person |
| + | IN the Right Way |
| + | AT the Right Time |
| + | TO the Right Person |
| = | Loving Confrontation |

## The Right Word

The first criterion for speaking up is the right word. Is what you are about to say true? Or better stated, is what you are about to say consistent with the Bible? Proverbs has clearly stated that true wisdom comes from the mouth of God (2:6). Therefore, we do not need to advise people with our opinions; we need to advise them from the Bible. Too many people—when they actually do speak up—speak out of what they think rather than from what God has said. On social media you can see all kinds of confrontation about how to give birth to a child, how to discipline a child, or how to date your wife, and much of it seems very dogmatic—even the advice that is blatantly wrong. If you are going to speak up, you need to be sure that what you are saying is consistent with the Bible, so take the time and do the work to make sure!

## From the Right Person

To figure out if you are the right person, you need to be able to positively answer the question, Is this my fight? To figure out if that is the case, ask questions like, Am I the offended party? Am I accountable for the offended party? Am I accountable for the offender? Proverbs puts it this way: "A person who is passing by and meddles in a quarrel that's not his is like one who grabs a dog by the ears" (26:17). As Longman points out, "It is obviously stupid to pull the ears of a dog." Therefore, the verse "ridicules those who would get involved in a fight in which they have no part" (*Proverbs*, 469).

Do not be the "confrontation police." Some people love to do this kind of thing. They love calling people out, putting them in their place, or getting in their business. Some people think their calling in life is to be an Old Testament prophet. They love telling their friends how they told someone off. They love jumping in and trolling on Facebook or Twitter.

Proverbs says that jumping into someone else's argument is like slapping a pit bull in the face. It's not going to go well for you! Do not jump into someone else's fight. Do not speak up if it is not your place. Some fights need to be had, but they need to be by the right person. On the other hand, do not use this as an excuse not to act if you are the right person. Do not convince yourself, "They will never listen to me." If it's not your place, stay out of it, but if it is your place, kindly and directly speak up!

## In the Right Way

True forgiveness and kindness must be present before any confrontation. It is easy to confront a wrong done you if you are hurt, but you usually do not go about it in the right way unless you have moved toward forgiveness. Without forgiveness, there will not be conflict resolution—only revenge.

There cannot be the slightest bit of bitterness or a desire to get someone back, or it will blow up in your face. Proverbs 24:29 says, "Don't say, 'I'll do to him what he did to me; I'll repay the man for what he has done.'" I have seen families in a church meet for conflict resolution, but each party merely wants their case to be heard and to win the day. It has driven families apart and out of the church. Resist a superiority complex where you look down on the person you confront as if you are not a sinner or could never have done what they did. Let go of your grudge before you talk.

If you dwell on what was done, turn it over in your mind often, and talk about it a lot with other people, then you are not going about it in the right way. Stop bringing it up! Proverbs 17:9 warns, "Whoever conceals an offense promotes love, but whoever gossips about it separates friends." Be willing to let it go. Overcome evil with good, since judgment ultimately belongs to God, not you. Forgive as God in Christ has forgiven you (Eph 4:32)! Longman reminds us that "a person who harps on problems will drive another away, robbing people of the opportunity to develop a relationship," but love "keeps no record of wrongs" (1 Cor 13:5) (*Proverbs*, 345).

Only after you have worked through forgiveness can you then confront. Proverbs 10:12 states, "Hatred stirs up conflicts, but love covers all offenses." If your confrontation is motivated by a desire to get someone back, it will not work. In fact, it will only make it worse. There are some things that you just need to let go. But if your desire is forgiveness and reconciliation, there is hope!

Also, the right way to confront someone is to do it with gentleness and love, or what Paul calls, "speaking the truth in love" (Eph 4:15). Proverbs 15:1 says, "A gentle answer turns away anger, but a harsh word stirs up wrath." The temperaments we bring to the confrontation will make all the difference (Garrett, *Proverbs*, 150). Do you have the self-control to give a reasoned response? (Waltke, *Proverbs, Chapters 1–15*, 612–13). Gentleness does not imply mealy mouthed or indirect—it can be a tough gentleness! The question is, Are your words motivated by love for her or by a desire to put her in her place? Are you genuinely concerned for the person, and therefore you will confront her kindly? Or do you just want to prove her wrong? If it is truly done gently, the hearer can say in her heart, "I do not want to hear this, but I at least know this person loves me, and it kind of hurt him to have to say this to me." That kind of attitude can help in persuading someone of his or her need to change. Slamming that person or being sarcastic will not help bring about change. After all, Proverbs 16:21 states, "Anyone with a wise heart is called discerning, and pleasant speech increases learning."

Finally, speaking up in the right way means speaking directly. Do not beat around the bush. Do not try to use spin. Do not be passive aggressive. Proverbs 24:26 says, "He who gives an honest answer gives a kiss on the lips." Being honest and straightforward is beneficial to the hearer. That said, let me give you a word of caution. Often those good at directness are bad at gentleness. And those who are good at gentleness can struggle with directness. We need both in our speaking.

## At the Right Time

It is crucial that you speak up at the right time. Proverbs 25:11-12 states, "A word spoken at the right time is like gold apples in silver settings. A wise correction to a receptive ear is like a gold ring or an ornament of gold." You have to speak at the right moment (Murphy and Huwiler, *Proverbs*, 126).

You may have the truth and say it in a gentle way, but it will not be well received because you do not speak up at the right time. Proverbs does not give us a "how-to" manual to know when is the right time.

Knowing the right time requires discernment. Thankfully, God promises that if we lack wisdom, we can ask him and he will give it to us (Jas 1).

A fool, on the other hand, speaks with no regard to the circumstances. He comes in when his wife looks frazzled and is complaining about how the kids have been a handful all day, and he says, "Honey, we need to have a talk." Or the fool wants to criticize the church to the pastor right after the pastor gets done preaching his heart out to his people.

Proverbs 15:23 says, "A person takes joy in giving an answer; and a timely word—how good that is!" Goldsworthy notes, "There is great satisfaction in being able to give a wise word at the right time" (*Tree of Life*, 116). Too many people who actually do speak up have the mentality, "I told them the truth. If they do not receive it, that's their problem." No! Proverbs says that it is your problem. Truth that is not delivered at the right time will not be received. Sometimes you need to wait. At other times you need take courage and speak immediately. Ask the Lord to help you with discernment.

## To the Right Person

Some people will never respond rightly, nor will they receive what you say no matter how gentle you are or how timely you are. Proverbs describes these folks as "mockers" when it says,

> *The one who corrects a mocker will bring abuse on himself;*
> *the one who rebukes the wicked will get hurt.*
> *Don't rebuke a mocker, or he will hate you;*
> *rebuke the wise, and he will love you.* (9:7-8)

The mocker will not listen to your correction no matter how you go about it. On the other hand, the wise person will receive correction and will want to grow and change.

This does not mean that people—even wise people—will always immediately receive your confrontation well. Sometimes it will take a while for them to see why what you are saying is good for them. It will require the work of the Holy Spirit. Proverbs 28:23 states, "One who rebukes a person will later find more favor than one who flatters with his tongue." Yes, you can flatter people and tell them what they want to hear, but that is ultimately unloving and unhelpful. The verse observes that a good reception may not happen immediately, but it will happen ultimately—"later." Longman writes, "Although it is true that initially people are likely to get a bad reaction from those whose faults they are highlighting, this proverb indicates that favor, gratitude for the advice, will come not immediately but 'afterward'" (*Proverbs*, 496).

Unfortunately, we often do not confront because we prefer the short-term comfort to the long-term hard work. That is true with disciplining our children as well. Correction and confrontation may hurt in the short term, but it is better in the long term. You may have to risk a friendship, only to get it back later!

Early in ministry I (Jon) was discipling a guy who had a particular struggle with pornography. One time when we were hanging out, I confronted him very directly about his struggles and his excuses for them. He got up and walked out on me. It strained our relationship, but thankfully God used that and some other things to get this guy's attention. Several years later he wrote me a thank-you note on Facebook:

> I realize it's been a while since I talked to you but want again to thank you for something you did for me several years ago. Remember probably in 2000–2001 maybe when you confronted me about some sin and I walked out on you? Thank you so much for being strong in that moment. I am involved in conversations with a person who used to attend our church that has done some pretty bad things and I've been able to repeatedly share God's love with him as well as his imminent danger should he not repent. I honestly believe that had you not gotten into my business then and confronted me, I would be in a different place in life. You have my utmost respect for being strong in the faith and confronting me. My own experience from this tells me that your job can be both fantastically awesome and heartbreaking in the same day. I pray for you.

Change may be slow in coming, but trust the Lord to do good work as you are faithful to speak up.

Finally, we need to be the kind of people who can receive a confrontation and respond well. That is what wise people do. Proverbs 17:10 says, "A rebuke cuts into a perceptive person more than a hundred lashes into a fool." Do not get mad when confronted. Ask, "What can I learn from this?"

## Conclusion

Proverbs 27:5-6 says, "Better an open reprimand than concealed love. The wounds of a friend are trustworthy, but the kisses of an enemy are excessive." These verses point us to the gospel, not merely because Jesus was kissed by an enemy whom he thought was his friend but also because Jesus was wise enough to know how to confront. Jesus is the Son who grows in wisdom, and he is the Wisdom of God. He lived out these truths, and he can empower us to live them out as well.

Whether or not you can give or receive a confrontation reveals whether or not the gospel is central in your life. If you are too scared to confront or too prideful to receive a confrontation, you have a problem with Jesus. The cross should not merely be a hoop you jump through to get into the Christian life; the cross transforms your life if you really rest in it! If you truly rest in the gospel, you can give a rebuke and receive one without getting mad like people usually do.[38]

When someone confronts us, they can be right or wrong, they can do it for the right reason or the wrong reason, and they can go about it in the right way or the wrong way. Our typical—sinful—response is to get angry and say things like, "Oh, no I didn't!" We get angry because in our pride we want to be right all the time. Therefore, in order to be seen as right we lose relationships or surround ourselves with yes men. But Proverbs tells us that confrontation is for our good. And if we truly believe the gospel, we can see how that is true. If I believe in the cross, I am crucified with Christ, and I died back there at Calvary. If I believe in the cross, it means that I agree with God's judgment of me and admit, "I am a sinner!" So I can say to any rebuke—fair or unfair—that it is just a fraction of my sin. And if I believe in the cross, I also agree with God's justification of my life—that God sees me now as he sees his beloved Son. I have God's approval. Since pride starts fights out of a desire to justify myself, God's verdict can alleviate that. I do not have to justify myself because God has done so in Christ.

Therefore, you can handle and receive any criticism because no one can criticize you more than the cross. God has criticized your shortcomings in the cross far more than anyone else can. You can thank the person for their correction, even if it is wrong, because it reminds you of your true faults that led to the crucifixion of Jesus. You are now free to

[38] The conclusion is dependent on Poirier's fantastic article, "The Cross and Criticism."

consider, "Is there anything valid here that I need to listen to?" And you can handle any confrontation without getting crushed or angry because you do not need man's approval since you have God's in Christ!

If you can take confrontation well, then you can learn to confront with gracious intent. You do it for the right reason, not to be seen as right or to get others' approval but because you have God's approval in Christ. Giving and receiving confrontation in a wise manner comes down to the gospel.

## Reflect and Discuss

1. Why is it difficult for us to be critical of others and confront them face-to-face?
2. Why does the Bible not give us the option of isolating ourselves from conflict with other people?
3. How can we create an open culture of confession and accountability in our churches?
4. Why do you need a friend who can get in your face and tell you that you are in the wrong? How can you be that kind of friend to someone else?
5. How can you discern if you are the right person to confront someone else?
6. What are some things that typically motivate us to confront someone else? What should our motivation be?
7. What does it mean to speak up at the right time?
8. How does knowing that change may not be immediate help you?
9. What should your first course of action be when you are confronted?
10. How does the gospel empower us to confront and be confronted?

# Pray Up!

## PROVERBS 15:29

**Main Idea:** You can only pray to God through Jesus Christ.

---

**I. Who Can Pray to God? Only the Righteous Can (15:29).**
**II. How Do We Pray to God? We Humbly Confess (28:13).**

---

Everyone—even those outside the church—think that God hears every prayer. Most people, some of whom do not even believe in Jesus or practice Christianity, pray. They pray for their children, their health, and their families. Many people can even tell you that God "always answers your prayers," but the answer could be yes, no, or maybe later.

That is why people got so enraged when a Southern Baptist Convention president had the audacity to say, "God Almighty does not hear the prayer of a Jew" ("Baptist Leader"). There were all kinds of reasons that the comment sparked controversy and outrage in a world with multiple religions and a fondness for cultural pluralism. But one of the biggest reasons people were upset was not because of the perceived offense to the Jewish faith specifically but rather because anyone, especially a pastor, would dare suggest that God does not hear someone's prayer. Everyone believes that God hears and responds to our prayers.

Is it possible that God would give someone "the silent treatment"? Honestly, the Bible says yes to this question. God does give the silent treatment to some people. That might be alarming for many people. If that is true, some important questions need to be asked like, Whose prayer does God hear? Why might he not listen to mine? How can I pray in such a way that God will answer me?

Let's look to the Proverbs and see the answers to these questions, so that our prayer lives can be radically changed. Proverbs 15:29 says, "The Lord is far from the wicked, but he hears the prayer of the righteous." What does this mean?

## Who Can Pray to God? Only the Righteous Can

### PROVERBS 15:29

This verse uses Hebrew poetic parallelism. There are several kinds of parallelism: sometimes the second line says something similar to the first; sometimes it says the opposite. In this case, one line can be looked at to fill out the other. So when the first line says that the Lord is far from wicked people, we can conclude that he is near righteous people; and when it says he hears the prayer of the righteous, we can surmise that he does not hear the prayer of wicked people.

When the text says that he does not hear their prayer, it does not mean that he does not audibly hear it. He hears the words because he is an omniscient God, but he does not respond to them (Longman, *Proverbs*, 322). He will not do anything about the prayer. We understand what that is like. Sometimes we are in a conversation with someone and we tune him or her out, or we hear what they are saying as background noise but do not respond.

God is not with the wicked in crisis like he is with the righteous. The Bible is clear on this point. Isaiah 59:2 says, "But your iniquities are separating you from your God, and your sins have hidden his face from you so that he does not listen."

The problem for many of us is that we assume we are righteous. We think to ourselves, "I am basically a good person," and we assume that God hears us. But the question must be asked, Who are "the wicked"? The Bible indicates that *we* are! The wicked are those who reject God's law and instruction—those who disobey his word. We have all sinned and fallen short of God's glory (Rom 3:23). We are all wicked, and that is why Proverbs 28:9 says, "Anyone who turns his ear away from hearing the law—even his prayer is detestable." If you do not listen to Yahweh's word to you, he will not listen to your words to him! Murphy and Huwiler refer to the "deafness of a person" and the "deafness of God" to their prayer (*Proverbs*, 138). Yahweh finds the prayers of sinners—all of us—detestable. He finds them repugnant (Waltke, *Proverbs, Chapters 15–31*, 413).

Therefore, if you do not listen to God's word (i.e., obey it), God will not listen to you. This includes sins of commission and omission—doing what you are not supposed to do and not doing what you are supposed to do. So if you lie, take God's name in vain, or take something that does not belong to you (sins of commission), then God will not hear your prayer. And if you can't let go of a grudge, you are selfish, or you do not serve your wife (sins of omission), then God will not hear your prayer. For example, Proverbs says that the wicked are those who refuse to be generous to the poor, and thus God does not hear their prayer: "The one who shuts his ears to the cry of the poor will himself also call out and not be answered" (21:13). If you are not generous to your neighbor, God will not hear your prayers. Murphy and Huwiler argue that it could be either man or God here in this verse (*Proverbs*, 105).

In some ways, this truth may not seem all that shocking. Many people think, "If you are a good person, God will listen to you; and if you are a bad person, God will not listen to you." We tend toward a works-righteousness approach that believes God is always more favorable to good people.

So at this point you may be thinking, "God will never accept me or listen to me because of all the sinful things I have done . . . he only hears good, church-going people." We think he only listens to pious people who pray in King James English using "thee and thou." So you might be thinking you are going to have to clean up your act and start doing what God wants you to do so that he will listen to you; and by that you mean things like get back in church, start giving, and be part of Bible studies. Wrong! Proverbs 15:8 says, "The sacrifice of the wicked is detestable to the LORD, but the prayer of the upright is his delight." Goldsworthy writes, "The folly of the wicked is to think that formal and outward adherence to the law can benefit them in any way at all" (*Tree of Life*, 115). The issue is the "sacrificer," not the sacrifice; it's the one doing the ritual, not the ritual itself. God cannot stand mere religious ritual because it is an attempt to manipulate God. Religious ritual that is not accompanied by heart change is worthless. This type of religion says, "If I am good and do what God says, he will owe me some favors." That is manipulation. Mere behavior modification is not the answer; God detests it!

People in the Old Testament were sinners just like us, so sacrifices were performed—similarly to the cross itself—to atone for sin and bring forgiveness. The problem is that God says the wicked are not really repentant or humbly dependent on God. They think if they just perform the ritual then God owes them, like people today think if they just go to church, give, and have a quiet time, then God has to answer them. Without accompanying faith and dependence, these rituals are a waste of time.

In every generation people have tried to do religious rituals in an attempt to manipulate God's favor—to put God in their debt as if he owes them. At least three times in my life a ministry group has mass-mailed me a "prayer rug." The so-called prayer rug is a picture of what people think Jesus's face looks like, and the note with the rug promises that if you will pray with your knees on this rug, God will give you $47,000 like he did with some poor soul under a mountain of debt. This ministry promises that if you do this prayer act, God will give you what you want. That's not Christianity; that's paganism!

The problem is that we can comfort ourselves by saying, "I'm not like that," but we do the same kind of thing. We think if we are good or if we do certain things, God will listen to us and act on our behalf. It may not be a prayer rug; it might just be bargaining with God: "God, if you get me out of this jam, I promise I will walk more closely with you." Or we think if I just give up my besetting sin—pornography, profanity, or my temper—then God will finally listen to me. If I can just turn over a new leaf, God will stop giving me the silent treatment. If I can just get this lust or this arrogance out of my life, maybe God will let us win the game, ace the exam, or get the job!

This approach to God is revealed clearly in our reluctance to approach God when we feel like we are in the valley. I (Jon) remember going through a period of rebellion in my freshman year of college and thinking, "I can't even pray to God for forgiveness right now because I don't deserve for him to listen to me. He must be so angry with me right now." Because of the sin in your life, you feel like you cannot pray or that it will not do any good. You think you must clean yourself up first. That is also manipulative paganism, not Christianity.

Therefore, no matter who we are, we have a huge problem. If you think you are good and God definitely answers your prayers, then you have a reality problem because the Bible says you are a sinner. And if you think you are bad and God will not listen unless you clean your act up, then you have a religion problem because God is not manipulated by ritual!

We have a big problem: God does not respond to the prayers of the wicked, and that is us. And if religion is not the answer, how can we pray at all? Humanity has had this problem since the garden of Eden—we have been separated from God. In Psalm 24 the psalmist asks a key question about who can approach God. The answer: "The one who has clean hands and a pure heart" (24:4). Clearly that is not us; only one man in history fits that description—Jesus of Nazareth, the King of glory (Ps 24:7).

Jesus lived the perfect, righteous life that we could never live; then he died the death we should have died, and God accepted his sacrifice because he is the righteous one (cf. Prov 15:8). Jesus was cut off from God—separated from the Father for us. He was the one who cried out and was unanswered because he bore our sin in his own body on the cross (Matt 27:46; 1 Pet 2:24). And it is through his atonement that the relationship with God that humanity lost in the garden is finally restored. His death tore in two the veil separating humanity and God so that now we have bold access to the Father (Matt 27:51; Heb 10:19-22).

God heard the cries of his righteous Son on the third day and rescued him from death. Then Jesus ascended the hill of the Lord to sit at the Father's right hand. Now he always lives to make intercession for us (Heb 7:25). We have access to boldly approach the throne in prayer and not shrink back (Heb 4:16). Our prayers are heard by God because Jesus is our righteous mediator before the Father, and through his righteousness—not ours—God answers our prayers!

## How Do We Pray to God? We Humbly Confess

**PROVERBS 28:13**

Since we are wicked and do not deserve for God to hear us, and since the only way we have access is through Jesus, then the only manner in which we should come before God is humble dependence. We recognize that it is only through Jesus that we have access. That is what it means to pray in Jesus's name. It is not a magic formula to tack on at the end of the prayer; it is acknowledgement that Jesus is the one who grants us access to the Father so that he hears us!

Since we are sinners, the first step in our prayer life should be to admit our sin and confess it to God. Proverbs 28:13 says, "The one who conceals his sins will not prosper, but whoever confesses and renounces them will find mercy." Proverbs says not to hide or deny our sin but to confess it and abandon it. Adam and Eve attempted to hide their sin in the garden (Gen 3); we are called to do the opposite. We cannot minimize our sin, act like it is not there, or attempt to cover it. Also, confession is more than simply being sorry that we got caught or the fear of the consequences of our actions. Confession is admitting that you have sin in your life, agreeing that it deserves judgment, crying to God for mercy, and agreeing that you need to abandon it altogether. Some people try to confess their sin without forsaking their sin. They feel bad about it, but they do not take measures to kill it in their life. You must fight against your sin! You must be killing sin or sin will be killing you.

If you think you are good enough, you are dead wrong. The only way to come into God's presence is to admit that you do not belong. Righteousness is found in repentance. As Proverbs has indicated, rituals that are not accompanied with penitent piety are detestable. We do not try to manipulate God; we humbly depend on his mercy through Christ.

The problem is that even Christians who know the good news start to act like pagans. We start to believe the lie that we have to clean up our act for God to respond favorably to us, and that if we do not clean up our act, God will zap us. That is not grace. We humbly and simply plead for the mercy of God through the cross of Christ. In Christ, God is always for us and never against us. He may discipline us for our good (Heb 12:5-13), but he will not condemn or judge us. So come to God in humble confession in prayer!

## Conclusion

Jesus told the story of two men praying—a Pharisee and a tax collector. God accepted one man's prayer and rejected the other man's prayer. The shocking turn of events was that the story did not follow expected patterns. Everyone listening to Jesus expected the righteous-looking, religious Pharisee to be heard; and they expected the sinful tax collector to be given the silent treatment. But Jesus said the tax collector was heard because he was too ashamed to even lift his eyes to heaven as he said, "God, have mercy on me, a sinner!" (Luke 18:13). God did not only hear that man, but God also justified him. If you want to be heard by the King of the universe, then come humbly as a sinner and plead the mercy of Christ.

## Reflect and Discuss

1. What answers do most people think God gives to everyone's prayers?
2. What do you think about the statement, "God does not hear everyone's prayer"? How does it make you feel?
3. Who does Proverbs say that God listens to?
4. Who are the "wicked" according to the Bible? Why?

5. According to Proverbs 21:13, what is considered a wicked act that will lead to your prayer being unheard?
6. Why can religious ritual be a form of manipulation?
7. Have you ever had a rough patch in your life where you felt like you could not pray to God? Why did you feel that way?
8. What does it mean to pray "in Jesus's name"?
9. Why do we have a tendency to limit our confession to simple regret of the consequences?
10. What does true confession look like?

# Section 5—Seven: The Deadly Follies

# Envy

## PROVERBS 14:30

**Main Idea:** Faith in Jesus saves you from destructive envy.

---

**I. Avoid Jealousy and Envy Because They Are Deadly.**
   A. Envy is deadly because it hurts you.
   B. Envy is deadly because it hurts the people around you.
   C. Envy is deadly because it leads to other sins.
   D. Envy is deadly because it will be judged by God.

**II. Faith in Jesus Will Save You from Envy.**

---

I (Jon) am a huge Dallas Cowboys fan. When I was younger, I would get really angry when they lost football games and would often slap my hand on the carpet as hard as I could. My dad would look at me and say, "Why are you doing that? What do you think that will do? You are only hurting yourself, and you might break your hand."

The Bible seems to say the same thing about envy. Envy never helps the situation, and it ends up hurting you. We see examples of this throughout pop culture. In the movie *Gladiator*, the jealousy of the emperor toward Maximus was the emperor's undoing. In the movie *Toy Story*, Woody's jealousy toward Buzz ended up hurting Woody. In our own lives, our jealousy of others can lead to depression, low self-esteem, anger, bitterness, and other issues. That is exactly what Solomon tells us through the Holy Spirit about jealousy and envy. Jealousy does not help; it only hurts. Proverbs 14:30 says, "A tranquil heart is life to the body, but jealousy is rottenness to the bones." Jealousy has psychosomatic effects on you (Murphy and Huwiler, *Proverbs*, 71). It is like a cancer in your soul.

### Avoid Jealousy and Envy Because They Are Deadly

When I (Jon) was a freshman in high school, I was cut from the school's junior varsity basketball team. I got extremely jealous because the principal's nephew made the team while I got cut from it. Instead, I played in a city optimist's league, where anyone who paid the fee could play. I thought that winning the city league championship (which we did) would make things right because I would prove that I was a better basketball player than the principal's nephew. However, Solomon is right. Winning the city league did not make getting cut from the team hurt any less, it did not put me on the team, and it led to a very depressed year of school.

Envy—wanting something someone else has—is destructive. So many of us want things that other people have. We envy their clothes, their car, their house, their bank account, and their popularity. That attitude is destructive, but the reverse attitude can be as well. Jealousy sometimes looks like the craving to keep what is ours and not let it become someone else's. Longman explains both of these and makes his own distinction between jealousy and envy when he writes, "Jealousy is the angry desire to keep what we possess and are afraid someone else wants," whereas envy "is the angry desire for what someone else possesses" (*Proverbs*, 476).

Though none of us really want to admit this because it lets other people gain even more power over us, we have all felt jealousy and envy. We have all felt spite or resentment when our peers succeed over us. We get jealous when people out-achieve us. Even pastors deal with this. Why is his church bigger? Why are they growing while we are declining? Why do they have so much money for ministry, while we are drowning in debt?

People get jealous for all sorts of reasons. People get suspicious that they might be replaced at work, or maybe a new friend has entered the picture and they are worried their relationships will never be the same. Or your single friend got married and is not spending as much time with you anymore. You are having a hard time dealing with it.

Jealousy happens in all kinds of situations in our lives. Jealousy is common with romantic relationships. You cannot believe that he likes another girl, so you are mean to her all the time. Or you compete for his affection because you want it all for yourself. This kind of jealousy also can happen in corporate life. When your rival has some kind of success, it eats you up; or when he fails, it makes your day. It happens in church life as well. Church members get worried that if the church grows too much they might lose their seat, so they become resentful toward new folks. People get jealous when it comes to their looks. You look at yourself and wish you had muscles like him; or you wish that you had her looks, so you find yourself badmouthing her to other people to compensate for your jealousy. At some point we all find ourselves wishing that we were as strong, as smart, as popular, as successful, as wealthy, as athletic, and as competent as others. Social media can take this to new heights when people post all about their lives and families, which causes even more comparison and jealousy.

The Bible condemns that kind of jealousy, but it is a bit complicated because according to the Bible jealousy can also be a legitimate emotion (see discussion on this in Longman, *Proverbs*, 307). Like anger, jealousy is not always a bad thing. Jealousy is not wrong when it involves an exclusive relationship being threatened. For example, God is jealous for his people and their exclusive devotion to him (Zech 8:2; Jas 4:5). God is also jealous for his glory (Num 25:11). There should be a positive jealousy and passion for exclusive devotion to God.

The same can be said for our mate in marriage! Some guys are real idiots when it comes to their wife's jealousy for their relationship. Oftentimes when a wife questions her husband about a relationship with another woman out of love for her husband and concern for her marriage, the husband will get angry and defensive and try to make his wife feel like a moron—like she does not know what she's talking about. That is ridiculous and foolish. Your wife's concern for your marriage and her willingness to ask you about it is a gift from God.

However, when it comes to non-exclusive relationships or anger over what belongs to someone else, jealousy is wrong. Not only is jealousy wrong, it is destructive and deadly.

### *Envy Is Deadly Because It Hurts You*

Envy damages you emotionally, mentally, and physically. Proverbs 14:30 says that jealousy has harmful psychosomatic consequences, whereas being content in your heart will lead to physical, mental, and emotional well-being. This verse alludes to the covenant curse of physical decay for those who violate the law, including God's command that we be content with what we have. Jealousy is a cancer of the bones. It eats away at you (Longman, *Proverbs*, 307). When you are jealous it can lead to being angry all the time, hives breaking out, eating disorders, uncontrolled rage, or simply not thinking straight. When you walk around jealous and angry, it ruins you emotionally. Jealousy that finds its roots in checking out other people on social media can not only discourage you, it can also cause you to not be thankful for the life you have.

### *Envy Is Deadly Because It Hurts the People around You*

Proverbs 27:3-4 says,

> *A stone is heavy and sand, a burden, but aggravation from a fool outweighs them both. Fury is cruel, and anger a flood, but who can withstand jealousy?*

The theme of these verses is unbearable behavior that other people cannot endure (Waltke, *Proverbs, Chapters 15–31*, 374). Do you get what the wise man is saying? Violence is bad, and a temper is bad. They are harmful to people, but jealousy is even more destructive! Jealousy cannot be endured. When you are a jealous person, no one wants to be around you and all the drama. It destroys friendships because "fury that stems from jealousy is not open to reason or moderation" (Garrett, *Proverbs*, 216).

### *Envy Is Deadly Because It Leads to Other Sins*

We see an example of this in the Bible in the way Saul feels about David. His jealousy of David causes him several times to try to kill David (1 Sam 18:9-11; 19:9-11) (Waltke, *Proverbs, Chapters 15–31*, 375). Jealousy leads to other sins because at its root it is a belief of the heart that what God has given you is not enough. God is withholding his best from you. That dissatisfaction and feeling of inadequacy causes you to lash out in all kinds of ways: violence, gossip, theft, and more.

Another way that envy leads to other sins is when you copy the behavior of the prosperous, wicked person. The Bible says that envy of sinful people—who seem to prosper—leads to imitating their behavior. Proverbs 24:1-2 says, "Don't envy the evil or desire to be with them, for their hearts plan violence, and their words stir up trouble." Jealousy of sinful people who are successful will lead you to adopt their behavior to get what they have. Instead, you should see that their behavior is despicable and you should not want to lower yourself to their level. Being repulsed by their angry, badmouthing, and bitter attitudes should be a motivation to avoid jealousy (Waltke, *Proverbs, Chapters 15–31*, 268).

### *Envy Is Deadly Because It Will Be Judged by God*

Several passages of Scripture warn us not to envy sinners who prosper, since God will judge them. Wisdom says not to join them. Proverbs 3:31-32 states, "Don't envy a violent man or choose any of his ways; for the devious are detestable to the LORD, but he is a friend to the upright." The application of the verse is clear: do not be envious of and thus copy the practices of a sinner. It is tempting to be jealous of those who succeed despite their sinful behavior. If it was not tempting, then so many people would not find it appealing. When ungodly people find themselves having all that they want while godly persons have very little, then godliness can seem like it does not benefit much. But we are told to avoid this, and one of the big reasons is that the Lord will condemn the wicked. The tables will turn. The "prospering sinner" will lose all that he has, and the righteous will be rewarded in the end. God's approval abides on the content person, and that approval is worth so much more than those good-looking things the sinner has. God tells you to trust his Word rather than your experience because the prosperity of the ungodly is only apparent; it will be short lived.

Proverbs 24:19-20 adds the eternal perspective: "Don't be agitated by evildoers, and don't envy the wicked. For the evil have no future; the lamp of the wicked will be put out." Do not be jealous of sinners, since the tables will be turned at judgment. The sinner has no future. So it is foolish to adopt his ways for a few decades of pleasure and seeming prosperity in light of eternity.

It is clear from Proverbs that the wages of jealousy is death: it rots your bones, it destroys your relationships, and it will send you to hell! So jealousy is a matter of life and death. Envy causes you to shrivel up, it eats away at you, and it casts you into darkness. The apostle Paul says about jealousy that those who practice such things will not inherit the kingdom of God (Gal 5:19-21).

## Faith in Jesus Will Save You from Envy

Proverbs 24:19-20 gave the negative warning, but Proverbs 23:17-18 gives the positive promise, "Don't let your heart envy sinners; instead, always fear the LORD. For then you will have a future, and your hope will not be dashed." We see in these verses a positive strategy for dealing with our jealousy, and it just happens to be the theme of Proverbs: fear the Lord. That means to fight off envy and jealousy in your life is to trust in the Lord—to have whole-hearted confidence in him! Again, there is a temptation to be jealous of prosperous wicked people in such a way that you copy their actions. What is the antidote? The antidote to jealousy is contentment in the Lord. What is the motivation for this contentment? The future reward of eternal life is the motivation to be content in the

Lord. Again, you must have an eternal perspective (Col 3:1-2). In light of eternity, if you fear the Lord, you will experience eternal blessings. In contrast, the wicked will lose everything that they have.

Proverbs 24:20, interpreted canonically, may refer to the preservation of the messianic line because the "lamp" often refers to progeny (Fox, *Proverbs 10–31*, 564). The lamp is connected to the Davidic dynasty because David's life is referred to as the "lamp of Israel" and God is concerned that David always has a lamp in Israel (i.e., an heir; 2 Sam 21:17; 1 Kgs 15:4). Psalm 132 applies the same lamp imagery to the Messiah. The hope is to preserve the messianic line until Messiah comes by not envying the wicked. The promise of an eternal kingdom ultimately brings an overlap of posterity with eternal life. There either had to be an eternal succession of faithful posterity or eventually an eternal son who lives forever. The resurrection of Jesus is where the two ideas meet. We can enter this eternal kingdom if we trust in the King and thus turn away from jealousy toward him!

Believing the gospel brings eternal and abundant life—the life that God meant for you to live. That is what the book of Proverbs is all about. The gospel story itself is a story about jealousy. Jealousy killed Jesus. His influence over the people drove the Jewish leaders to insanity. After all, the Bible says the Jewish leaders handed Jesus over to the Romans "because of envy" (Matt 27:18). Not only was it the jealousy of the Jews that caused the death of Jesus, but our own jealousies killed him. He hung on the cross to pay the penalty for our jealousy. Every time you resented someone else's promotion, got green-eyed at someone else's popularity, or raged at another person's good looks, you added your sin in killing Jesus.

But the good news is that God's jealousy to have an exclusive relationship with us motivated him to send his Son to die for our sins. Even though his bride had satisfied herself with so many idolatrous lovers, God was zealous to purchase her and satisfy her with himself alone. He loves you and wants you to be his. So say this to yourself when you feel jealousy rising in your heart: Jesus drowned in his own blood so I can be satisfied in him. I don't need those things that I so jealously want because I have Jesus, and he is all I need.

## Conclusion

We have been jealous and envious; but Jesus, who never was, died for us to forgive us and save us. He is the one who can not only forgive you for your jealousy, but he can also empower you by his Spirit to live a life that is free from envy. As we have seen throughout Proverbs, foolishness is a faith issue. The problem is not one of effort but of belief. Foolishness in our lives shows us that we are not believing in Jesus, and that is so true when it comes to the foolishness of jealousy. You are jealous because you are not satisfied and happy in all that he is for you. Faith in Jesus will free you from that jealousy. Your future hope in Christ is much greater than whatever that alluring thing is that someone else has right now.

## Reflect and Discuss

1. What are some classic stories of jealousy and envy? What do they reveal about jealousy and envy?
2. What are some ways that we get jealous?
3. What are some ways to be rightly jealous?
4. Practically, how can we jealously protect our marriages?
5. What are some ways that jealousy and envy hurt you?
6. How does jealousy affect your family?
7. What are some ways that jealousy and envy lead to other sins?
8. How can we fight against being envious of wicked people?
9. How can having an eternal perspective help you battle envy in your life?
10. How does believing the gospel help free you from envy?

# Gluttony

## PROVERBS 23:19-21

**Main Idea:** Jesus can rescue from gluttony.

---

**I. Overindulgence Is Deadly (23:19-20).**
**II. Jesus Can Free Us from Overindulgence (23:20-21).**

---

Dr. Bill Cutrer was one of my dad's best friends, and he was also my mom's OB-GYN. He delivered my three brothers and me (Jon). In fact, when my mom was pregnant with my twin brother and me, she had to be put on bed rest. My parents stayed at the Cutrers' house during that whole time. He also showed my wife and me an ultrasound of our daughter Maddy before she was born. He was a great friend to our family, and he died a couple years ago from unexpected heart failure. But one of the things I found out at his funeral that I did not know was that when my dad first met Bill, it was at a men's dinner at the church where my dad was the associate pastor. My dad just so happened to sit at the table where Bill was sitting, and they struck up a conversation. Bill was a very funny guy, and he liked to pick at you a little. So the first thing that Bill ever said to my dad—who was in seminary at the time and a little bit heavier than he should have been—was, "You know, I noticed that Baptist preachers love to preach against alcohol and smoking, but you never talk about gluttony. Why is that?" That eventually led to a friendship where they began to run together and train for a marathon.

What Bill said jokingly is actually pretty accurate. Most people have never heard a sermon on gluttony, but most people have heard sermons on the evils of smoking, gambling, and alcohol. This study will address the alcohol and gluttony issues. The Bible says in the book of Proverbs that a lack of self-control when it comes to your appetite for food or drink is foolish and destructive.

When was the last time you heard a sermon on gluttony? Fundamentalist Christianity, especially in the South, really loves to bash alcohol but does not want to touch gluttony. Why? Well probably because gluttony hits a little too close to home. After all, it is so well known that Baptists love to eat that people often make jokes about it. If you asked somebody on the street, "What are Baptists known for?" you would probably get two responses: fighting and potlucks! One man said at the Southern Baptist Convention a number of years ago that the SBC is the only convention where you find the donut vendor right next to the sermon tapes! We joke about that, but one of the big problems of fundamentalism has been condemning the sins of others while ignoring our own sins. Often we are unable to inspect ourselves the way we inspect the world. It is a massive issue, and preachers are guilty of playing into it. A pastor can stand in a pulpit every Sunday and preach hard—really hard—against sin, and everyone says of the pastor things like, "He tells it like it is." "He is a hellfire and brimstone preacher." "He's not afraid to call sin, 'sin.'" And the preacher can get a lot of "amens" doing that. And yet, he really is a coward because he does not touch the sins of his congregation but only those of the people outside his religious community. We can give the impression that what God really cares about is homosexuality, drug addictions, and wild partying, but he is not all that concerned about judgmentalism, self-righteousness, and gluttony!

Gluttony is a major problem in America and in the church. It is often an avoided topic because so many of us struggle with it. We also tend to think it's just a physical issue, not really a gospel issue. Unfortunately, it seems that Michelle Obama and *The Biggest Loser* have taught Americans more biblical principles about food than the church has. Preachers notwithstanding, the Bible is absolutely concerned with overindulgence and gluttony.

We like to bash alcohol and its dangers; and rightly we should because it destroys family ties, social lives, physical health, and even life itself. Yes, we should talk about the dangers of alcohol, but we should be honest about the fact that gluttony is also a big a problem in America. It can be just as deadly. We are eating ourselves to disease and death. Let's look at some stats to back that statement up—some are humorous, but others are not quite so funny.

In 1957 a fast food hamburger weighed one ounce and was 210 calories. Today a fast food hamburger averages about six ounces and 618 calories. In 1957 a McDonald's burger, fries, and Coke totaled 590 calories; today a "supersized" Quarter Pounder meal notches 1,550 calories. If you eat a Big Mac and large fries and drink a large Coke, you will have to walk non-stop for six hours to burn off the calories. In 1957 a box of movie theater popcorn was three cups and 170 calories; currently it averages sixteen cups and 900 calories. There are more than 160,000 fast-food restaurants in America. Fifty million Americans eat fast food daily, and $110,000,000 is spent on it annually.

What is the result? Women are at a double risk for heart failure. There has been a 50-percent rise in Type 2 diabetes that is primarily caused by obesity. A survey done of 813 overweight Louisiana school children showed that 58 percent had at least one heart disease risk factor such as high blood pressure, cholesterol, or insulin levels (D. Akin, "Vanity of Happy Meal Christianity"). In the 1950s, 9.7 percent of American adults were considered clinically obese; today the United States leads the world with an obesity rate of more than 30 percent—yes, we are number one! We have the highest rate of calorie consumption per capita in the world. Childhood obesity has more than doubled in children and tripled in adolescents in the past thirty years. In 2010 more than one third of children and adolescents were overweight or obese. Let that soak in. Why is this happening? The CDC says it is a result of "caloric imbalance." Translation: we eat too much and are not active enough! Obese youth are more likely to have risk factors for cardiovascular disease, high cholesterol, high blood pressure, prediabetes, bone and joint problems, and sleep apnea, and as adults increased risks for types of cancer ("Childhood Obesity Facts").

We are literally eating ourselves to death. We are unable to control our appetites. Our lack of self-control with money, sex, drink, and food will kill almost every American before any terrorist or foreign army. If we would just listen to God's Word we could be instructed in wisdom in this vital area.

> *Listen, my son, and be wise;*
> *keep your mind on the right course.*
> *Don't associate with those who drink too much wine*
> *or with those who gorge themselves on meat.*
> *For the drunkard and the glutton will become poor,*
> *and grogginess will clothe them in rags.* (Prov 23:19-21)

## Overindulgence Is Deadly

### PROVERBS 23:19-20

God created the world good, and everything in it worked right. The Creator gave good gifts to his creation for people to enjoy with grateful and worshiping hearts. He gave us things like food, drink, and sex to be enjoyed in the right context and to move us to worship him. The problem is that humanity rebelled against God's word and departed from God's design, which led to brokenness. In our brokenness, our affections focus on the gifts rather than the Giver! So now we do not use God's gifts in ways he intended, but rather we use them in ways that he forbids because he knows it will be harmful to us. Food becomes gluttony, drink becomes drunkenness, and sex becomes fornication and adultery. The gifts in and of themselves are not bad things—they are good things—but we turn them into ultimate things, and they become bad for us. Food is not bad thing. You have to eat to live, and there are times of feasting that are a means of worshiping God. Sex is not a bad thing. It is a great gift to be enjoyed rightly in heterosexual marriage. Drink is not bad in and of itself, but these things become bad when we use them in ways God did not intend—namely, overindulgence.

The subject is complicated by the fact that it is hard to define gluttony. It is not bad to eat or even to want food because we need it to survive, and God gave it to us for our enjoyment! But it is bad to overeat or to eat a wrong thing or to lack self-control when it comes to eating. Balance is needed. The normal routine is to eat in moderation with times for fasting and feasting. It is not only difficult to define gluttony because eating is a good thing, but it is also difficult because the Bible does not equate gluttony with being overweight. There are numerous reasons why someone might be overweight that are not necessarily linked to gluttony or overeating. Some people are predisposed to certain things. Furthermore, you may be as skinny as a rail and still be a glutton—just a glutton blessed with a fast metabolism.

So how do you know when you have crossed the line? John Piper defines gluttony as a craving for food or drink that masters you ("How Can I Conquer Gluttony?"). If I (Jon) am completely honest, that is me! I am mastered by food. So gluttony can be eating too much or drinking too much. An addiction to food or drink that you cannot control is gluttony. Gluttony—and we will walk through some of this in Proverbs—can be eating food that is too rich or costly (too often), or it can be eating too soon or at inappropriate times. I used to frequently have a "fourth meal" at Taco Bell, and I like the Hobbits' idea of "second breakfast" and "elevensies." Gluttony can be eating bad food coupled with inactivity. Gluttony can be eating too fast so that your stomach doesn't catch up with your eyes. Or gluttony can be eating without gratitude to God for his provision.

Therefore, the issue is not when we use these things in moderation—even beverage alcohol according to the Bible. The issue is overuse. As we have said, many in modern Christianity bash alcohol while practicing gluttony; but these verses place meat in the same category as wine. The warning is about the overuse of alcohol and its hazards as well as the danger of overusing food. And if we miss how great the temptation to overindulge food is, it might be helpful to know that the word for meat here literally refers to "the meat next to the bone" (Waltke, *Proverbs, Chapters 15–31*, 256)—the yummiest part!

As we walk through these verses let's be honest about what the Bible says and submit to it. The Bible does not condemn the consumption of alcohol in moderation (though the principles of wisdom and witness in our cultural context may lead us to abstain); it condemns the overuse of it. And we should not make unsustainable arguments like saying the wine in the Bible was just grape juice. There would be no warnings against drunkenness if the drink was not fermented. We think it is safe to say that the alcohol content was not as high then as many drinks today, but it was actual wine (Stein, "Wine-Drinking in New Testament Times"). Every word for wine in the Old Testament and the New Testament referred to an alcoholic drink (i.e., what Noah drank in Gen 9:21, the new wine in Hos 4:11, the sweet wine in Isa 49:26, or the communion wine that congregants got drunk on in 1 Cor 11:21).

So, as with food, there are two sets of texts in the Bible on wine: warnings and commendations. Proverbs has many warnings about the dangers of alcohol and its consequences. Proverbs 23:29-35 gives a vivid description of this, even describing the spinning sensation of drunkenness.

> *Who has woe? Who has sorrow?*
> *Who has conflicts? Who has complaints?*
> *Who has wounds for no reason?*
> *Who has red eyes?*
> *Those who linger over wine;*
> *those who go looking for mixed wine.*
> *Don't gaze at wine because it is red,*
> *because it gleams in the cup*
> *and goes down smoothly.*
> *In the end it bites like a snake*
> *and stings like a viper.*
> *Your eyes will see strange things,*

*and you will say absurd things.*
*You'll be like someone sleeping out at sea*
*or lying down on the top of a ship's mast.*
*"They struck me, but I feel no pain!*
*They beat me, but I didn't know it!*
*When will I wake up?*
*I'll look for another drink."*

The Bible warns that alcohol will destroy you, and it is right. Sadly, there are too many instances of this reality to count. My (Jon's) mother, Charlotte, grew up in a Baptist children's home because of an alcoholic dad and mom who could not care for her. My adopted cousin was born with fetal alcohol syndrome because of a biological mother who drank throughout her pregnancy. When she was little, my cousin would sit and bang her head against a wall for an hour as a result of the disease. These biblical warnings and sober tales need to be told in the midst of a culture that celebrates and laughs at drunkenness. Brad Paisley's song "Alcohol" giggles at how with alcohol you have had some of the best times you won't remember and that it teaches white people how to dance. Even in some Christian circles there is the expectation that children will go wild in college. The Bible says that what overindulging in alcohol can do is not funny, and tragically we know that all too well in our society.

And yet, we must be honest that the Bible also commends wine in a certain context. Exodus 29:40 refers to a drink offering, and Deuteronomy 14:24-26 describes a party with food and wine as a means of worship. Psalm 104:14-15 says,

*He causes grass to grow for the livestock*
*and provides crops for man to cultivate,*
*producing food from the earth,*
*wine that makes human hearts glad—*
*making his face shine with oil—*
*and bread that sustains human hearts.*

Sex, we all admit, can be used rightly or wrongly. Sex in heterosexual marriage is good, while adultery is condemned as sinful. Too many people view wine like adultery (i.e., sinful sex) instead of viewing it like sex itself, which can be used rightly or wrongly. Not every use of alcohol is sinful. Discernment is required. You must know yourself. Some need to avoid wine at all cost because of possible addiction or because they are underage. In many situations and contexts it is not a bad practice to abstain from alcohol as a matter of wisdom. After all, you will never get addicted if you never take the first drink. Or one might abstain as a matter of witness—not wanting others to stumble. Paul tells the church at Rome to consider witness, but he also tells them to be charitable to each other. Let people make their own choices and do not judge them. We have freedom here to make different choices (Rom 14), but they need to be wise choices.

Overindulging food (gluttony) or drink (drunkenness) is always unwise and deadly. Proverbs says it leads to poverty (23:21), and we also can observe this in our culture. Gluttony leads to poverty for all kinds of reasons. Some people get fired because of an addiction that affects their work. Others perform poorly at work because they are lethargic after eating a huge lunch, and their supervisors notice their lack of productivity when reviews come around. Others overspend on food they want—eating out at restaurants constantly or going to bars—which leads to financial troubles. Some have to spend lots of money on health costs because of their unhealthy lifestyle. The sage knew what he was talking about!

Gluttony is also deadly because it hurts you in social contexts. Proverbs 23:1-3 says,

> *When you sit down to dine with a ruler,*
> *consider carefully what is before you,*
> *and put a knife to your throat*
> *if you have a big appetite;*
> *don't desire his choice food,*
> *for that food is deceptive.*

This refers to a social context that we are unfamiliar with—eating with the royal family. But we can imagine that it would be nerve-racking! No doubt one would be tempted to overeat when presented with the delicacies that royalty can afford. But I think these verses can have application for eating with an employer today. Longman argues for a broader application as well and explains how the "false" food is a potential trap (*Proverbs*, 422–23). The food is referred to as deceptive or false because it is possibly a test, or at least an opportunity for the ruler to discern the young man's character. The ruler—or boss—may be observing to see if the young man lacks self-control and cannot be trusted with key matters, so the scarfed-down meal ends up ruining the career of the young man

(Waltke, *Proverbs, Chapters 15–31*, 238–39). If he overindulges it could be a sign to the king that his appetites are uncontrolled and therefore he cannot really be trusted. That would also be something a boss might observe at a business lunch. Are you able to restrain yourself, or do you seek immediate or over-gratification? If you cannot control yourself, it might cost you the trust of your boss or a possible promotion. The sage says if you struggle in this area, take drastic measures to control it.

I think it can have even broader application. Don't have eyes that are too big. You sit down to eat and you are starving, so you order way too much. My (Jon's) dad always used to get onto me about that. Be self-controlled at meals and enjoy them in moderation, or it will hurt you in social relationships.

Theses verses also seem to indicate that an uncontrolled appetite for delicacies can be a form of gluttony—that is, eating food that is too rich. You have a taste for the best, most expensive foods. As the saying goes, "You eat like a king."

These verses say that gluttony is to be taken so seriously that you take drastic measures to avoid it, like stabbing a knife into your own gullet! Jesus says something very similar about lust—gouge out your eye (Matt 5:29). It is a hyperbole that urges you to do whatever it takes to curb your tendency to overindulge.

Another reason that gluttony is deadly is because it will make you sick. Proverbs 25:16 says, "If you find honey, eat only what you need; otherwise, you'll get sick from it and vomit." The principle of this verse applies to all food (Longman, *Proverbs*, 455). Eating in moderation is good, but if you eat more than you need or too many sweets, you can get sick. Contrary to what the "theologian" Alan Jackson says, too much of a good thing is a not a good thing. If you eat too much you will be uncomfortable, feeling like you have a cinderblock in your chest because you are so overstuffed. You might vomit. You certainly run into health risks, as seen above. The key is knowing when to stop and having the control to be able to do it. Everybody is different, so eating "what you need" is an important clarification. That requires discernment because it may be different from what someone else needs.

The problem here is that we train ourselves to be gluttons. The first time you eat two Big Macs you might feel sick. And you will probably feel sick the second and third times, but by the seventh time you get used to it. Instead of keeping on until you can handle the gluttony, you need to know when to stop!

Proverbs 28:7 says, "A discerning son keeps the law, but a companion of gluttons humiliates his father." Let's pick this verse apart. Keeping the Torah is equated with wisdom in the Bible (Deut 4:6). God gives us commands for a reason—he knows what is best for us, so following them is wise. The law commands moderation rather than a lack of self-control when it comes to our diet, and it does so for our good. The lines of this verse are parallel. Therefore, a wise son keeps the law and does not associate with gluttons, whereas a foolish son breaks the law and associates with gluttons, thus dishonoring his family. You disobey God's law if you are a glutton, which is implied by the fact that the foolish son associates with them. The wages of gluttony according the law is death.

> *If a man has a stubborn and rebellious son who does not obey his father or mother and doesn't listen to them even after they discipline him, his father and mother are to take hold of him and bring him to the elders of his city, to the gate of his hometown. They will say to the elders of his city, "This son of ours is stubborn and rebellious; he doesn't obey us. He's a glutton and a drunkard." Then all the men of his city will stone him to death. You must purge the evil from you, and all Israel will hear and be afraid.* (Deut 21:18-21)

God's apparent abhorrence for gluttony is bad news for us because we have all fallen short here. Who has not eaten more than they should? And it is deadly. Gratifying our appetites is disastrous and condemnable.

## Jesus Can Free Us from Overindulgence

### PROVERBS 23:20-21

Gluttony is a spiritual issue, not merely a physical one. Proverbs 9 has shown us that wisdom is personal. Whether or not you walk in the wisdom of Proverbs reveals whether or not you are following Jesus. And foolishness is personal. If you walk in foolishness, it reveals that you are following idols. Gluttony or drunkenness reveals that you have a problem with Jesus and shows that you are following Folly!

If you have a relationship with the Wisdom of God—Jesus—it means Jesus's Spirit lives inside of you. The fruit that Jesus's Spirit produces in you includes self-control (Gal 5:22-23). If you have no self-control in the area of sex, food, or drink, it shows you are not following Jesus—not believing the gospel rightly. It is a worship issue. You find your satisfaction in created things rather than the Creator God. That is why Paul describes idolatry as worshiping the stomach as a god (Phil 3:19). You live to eat instead of eat to live. Paul says the destiny for that is destruction.

Since gluttony is a worship or belief issue, it cannot be dealt with merely at the level of behavior modification. There is some value in modifying behavior. Go on a diet, start exercising, and eat smaller portions. But you have to go further than that because without right belief the change will be short lived. That is why so many make New Year's resolutions to go on a diet and start working out, but by February the treadmill is already collecting dust in the corner.

Our failure should drive us to Jesus and satisfaction in him. Jesus knew when to fast in the wilderness, when to feast at the wedding in Cana, and how to balance! Jesus perfectly kept this law because he knew man does not live by bread alone but by the Word of God. His appetites did not control him; rather, he controlled his appetites. In Matthew 4, when Satan tempted Jesus, he refused to give in to his hunger pangs. What is it like to be really starving and have bread at your fingertips and say, "No!"? Jesus had self-control.

And yet, Jesus was accused of gluttony and drunkenness because of his association with a certain kind of crowd. Proverbs 23:20-21 says not to associate with them, but Jesus was a friend to gluttons and drunks (that's good news for us)! Luke 7:34 says, "The Son of Man has come eating and drinking, and you say, 'Look, a glutton and a drunkard, a friend of tax collectors and sinners!'" Jesus wrongly was accused of being the rebellious son of Deuteronomy 21, and he was condemned to death. Jesus took in our place the punishment we deserved. He was condemned by the elders and executed outside the city—hung on a tree (Deut 21:22-23). Why? Galatians 3:13 says, "Christ redeemed us from the curse of the law by becoming a curse for us, because it is written, Cursed is everyone who is hung on a tree." His death provides forgiveness for when we fall short, and his Spirit is given to us to produce self-control.

So the positive strategy for battling gluttony and drunkenness is to feast on Jesus—the living water and bread from heaven. If you do that, you will live forever. Satisfaction in Christ will produce self-control so you are able to have a well-balanced diet, feast at appropriate times as a means of worship, and yes, fast to show your dependence on God rather than on bread!

## Conclusion

Aren't you glad that Jesus came to eat and drink with sinners, drunks, and gluttons? He offered himself to save us from our uncontrolled appetites. Feast on and be satisfied in him alone!

## Reflect and Discuss

1. Why do we so often avoid the topic of gluttony?
2. In what ways are we eating ourselves to death?
3. In what ways does the culture's celebration of alcohol obscure its dangers?
4. How would you define gluttony?
5. What does the Bible say about beverage alcohol? Drunkenness?
6. In what ways can gluttony hurt you socially?
7. In what ways does a lack of self-control reveal a problem in your relationship with Jesus?
8. How can Jesus free you from gluttony?
9. What are some things you can practically put in place to modify your behavior in this area?
10. What are some times to feast?

# Greed

## PROVERBS 11:24-28

**Main Idea:** Greed reveals unbelief.

---

**I. Greed Is Foolish (11:24-28).**
- A. Greed is foolish because it hurts you (11:24-26; 28:22).
- B. Greed is foolish because it hurts the people around you (15:7).
- C. Greed is foolish because money doesn't last (23:4-5).

**II. Greed Is Deadly Because It Is Unbelief (11:28; 28:25).**

**III. The Antidote to Greed Is Believing the Gospel (11:28).**

---

"He got greedy" is a modern proverb of sorts that we use when people go for a little bit more than they should and things go bad. This kind of greed is often easy to recognize in others, but it is hard to recognize in ourselves. We think greed is a rich man's problem. The Bible, however, says it is everyone's problem, including those who follow Jesus. The great Baptist preacher Charles Spurgeon understood this, and he offered up this prayer for himself and his people:

> O, my Lord, let me not merely talk thus, and pretend to despise earthly treasure, when all the while I am hunting after it; but grant me grace to live above these things, never setting my heart upon them, nor caring whether I have them, or have them not; but exercising all my energy in pleasing thee, and in gaining those things which thou dost hold in esteem. Give me, I pray thee, the riches of thy grace that I may at last attain to the riches of thy glory, through Christ Jesus. (*Illustrations and Meditations*, 263)

However, that kind of attitude Spurgeon prays for is not in all of us. So often we are not content with what we have. We want just a little bit more. It starts when we are young with whatever we see on television. I (Jon) remember my girls seeing a commercial for "seat pets"—stuffed animals that connect to the seat belt in your car. They said, "We have to have those!" They had ridden in the car from place to place just fine up until then, but all of a sudden they just had to have what they saw on TV! The problem is that we never grow out of that. Expenses always increase to meet the income because we want more, more, and more. We think we have to have a bigger TV, a nicer home, and a newer car. We always crave just a little more.

That is why total debt has increased from about $1,200 per person in 1948 to $10,168 per person in 2010, and that does not include real estate debt. Americans now average $3,480 in credit card debt per person. That is an increase of 285 percent since 1980 (Indiviglio, "Americans' Love Affair with Debt"). Half of Americans spend more than they make annually (Kavoussi, "Half of Americans"). Think about that. Half of America spends more money than they make year after year. That shows a lack of contentment with what we have and a craving for more.

The problem is complicated by the fact that greed is hard to define. After all, it is not wrong in and of itself to want money, a house, provision for your family, and other things. But at any moment these desires could become greed or covetousness. John Piper defines greed as "desiring something so much you lose your contentment in God" ("Future Grace, Part 5"). Therefore, greed is thinking that you need this or that to be happy. It's thinking, "For me to be happy I need God plus _________." Once you fill in that blank, you travel the road of greed into the world of unbelief. God is no longer enough. Jesus no longer satisfies your soul. This distinction made by Piper is really important because Proverbs is not against money. In fact, Proverbs often links God's financial blessings with wise behavior. But desire for more becomes a very bad thing if you love, trust, or find your satisfaction in money or things rather than in God.

Greed is a temptation for all of us, and the Bible says it is deadly. Greed will destroy you. We can see this destruction all around us. The problem is that we think we do not really struggle with greed because we do not have a lot of money. But the apostle Paul reminds us in 1 Timothy 6 that just to want to be rich and have stuff is deadly (v. 9). You do not have to be rich to crave riches, and a greedy heart shows a life that is walking away from satisfaction in Jesus. And what Paul tells us in the New Testament is echoed throughout the book of Proverbs—greed is deadly. We see this truth clearly in Proverbs 11:24-28.

## Greed Is Foolish

### PROVERBS 11:24-28

Proverbs argues that greed is foolish and deadly, and you should be able to observe that in everyday life. There are too many modern examples of this to count. Dr. Seuss's story "The Lorax" reveals the deadly effects of greed on the environment. The main character abuses natural resources for his own gain. Or one can look at the economic crisis in America a few years ago and see how greed not only destroyed the economy but also people's lives.

*Greed Is Foolish Because It Hurts You (11:24-26; 28:22)*

Greed hurts us in all kinds of ways. Greed might make you a workaholic who misses out on time with family, or it might make you a miserly kind of person who refuses to be kind to others. The Bible says that kind of lifestyle will injure you personally. We see this truth in Proverbs 11:24-26.

> *One person gives freely,*
> *yet gains more;*
> *another withholds what is right,*
> *only to become poor.*
> *A generous person will be enriched,*
> *and the one who gives a drink of water*
> *will receive water.*
> *People will curse anyone who hoards grain,*
> *but a blessing will come to the one who sells it.*

These verses sound counterintuitive to us. We think that holding on to our money and stuff will mean that we have more of it, but the Bible says hoarding what you have does not mean more; it means less. While it may seem counterintuitive, we can observe this truth in nature. Generously sowing seed and generously watering the ground will lead to much fruit (Murphy and Huwiler, *Proverbs*, 56). Therefore, one major sign of greed is hoarding and stinginess, and that hurts you and others around you.

People are even able to justify hoarding in their minds. They say things like, "I can't tithe right now because we just bought a new house." But this attitude is foolish because the Bible says it leads to poverty. Proverbs 28:22 says, "A greedy one is in a hurry for wealth; he doesn't know that poverty will come to him." We might be tempted to say, "Is this true?" (Johnson, *Him We Proclaim,* 303–13).[39] After all, we know stories of greedy misers who prosper and generous people who are poor. The point of Proverbs is that God's wisdom will work out ultimately even if it does not work out immediately in this life. There will be a reversal. God will see to it. We see examples of this all over Scripture. Ahab and Jezebel looked like they prospered from their murderous greed for another vineyard, but the tables turned on them in the end (1 Kgs 21; 2 Kgs 9). The rich man in Luke 16 prospered while the poor man languished with the stray dogs, but in the end the poor man was comforted in paradise while the rich man was tortured in hades (Luke 16:19-31). The consequence of greed will be that the poverty you dread is what you will end up with—sometimes now and sometimes later. In contrast, the generous will be given even more. Reject greediness because it hurts you.

### *Greed Is Foolish Because It Hurts the People Around You (15:7)*

Your desire for more hurts those around you—the people you love. Greed might cause you to fail to meet people's needs or drive your family into the ground. Proverbs 15:27 says, "Whoever is greedy for unjust gain troubles his own household" (ESV). Craving money and going after it by any means necessary always has repercussions on those closest to you. If you are a workaholic, cheat on your taxes, or misuse petty cash at work, inevitably it will have consequences on those you love. You hear story after story of people who had everything by worldly standards and were still miserable. Not only were they miserable, but so were their families. We see biblical examples of this with Achan in Joshua 7 or Ananias and Sapphira in Acts 5. Greed brought down the wrath of God. We can see modern examples of this all around us. As I (Jon) have mentioned earlier, I had a friend in high school who was rich by the world's standards. He drove a BMW at age sixteen, but when I stayed over at his house I noticed his mom would pass out drunk at night because her husband never came home. Having riches and possessions does not lead to happiness!

### *Greed Is Foolish Because Money Doesn't Last (23:4-5)*

Proverbs 23:4-5 says,

> *Don't wear yourself out to get rich;*
> *because you know better, stop!*

---

[39] Dennis Johnson's great discussion on this issue shaped my thinking here.

*As soon as your eyes fly to it, it disappears,*
*for it makes wings for itself*
*and flies like an eagle to the sky.*

Proverbs tells us to be wise enough to exercise restraint in our pursuit for money. It does not say, "Don't work hard," but rather it teaches that there should be a rhythm of work and rest in your life. There comes a time when enough is enough (Longman, *Proverbs*, 424). Do not neglect your family, lose your relationships, or let your happiness fluctuate in pursuit of something that is fleeting. Have the wisdom to recognize that there are things that are more valuable than money. Do not waste your life on things that do not last! Money has wings, and it flies away!

Once my wife and I (Jon) bought our daughters butterflies to raise. We got them as caterpillars and tended to them and nurtured them until they grew to be butterflies in a net, but at some point we had to let them go. The girls were so sad because they wanted to hold on to them as long as they could, but they could not hold on to them forever. Money is the same way. The saying goes that you never see a hearse pulling a U-Haul trailer.

The fact that you cannot take money and stuff with you should change your perspective on it. Why do we spend so much energy acquiring the stuff of future garage sales? Sure, it shimmers and shines when we get it, but it fades quickly and then we think we need a new one. One big example of this is the story my youth pastor told me about taking his children to Graceland. Elvis had things in his day that were considered unbelievable and decadent. He had a television and a mobile phone in his car. My youth pastor told me when he showed those things to his young sons they were not impressed at all. They were saying, we have a mobile phone and can play Pacman on it, and we have a TV in our car and it plays DVDs. Elvis's possessions were so exceptional and valuable at the time, but now they have lost their shine. That is why Jesus says that moths and rust will destroy the things that we work so hard for, and we cannot take them with us when we die (Matt 6:19-21).

## Greed Is Deadly Because It Is Unbelief

### PROVERBS 11:28; 28:25

Proverbs 11:28 says, "Anyone trusting in his riches will fall, but the righteous will flourish like foliage." Greed is trusting in and finding happiness in money rather than in God. The problem is not wealth but rather our attitude toward it. The parallelism of this verse implies that the person who relies on wealth is unrighteous. How then do you assess whether or not you are trusting in wealth? Ask questions like, "Does my joy or anxiety rise and fall with my bank statement? Am I constantly anxious about money and provision?" The answers to those questions might reveal you have made money or stuff an idol. If your joy is determined by your money and possessions, you are falsely worshiping something other than God. If you are constantly anxious about provision, it reveals that you believe you need something other than God to be happy. When money and stuff are seen as the path to a happy life, you are in idolatry. Jesus says that you cannot serve both God and money (Matt 6:24), and Solomon says the exact same thing.

We see the contrast between greed and belief again in Proverbs 28:25: "A greedy person stirs up conflict, but whoever trusts in the LORD will prosper." Here's the bottom line: those who are greedy do not trust God. They trust in money instead of Jesus. That reality is why Jesus said that it is hard for a rich man to enter the kingdom of God (Matt 19:23). The rich do not see their need for God. In contrast, those who trust the Lord are content, they do not grasp for other things to make them happy, and they wait for the true blessings that come from God alone.

Trusting in money and possessions will send you to hell because it is unbelief, and we are only saved by grace through faith. Proverbs 11:4 states, "Wealth is not profitable on a day of wrath, but righteousness rescues from death." God's wrath will be poured out on the greedy. We will stand before a judge who has access to the hidden cravings of our hearts. On that day, what will it profit you to gain the whole world and lose your soul (Mark 8:36)? It's not just that greed will cause things to go badly for you in this life, although it will; but even more than that, greed will send you to hell.

## The Antidote to Greed Is Believing the Gospel

### PROVERBS 11:28

Here's the bottom line: greed is a belief and worship issue. You believe and worship your way into greed, and you must believe and worship your way out of it. It's not just that greed makes you a Mr. Scrooge; it's that greed shows that you are walking away from Jesus, the Wisdom of God. Proverbs reveals that foolishness is idolatry, and thus the foolishness of greed reveals a heart that does not believe or follow Jesus.

Jesus perfectly avoided greed; he was never greedy, even one time. Satan tried to bribe Jesus with the kingdoms of the world if he would bypass the cross and its suffering, but Jesus perfectly controlled his appetite and refused idolatry. Everything he refused from Satan—and more—was given to him by God later. After all, after his resurrection from the dead he looked at his disciples and said, "All authority has been given to me in heaven and on earth" (Matt 28:18). Jesus refused the fleeting pleasures of this life so that he could enjoy eternal ones. He knew what we do not seem to understand—our cravings will never be satisfied in this life. Man does not live by bread or flat screen TV alone; he lives by God alone (Matt 4:4).

Even though Jesus was never greedy, he died because of the greedy and for the greedy. Judas's greed for silver led him to betray Jesus and enrich himself (Matt 26:15). And yet, if you only look at the death of Jesus from a short perspective, you might be led to ask, Is Proverbs right? The greedy person was enriched while the generous person was killed. But from the post-resurrection perspective, we see that by Sunday morning the tables had turned—righteousness delivered Jesus from death!

Jesus, through his death, provides forgiveness and salvation to those who repent of greed and believe in him. He also grants his perfect record of contentment to those who believe in him. If you are in Christ, this is who you are: the perfectly content son or daughter of God. Now live like it!

Jesus, through his gospel, now empowers us to be content and generous people. The promises of money are powerful, and they are only broken by the power of the gospel's superior promises—like the fact that God is now for you and no good thing will he withhold from you (Ps 84:11). Do you believe that? Believing that is the means to be content and generous.

According to Hebrews 13:5-6, the only way you will be content is if you believe that God is for you:

> *Keep your life free from the love of money. Be satisfied with what you have, for he himself has said, I will never leave you or abandon you. Therefore, we may boldly say, The Lord is my helper; I will not be afraid. What can man do to me?*

If you are not content, it is because you do not trust God to help you. This is a belief issue. You do not trust that your God will supply all your needs according to his riches in glory in Christ Jesus (Phil 4:19). But when you place your trust in God and find your satisfaction in him alone, you can be content with what you have and praise God for what he has given you.

Not only does the gospel lead you to be content with what you have, it also leads you to be generous toward others. Second Corinthians 8:9 says, "For you know the grace of our Lord Jesus Christ: Though he was rich, for your sake he became poor, so that by his poverty you might become rich." The gospel turns us from takers and hoarders into generous and joyful givers because what we have in Christ is vastly superior to material riches. When God got hold of my dad, he (Danny) sold his car to give more money to the church. You do not have to be rich to be generous; you just have to be changed by Jesus. I remember leading a young couple to the Lord who had nothing and barely scraped by, but they gave away their crib and some baby clothes to help other people. Once you grasp the gospel of Jesus leaving his throne in heaven, then you can let go of the things you hold so dear and give them to others generously.

## Reflect and Discuss

1. Why do we think that only rich people struggle with greed? Is that true?
2. Why do you think we crave what we see?
3. It is obvious that you should not spend more than you make, so why do so many of us do it?
4. How would you define greed?
5. Give some examples of how greed hurts people or those around them.
6. How can the perspective that money and possessions are temporary help you fight against greed?
7. Did you ever get a new possession that you just "had to have" but quickly got tired of? What does that teach you?
8. In what ways does greed reveal our unbelief?
9. How does the gospel help you be content?
10. How does the gospel help you be generous?

# Lust

## PROVERBS 23:26-28

**Main Idea:** The antidote to lust is the gospel of Jesus Christ.

**I. Lust Will Ruin Your Life.**
**II. The Gospel Will Save Your Life.**

When people go deer hunting, they put out bait to lure the deer in and they put on camouflage to disguise themselves so the deer cannot see them. The deer is not suspecting anything as it walks toward what looks like a good meal; then BAM! it gets shot through the heart. As graphic as that image might seem, that is exactly the picture that Proverbs paints when it comes to the issue of lust. You are prey being hunted down by a predator.

This wisdom principle is observable. Even non-Christians can sense this truth. I once counseled with an atheist who lost his marriage because of pornography. He and his wife were not believers and did not have the ethical code of the Bible, but his uncontrolled lust for pornography still destroyed his marriage and brought great devastation into his life. He, an unbeliever, saw up close and personal the horrible consequences of uncontrolled lust.

Lust is deadly for all of us! Lust is a predator stalking its victim, and we must be able to see it. The problem is that we are often like that deer that does not see the danger until it is too late. Granted, some of you do see it, but the only reason you see it is because it has already ruined you or gotten its clutches into you. Others of you do not think you have a problem with lust because you do not act on it, but Jesus says it is not just the act of sexual sin that condemns us. It is also the desire for sinful sex that condemns us. That is why Albert Mohler Jr. has said that everyone north of puberty is a sexual sinner.[40] Some of you fool yourselves into thinking that you are safe because your fantasies stay in your mind, but the Bible says that sexual sin starts with lust in your heart and mind.

[40] See similar remarks in Lillian Kwon, "Stop Separating Gays From 'Normal' People, Says Evangelical."

Even if you have never acted out in a sinful sexual way, you have thought about it and are therefore guilty of it.

Some people do not see how right now they are taking small steps in this area that will ultimately destroy their life. Some are training themselves for destruction right now and think it is no big deal. They think to themselves things like, "I just look at porn occasionally." "It's not hurting anyone." "I don't have a problem." "What's the big deal if I make out with my girlfriend?" "What's the big deal in giving an iPhone to my twelve-year-old?" Some folks are setting patterns in their lives right now—or in the lives of their children—that will cause them to do something one year, three years, or fifteen years from now that their children will remember at a funeral service.

Sexual lust is not something to play with; it is deadly! Proverbs 23:26-28 says,

> *My son, give me your heart,*
> *and let your eyes observe my ways.*
> *For a prostitute is a deep pit,*
> *and a wayward woman is a narrow well;*
> *indeed, she sets an ambush like a robber*
> *and increases the number of unfaithful people.*

## Lust Will Ruin Your Life

God gave sex as a good gift to be enjoyed in the context of the covenant commitment called "marriage." However, in our sinfulness we distort God's good gift and use it in ways he forbids. He forbids those ways not because he wants to rob us of fun but because he knows that using sex in a way that he did not design is harmful and destructive. This includes all sexual activity outside of heterosexual marriage. All of it. So God warns us about sexual sin and lust because enjoying sexual pleasure in the wrong context is deadly.[41]

The sage says, "My son, give me your heart," because he knows—like Jesus—that lust starts in the heart. Purity of heart is the goal because it will lead to a pure life. As Proverbs 4:23 has already told us, your heart determines your behavior, so you cannot simply modify your behavior. If

---

[41] For a New Testament perspective on this topic, see Daniel Akin's sermon, "My Body Belongs to God."

you are not pure at the heart level, you will find new outlets for your sin. For example, without a pure heart, you might put blocking software on your computer, but you will find ways around it, or you will just fantasize in your own mind. The battle against lust must be fought in the mind and heart because that is where this all starts. That is its origin.

Then the sage moves from the heart to the eyes because a lustful heart will drive eyes to look at things they should not look at. We cannot tell you how many people are killing themselves with pornography. They are warping their minds to view sexuality in a purely selfish and corrupt manner. This selfish view of sex destroys marriages and will destroy future marriages because the viewer's mind is twisted by pornographic images into seeing intimacy as something other than what it is, something other than God designed and intended. Looking at all kinds of things can drive lust: Internet porn, the wrong movies, the wrong sitcoms, the *Sports Illustrated* swimsuit edition, or just checking out women at the mall.

The sage says to the son, "Observe my ways." Imitate me. Can we say that? What if your son or daughter grew up to think just like you? Would that be good? Can you urge them to imitate you? Or is the fact that you check out women in public or talk about the beauty of other women, thereby putting down your wife's beauty, leading your son to death? I once ministered to a family with a young son who they would take to Hooters and get his picture taken with all the waitresses surrounding him. They would post his big smile on Facebook, but they did not understand the view of women and sexuality that they were planting in his mind with pictures that they thought were innocently cute. God designed sex for other-ness, not selfishness.

Solomon constantly warns his son on this specific topic because this is where Solomon fell and was destroyed (see 1 Kgs 11). He repeatedly said, "Listen to me," and warned his son of the wayward (foreign?) woman who leads to sexual sin. Here in Proverbs 23 the sage again warns that the immoral woman—a metaphor for sexual sin and lust—is a deep pit! The image is clear. Hunters would dig out deep pits in an attempt to trap their prey. They would then camouflage the hole so that their prey would not see it and would fall into the trap. That is what sexual lust does.

Also, the pit is a metaphor for physical and spiritual death. Proverbs talks about Sheol, or the grave, when it talks about the pit (Prov 5; 7; 9). Sexual lust will send you to hell. Sexual sin and lust is an enemy. Lust is a huntress or robber who wants to kill you and take everything you have. Just like the hunter's prey, you often do not see the trap until it is too late.

Proverbs has told us repeatedly that wisdom is not a set of ideas; Wisdom is a person. And the New Testament tells us that person is Jesus. But Proverbs also reveals that Folly is a person. Satan stands behind the wayward woman—sexual sin—seeking to kill you. The enemy is prowling around setting a trap to destroy you and take you to hell. How does he do it? He does it through things that are seductive and appealing. Satan is tracking you down, and he notices the things that turn you on, just as a hunter notices what bait attracts the deer.

Lust traps you and ruins your life. It is a waste of time and resources. It warps your idea of marriage. And it puts in place a pattern of behavior that in the future will cause you to hurt your spouse and betray your family. That is what verse 28 says. The predator increases the number of unfaithful people. So lust will ruin you. It will damage your reputation, or it will cause you to lose your family or your future family. Sexual sin is a break of the marriage covenant, even your future marriage covenant. Goldsworthy points out that this verse refers to those who are unfaithful in marriage (*Tree of Life*, 155).

The sage says that sexual sin is a pit. He said it earlier about the adulteress's mouth in 22:14: "The mouth of the forbidden woman is a deep pit; a man cursed by the LORD will fall into it." What does this refer to? The mouth is what often leads men and women astray (cf. Prov 5; 7). Flattery appeals to a man's vanity (Longman, *Proverbs*, 408), and words appeal to a woman's desire for intimate conversation. Sexual sin offers you pleasure, and it delivers for a little while. But then you realize too late that you fell into a trap. After all, Proverbs 7 and 9 say this woman's house leads down to the grave.

Interestingly, falling for this kind of sin will not just earn you future judgment; it is a sign of God's condemnation right now (22:14). A sign of God's judgment is the fact that he is handing you over to your fleshly desires. He removes his merciful, restraining hand from you. Not being able to control yourself, loathing yourself because one more time you have deleted the Internet history on your computer, losing your family because of pornography addiction—these are all just a foretaste of the judgment that is to come.

The problem is that we are all predisposed to this and have fallen short of God's glory in this area. It starts out small and sometimes seemingly innocent, but then BAM! you fall. All along you did not see how you were undermining your marriage or your future marriage. You thought it was harmless. You thought you had not really done anything "sinful," but you did not see how you were driving a wedge into your marriage. You thought things like, "It's just a little flirting. So what? He makes me feel appreciated in a way I don't at home." "What's the big deal? I'd never really do anything anyway." "She laughs at my jokes." "He's a better listener than my husband." Those thoughts, even unconsciously, plant a deadly germ in your marriage.

Facebook can be a big killer because you start to wonder about an old flame and what it would have been like if you had ended up together. Now you can attempt to recreate what you once had. For some women it is reading romance novels that make them desire intimacy with someone else. For some there are struggles with modesty, causing others to stumble. For teens it might be when they ponder, How far is too far? If you ask that question, it shows that you do not understand that you are training yourself to enjoy sexual contact outside of the covenant of marriage and you are cheating on your future spouse. So parents, it is foolish to let your kids be alone with someone of the opposite sex.

Again, we do not see how deadly some things, that we think are innocuous, actually are. I (Jon) once counseled with a couple where the husband had cheated on the wife. They were trying to put their marriage back together; and as I dug into their issues, they told me that they used to watch pornography together to spice up their marriage. I asked them why in the world they would do such a thing. I looked at the wife and said, "Don't you see that you are training him to be aroused by a woman that is not you? Is it any wonder that he went out of the marriage with another woman?" Often, the things that we think are not that big a deal are the things that destroy us.

Proverbs 30:20 says of the adulteress, "This is the way of an adulteress: she eats and wipes her mouth and says, 'I've done nothing wrong.'" What this verse means is that we find a way to justify our sexual sin. Some people justify themselves because their spouse isn't "holding up their end of the marriage." Some will even justify their sexual sin by saying it is God's will. I (Jon) remember riding to my brother's basketball game with his roommate's mother, who had stolen her best friend's husband. She left her second marriage to begin a relationship with her best friend's husband, and she said to me, "I finally found the person that God has for me."

We try to downplay and justify our lust and our sexual sin, but the Bible says they are deadly. The sexually immoral will not inherit the kingdom of God. So the question asked by Tim Challies is a good one: "Do you love pornography enough to go to hell for it?" ("Desecration and Titillation"). And we might add, Do you love lust enough to go to hell for it?

## The Gospel Will Save Your Life

Folly—Satan—wants you to follow him to hell. So the sage constantly warns us not to fall for lust because if you do, you are following Folly toward death. On the flip side, Jesus is the Wisdom of God and wants you to follow him on the path of life and wisdom. If you are falling into lust, it shows you have a problem with Jesus—that is, you do not believe the gospel rightly, even if you are a Christian.

In Tim Challies's article, he makes a great argument ("Desecration and Titillation"). God gave humanity a picture of the gospel long before Jesus died and rose again when he gave us the institution of marriage (Gen 2; Eph 5). Marriage is meant to point us to the relationship of Christ with his church. Our marriages should picture this: Christ's pure love for his bride that drove him to the cross to be united with her in one flesh. Sexual union is only right in marriage because only then can it point to the intimate love Christ has for his people. Sex outside of marriage—lust—lies about Jesus and the church. It makes a mockery of the gospel. "To tamper with sex is to tamper with the death and resurrection of Jesus Christ" (Challies, "Desecration and Titillation"). When you look at pornography, fantasize, or flirt with a coworker, you are mocking the gospel. In pornography, you are watching a violation of the gospel and being turned on by it. In contrast, a pure sexual relationship in marriage points to the purity of Jesus's love for you. So when you lust you are saying that you need a more satisfying and pleasurable love than the love of Jesus. That shows you have not rightly grasped the gospel.

Therefore, Proverbs tells us that the horizontal antidote to lust is marriage. Enjoy exclusive and repeated intimacy with your spouse rather than burn with lust. So guys, romance your wife, learn about her, become an expert on her, do getaway weekends without the kids, do not sleep in separate rooms, and pursue her your entire life. If you are not regularly intimate with your wife, Paul says you are in a danger zone.

After all, he mentions the same predators seeking to destroy marriage as Proverbs (1 Cor 7).

The vertical antidote to lust is Jesus and the gospel. Preach the gospel to yourself daily. Fight this war in your heart and mind. John Piper talks about imagining graphic images of Jesus dying on the cross—head pierced by thorns, lacerated back heaving up and down on the cross beam, and lungs struggling for breath—as you quote Titus 2:14: "He gave himself for us to redeem us from all lawlessness and to cleanse for himself a people for his own possession, eager to do good works." He did that for our purity; and if we yield to lust, we add to his already excruciating suffering by stabbing him with a sword. Because he died for our purity, we should not do that (Piper, "Future Grace, Part 4").

The sage warns us through the Spirit about lust, and we are called to heed the warnings and walk in wisdom—following after Jesus. That means gouging out your eye instead of going to hell (Matt 5:29). Flee from lust and do not even get close to it because it is so dangerous. Do not see how far you can go or how close you can get to the line. Do not ask, "How close to immorality can I get without actually committing it?" No! Run from it (1 Cor 6:18)! This might mean a community group where you are accountable to other guys, blocking software, joining a reporting program like Covenant Eyes, getting rid of your computer, or throwing your kids' iPhone in the trash. It means doing whatever you have to do. You might say, "Oh that's a bit much," but not if you look at it this way: there is a ferocious predator loose in your house trying to kill you, and it only makes sense to take drastic measures to take its life before it takes yours.

## Conclusion

We have all fallen into lust and earned the wage of descending into the chambers of hell (Rom 6:23). The good news is that Jesus went into the pit for you—he became the prey—and he came back alive on the other side. He crushed the head of the predator and offers you forgiveness and new life if you will turn to him. One day those things that you think no one else knows about will be uncovered, and you will have to look a man in the face who knows not only everything you have ever done but also everything you have ever thought. Miraculously, you can hear that man say to you right now, "There is no condemnation" for you if you will repent and ask me for mercy (Rom 8:1).

## Reflect and Discuss

1. Why does porn destroy marriages?
2. In what ways does sexual sin include more than physical acts?
3. What are some seemingly innocent ways that people fall into lust?
4. Why is God's design for sex the best?
5. Why is porn so destructive?
6. What are some ways that we express our lust?
7. How does sexual sin show you are under God's wrath right now?
8. How should marriage free you from lust?
9. How can you practically fight against lust?
10. What does it look like practically to "gouge out your eye"?

# Pride

## PROVERBS 16:18-20

**Main Idea:** The antidote to destructive pride is trust in Jesus.

---

I. **Prideful Trust of Self Is Foolish and Destructive (28:26).**
II. **Humbly Follow God and His Word (15:31-33; 16:18-20; 30:1-6).**
III. **Humbly Follow Godly Instruction and Counsel (10:8).**

---

The prevailing idea of our pop culture is "Follow your heart, and you can't go wrong." From Disney movies to *The Bachelor,* we are told to follow our hearts in order to make the best decisions for our lives. Whom should I date? Whom should I marry? Should I stay married? What career path should I choose? To answer those kinds of questions, you just need to ask, What does my heart tell me? Even "Christian" counsel often seems to be a mix of Bible verses and "follow your heart." Be true to you, or be true to who God made you to be—however you might define that—and things will always work out.

Such counsel is foolish. Charles Spurgeon was spot on: "The heart is a den of evil" ("Meeting of the Neighboring Churches"). Left to ourselves, we choose wrongly because we have sinful hearts. We do not see the world rightly, so we make decisions that ruin our lives. Proverbs reveals that wisdom and foolishness basically boil down to two issues of the heart: humility and pride. Those who are prideful and trust in themselves for decision making will fall, but those who are humble and trust in the Lord for decision making will be wise. Everything can boil down to pride and humility (16:18-20).

## Prideful Trust of Self Is Foolish and Destructive

### PROVERBS 28:26

The world calls us to pride and self-exaltation, but the Bible warns us about these companion sins. While the Disney Channel tells you to rely on yourself and follow your heart, the Bible says that is foolishness. Proverbs 28:26 says, "Whoever trusts in his own heart is a fool, but he who walks in wisdom will be delivered" (author's translation). The reason it is wrong to pridefully follow your heart is because your heart is sinful. Proverbs 20:9 asks, "Who can say, 'I have kept my heart pure; I am cleansed from my sin'?" The rhetorical question is posed in such a way that the expected answer is, no one! (Waltke, *Proverbs, Chapters 15–31*, 135). Because of our sinful and impure condition, we do not choose rightly. We do not see things clearly, and therefore following our hearts is deadly because we will not be "delivered" (i.e., saved). A pride that thinks we are always right and does not see things for the way they really are is a deadly thing.

Even though our pride clouds our vision of the world, there are still some wisdom patterns that we can see in our sinful condition, such as the fact that laziness generally leads to poverty. However, there are things that are wise to God that are foolishness to men, and there are things that are foolishness to God that we think are wise (see 1 Cor 1). Our logic is contaminated by sin, folly, and pride; and the biggest problem is that we cannot even see it. The wisdom of this age makes sense to us because it's all we know. Therefore, it's difficult for us to know what is truly wise and right in life. We pridefully think our view is the correct one.

There are plenty of examples where being wise in God's eyes will require the humility to look strange in the world's eyes. The world says you should sleep with your girlfriend before you marry her. After all, how else will you know if you like being romantic with her? God says that's destructive, and we can observe that in the pain that many experience as a result of premarital sex or in the higher divorce rate among those who live together before marriage. Still, we choose to ignore the evidence. Or the world says to get what you want now and pay for it later. Spend money you don't have! But God says that is foolish. Again, we can see that with the massive credit card debt of our culture and the heavy burden it brings. We choose to ignore the evidence because our hearts are sinful, broken, and prideful.

God's wisdom clashes with the wisdom of the world. Worldly wisdom says, "If you want to be rich, you need to be stingy and keep things for yourself." But godly wisdom says, "One person gives freely, yet gains more; another withholds what is right, only to become poor" (11:24). Worldly wisdom says, "If someone wrongs you, get back at them, hold a grudge, or revel in their failures." But godly wisdom says, "Don't gloat when your enemy falls" (24:17) and, "If your enemy is hungry, give him food to eat" (25:21). Do good to your enemy! Worldly wisdom says,

"Money will make you happy, so get as much as you can." But godly wisdom says, "Anyone trusting in his riches will fall" (11:28) and, "A righteous person eats until he is satisfied" (13:25). Be content with what you have! God says that often you will be happier with less: "Better is a little with the fear of the LORD than great treasure with turmoil" (15:16). While the world calls us to chase money with all we have, we can observe that riches often bring great sadness. As Matt Chandler said, "I've never met someone who came from a really poor background whose parents loved them and were around a lot, who was really bitter about the fact they drove a trashy car. . . . But I have met devastated young men and women with very expensive cars and very nice clothes whose daddy and mommy was [sic] never around" ("Mission of God").

The world says, "If you want to get ahead in life, you need to promote yourself." But God says, "Let another praise you, and not your own mouth" (27:2). The world says, "Be buddies with your kids. Don't discipline them or say no to them. You don't want them to be maladjusted, do you?" But God says, "The one who loves [his son] disciplines him diligently" (13:24). The world says, "Follow your heart when it comes to dating, the friends you have, the style of clothes you wear, or the lifestyle you lead. Don't listen to your parents or your pastors. Be yourself!" Proverbs says that listening to your heart is foolish. You need to submit to your parents and listen to godly counsel. Worldly wisdom says, "Go along to get along. Don't jeopardize friendships by having difficult conversations; it's not your business anyway." But godly wisdom says, "Better an open reprimand than concealed love" (27:5). God tells us these things because he loves us.

Some of the things the world tells us—if we take a step back—are easily seen as foolish, but others are not. We cannot see how bragging is self-destructive, but God says these things are foolish and will be called to account. Our big problem is not a lack of information but rather that we do not see the world rightly because of our heart condition; and the even bigger problem is that we do not even know it! We are wise in our own eyes, and Proverbs says that is the epitome of foolishness (21:2).

Foolishness is a lot like colorblindness, and I know a lot about colorblindness because I (Jon) am struck with this malady. At my house, one of our girls' favorite games is to hold up items and ask daddy, "What color is this?" while they giggle uncontrollably when I cannot answer! I cannot see colors rightly (neither can two of my brothers)—they look different to me than to most people. Proverbs says that is how foolishness is. You are not able to see things the way they really are. You cannot perceive the right order of things. For example, all of us have watched movies or sitcoms on network TV that our grandparents would have considered hardcore pornography. We don't consider them hardcore because we have grown up in a culture where seeing skin, lots of skin, does not shock us (Moore, *Walking the Line*). We are self-deceived and cannot see that we are thinking wrongly; so we go against the grain of how God designed the world, and we hurt ourselves and often others as well.

"There is a way that seems right to a person, but its end is the way to death" (14:12; 16:25). What seems like the right course to you actually will lead you to ruin and death because you are not seeing things clearly. Left to ourselves, we will pridefully choose the wrong way. Proverbs says, "Foolishness is bound to the heart of a youth" (22:15). Anyone who has children knows that this is true. A parent does not have to teach their kids to be stingy with their toys, but they do have to teach them to share. Wise choices—like sharing—do not come to us naturally. That is true for children, but it is also true for adults. We are just as self-deceived. As Proverbs says, "A fool's way is right in his own eyes, but whoever listens to counsel is wise" (12:15). It is foolish to think your way is always right and not to listen to counsel in your life, whether it comes from a parent, a pastor, or a godly friend. But again, wisdom requires humility whereas foolishness is the pride that refuses to submit to counsel.

We need to be called away from pride—trusting in ourselves—to trusting the Lord. Proverbs 3:5 says, "Trust in the LORD with all your heart, and do not rely on your own understanding." These are two sides of the same coin: trust God not yourself, walk in humility not pride. "Don't be wise in your own eyes," Proverbs 3:7 states. So foolishness consists of pridefully thinking that you are wise or that your way is always right; it's a lack of humility.

This kind of pride and self-deception is deadly dangerous. Proverbs 26:12 asks, "Do you see a person who is wise in his own eyes? There is more hope for a fool than for him." Wow! You are worse than a fool if you are cocky enough to think you are wise. You push back because you are sure that you are right, and you hurt yourself in the process: your plans fail because you did not seek advice, you wreck your family because you thought it was OK to step out on your marriage, you run your family into the ground because you thought life was all about money, or your kids are out of control because you thought discipline was outdated. If you trust yourself or you care too much about what others think of you, it can ruin your life. Proverbs 29:25 says, "The fear of mankind is a snare, but the one who trusts in the LORD is protected." If you fear man rather than God—if you want to be liked and accepted too much—it will lead to foolish and harmful decisions.

So if pride is essentially the epitome of foolishness, how and where do we look for wisdom in decision making?

## Humbly Follow God and His Word

### PROVERBS 15:31-33; 16:18-20; 30:1-6

Proverbs as a whole, and Proverbs 16 in particular, tells us that wisdom is found in humbly trusting God. After all, he made the world, and he knows how it works. Proverbs encourages us to look to God and his Word for wisdom. If one were to boil down the message of Proverbs, it might look like this: "Trust God, not yourself!" Or "Be humble, not prideful." This is what Solomon means when he says that the fear of the Lord is the key component to wisdom (1:7; 9:10; etc.). What does that mean? It means that there are two components to gaining wisdom: humbly look away from yourself, and look to God and his Word. The fear of Yahweh is reverent awe and dependence on him—as he has revealed himself in his Word—that leads to obeying him. This is a healthy fear of him who can cast both soul and body into hell (Matt 10:28). True wisdom entails the humility to know that you do not know it all!

So if the boiled-down message of Proverbs is to trust God with all your heart and not lean on your own understanding, then this requires humility, which is almost synonymous in Proverbs with the fear of Yahweh (see 15:31-33). The first step to wisdom is to realize that you are not wise. In order to have knowledge, you must first recognize that you do not know everything and you are not always right. Wisdom is being humble enough to admit that, and then submitting yourself to God and wise counsel. Proverbs 9:8-10 says that when you correct a wise man he will be wiser still. This means that you never arrive at the point where you are so wise that you do not need to humble yourself to correction. On the other hand, pride is the essence of foolishness in many ways. Proverbs 11:2 states, "When arrogance comes, disgrace follows; but with humility comes wisdom," and Proverbs 16:18-20 explains that "Pride comes before destruction . . . and the one who trusts in the LORD will be happy."

The fear of Yahweh and the knowledge of God seem to be parallel concepts (2:5). The bottom line is that a personal relationship with

God is the key to wisdom. We fear him because he is the one who gives wisdom—it comes from his mouth, which also points us to the Word of God (2:6; cf. 30:5-6). In order to fear God and be wise, we must go to his Word and submit to its authority for our lives.

In Proverbs 30:1-6 Agur acknowledges that he is not wise—since wisdom starts with recognizing your own ignorance—and that wisdom lies in heaven with God. No one has gone up to him to get wisdom. Wisdom belongs to him, and it belongs to his Son (30:4; Jesus!). Not only is wisdom found in the Son, but it is also found in God's words (30:5-6).[42] God's words are sufficient to shape our lives; one does not need to add to them. The problem for our lives is that we often try to add to God's Word. We think we need something else in addition to Scripture—something more relevant, practical, or helpful. "Proverbs is not sufficient to inform my parenting; I need to grab a book from Books-A-Million to supplement it." "Proverbs cannot really tell me how to manage my finances, so I need to let Dave Ramsey do that." I am not saying that you shouldn't read other resources, but the lack of confidence in the sufficiency of God's Word among Christians is tragic.

So we need God's Word to shape our worldview in order to observe the world through that lens. We need to view the world through the lens of the written Word and the living Word—Jesus of Nazareth (John 1:1-18) (Goldsworthy, *Tree of Life*, 187). Otherwise, we cannot see how corrupted the world around us is. We hear this throughout Proverbs as it exhorts us to keep the commands, look to the law, and look to the prophets (29:18). Hamilton points out that the words used in this verse connect Proverbs with the rest of the Old Testament (i.e., the Law and the Prophets) since the words used here refer to the law of God and the visions of the prophets (*God's Glory*, 272). God must write the Word on our hearts through conversion, but our responsibility is to actively bind the words of this book around our neck, write them on our hearts, and wrap them around our fingers, like Old Testament Israel (3:3; cf. Deut 6). One practical way to do this is to wear something on your wrist like a rubber band with a Bible reference written on it so you can be reminded constantly to meditate on it.

[42] The fact that wisdom is found in the Son and the Word should not be shocking because the New Testament reveals to us that the Word is a person—Jesus of Nazareth (John 1:1-14). See Goldsworthy's discussion of this in *Tree of Life*, 187.

Trusting God and his Word brings life. Proverbs 28:14 states, "Happy is the one who is always reverent, but one who hardens his heart falls into trouble." So there is blessing if you fear Yahweh, but if you reject him it will be disastrous. Trusting the Lord prolongs life, whereas folly can ruin your life or lead to a premature death (Fox, *Proverbs 1–9*, 143). Trusting Yahweh has positive consequences on the family because it gives your children a refuge (14:26). It leads to not having anxiety because you are satisfied in the Lord (19:23). Trusting Yahweh leads to a good reputation, joy in life now, and eternal life in the age to come. So recognize that prideful insistence that you always know what is right is actually wrong, and humbly submit yourself to the Lord!

## Humbly Follow Godly Instruction and Counsel

### PROVERBS 10:8

Proverbs tells its reader that godly wisdom is often mediated through human agents like parents. But it could also be applied to counselors, authority figures, or pastors. Foolishness means not submitting to these agents because you do not think that you need to, because in your pride you think you are always right. Wisdom means submitting to godly counsel that accords with the Word of God. You humbly submit to it because you know that you need it, need to learn more, and need to learn from your mistakes. Proverbs 10:8 states, "A wise heart accepts commands, but foolish lips will be destroyed." One must recognize that correction is in your best interest, and that it is not in your self-interest to ignore counsel (though many if not most people act as though it is).

The first place that a person is called to submit humbly is to their parents, as if they are obeying the Lord himself (1:8; 2:1; 3:1; 4:1,10; etc. cf. Eph 6:1-2). Proverbs 13:1 says, "A wise son responds to his father's discipline, but a mocker doesn't listen to rebuke." God has placed this authority in your life for your good. Wise children will recognize that and submit to their parents' authority, while fools will refuse to listen to their parents. Fools think their parents are unwise and outdated, but you will learn one day just how foolish that is. The following is attributed to Mark Twain, although its provenance is unclear: "When I was a boy of fourteen, my father was so ignorant I could hardly stand to have the old man around. But when I got to be twenty-one, I was astonished at how much the old man had learned in seven years."

Someone might object, "But I have ungodly parents!" The Bible says we are still supposed to submit to ungodly authority that he has placed in our lives. Paul exhorts the church at Rome to submit to a government run by Nero, who is turning Christians into human candles to light his garden parties (Rom 13). The Bible is clear that unless the ordained authority in your life is forcing you to disobey God, you are to submit to it (Dan 3; 6; Acts 4). So listen to your parents when you are in their home because they have more experience and wisdom than you do. And when you are grown and out of the house, seek their counsel on major decisions.

Outside of parents' authority over their children, there are people in our lives who are either authority figures or can be counselors, like pastors (Heb 13), bosses, teachers, and peer advisors in our church families. A great gift from God is a godly friend who will tell you what you need to hear, not just what you want to hear. We should all want people in our lives who can correct us because that is for our good. We are designed with a need for community—a church family. Proverbs 15:22 says as much: "Plans fail when there is no counsel, but with many advisers they succeed." Two heads are better than one; your own opinion on the situation is not sufficient. If you do not recognize this, the consequences will be ruinous. Pridefully refusing to listen to counsel harms you and the people around you. You will go astray, and you just might lead others astray as well by your foolishness (see 10:17).

## Conclusion

We are programmed to reject the voice of God and listen to the wrong voice—usually our own! It has been this way since Eden. The voice of the serpent deceived Eve into going after what her own eyes said was right instead of listening to the word of God (Gen 3). That's foolishness. That is pride! She rejected God's word, and instead she listened to the serpent's word and followed what her eyes said was wise. Trusting yourself and listening to Satan go hand-in-hand; after all, pride caused his fall (Ezek 28:17). Eve sought wisdom and knowledge apart from the word of God, and it was destructive because it led to death. She became the arbiter of what was good and evil instead of allowing God's word to determine those realities, and we've been doing it ever since. All of us have chosen to disobey God's word—we have chosen the wisdom of the world over God's word.

But there is one man who did not give in to the temptation in the garden. He said in his garden, "Not what I want but what you want," and he went to the cross. First Corinthians 1 tells us that act was foolishness to the world, but it's the wisdom and power of God. If we are going to be wise in God's eyes, that will mean looking strange in the eyes of the world. And if we are going to be wise, that means humble submission to the one who is God's wisdom and sanctification for us. It will mean having the mind of Jesus, who humbled himself to the point of death—even to death on a cross (Phil 2:5-11). So fear Jesus and humbly walk in wisdom!

## Reflect and Discuss

1. What are some examples from pop culture or anecdotally from your own life that demonstrate the culture's advice to follow your heart in order to make the right decisions in daily life? What do you think is the driving force behind that counsel?
2. Why is it a sign of pride to follow your own heart?
3. What are some examples of actions or conditions that are accepted in our culture that would have been outrageous a century ago? Which of these progressions are consistent with the Scriptures, and which ones are a departure from the Scriptures?
4. Give some examples of counsel that people give to others at work, to friends, or to their neighbors about marriage, parenting, work, finances, etc., that would be considered "worldly wisdom" by the Bible. What does the Bible counsel in those situations instead?
5. Give some examples of how pride can lead you to ruin and heartache in your life.
6. We are called to humbly look to God and his Word for wisdom. What are some practical ways we can do that in our daily lives?
7. Have you ever received counsel that was extremely helpful to you? What about unhelpful counsel? What was the difference between the two?
8. Why does it require humility to seek counsel?
9. Why does God tell us to submit to authority—even if it is not necessarily Christian authority?
10. What criteria should determine when you reject authority?

# Laziness

## PROVERBS 24:30-34

**Main Idea:** Our laziness points out our need for Jesus.

---

**I. Our Laziness Is Destructive.**
**II. Our Laziness Points Us to Jesus.**

---

In a song titled "Down the Road" by Mac McAnally, Kenny Chesney sings about a boy wanting to marry a girl and go through life together. In the third verse, her mother wonders if the boy is a genuine Christian, but her father worries whether the boy has a good enough job to make it through married life. We hear that and think those are two very different concerns: Momma's is a very spiritual (and godly) concern, whereas Daddy's is merely a material concern. Wrong! Wanting to know if a man has a good enough work ethic to provide for your daughter is a very spiritual concern according to the Bible. Work is not a secular or neutral matter; it has everything to do with your walk with Christ!

Proverbs says that sloth—laziness—is not just a character flaw, although it is. Proverbs mocks lazy people repeatedly as those who can't even bring their food to their mouths. But Proverbs also says that laziness is a spiritual problem! Proverbs warns the lazy and thereby calls them to repentance.

> *I went by the field of a slacker*
> *and by the vineyard of one lacking sense.*
> *Thistles had come up everywhere,*
> *weeds covered the ground,*
> *and the stone wall was ruined.*
> *I saw, and took it to heart;*
> *I looked, and received instruction:*
> *a little sleep, a little slumber,*
> *a little folding of the arms to rest,*
> *and your poverty will come like a robber,*
> *and your need, like a bandit.* (24:30-34)

## Our Laziness Is Destructive

This passage pictures a wise man who sees the field of an idler. Literally the text says that the man "lacks heart" (v. 30 translated by CSB as "lacking sense"). To lack a heart in the Bible is a serious spiritual problem since it's associated with an inability to obey the law (Deut 5:29). His laziness is revealed because the field is overgrown with thorns. This language reminds one of the curse language of Genesis 3:17-19 where sin makes it difficult to work and provide, and where the ground bears "thorns and thistles" rather than fruit.

Often, our sinful reaction to the curse is to take on as little responsibility as we can. Many become couch potatoes or lack the drive to work hard. The slacker gives in to this temptation. He is not sweating, and he is not providing. He just lets the weeds grow and allows things to fall apart.

The sage observes this and is instructed by it (v. 32). Wisdom teaches that there is an order to the world so that it works in a certain way. We see this in Proverbs 6 when the sage observes the ants' work ethic to provide and store. While you can observe the ant to see that a work ethic is helpful, you can observe the slacker in Proverbs 24 to see that lazy behavior has destructively negative consequences. Garrett says, "The anecdote invites the reader to recall similar observations of homes in disrepair and to draw the same conclusions" (*Proverbs*, 202). The sage is pleading with us to not live against the grain because if you live against God's design of the world, you can become the slob on the couch who is dependent on handouts (self-inflicted poverty). If you do not do what needs to be done, or if you sleep too much, then your life will be in chaos and more likely than not you will be poor and unable to provide. We need to be instructed by this as well and to be called to a strong work ethic that enables us to meet our family's needs.

But the problem for us is that when we read these verses we automatically think of the thirty-five-year-old sleeping on his mommy's and daddy's couch watching Jerry Springer while he stuffs his face with chips! Some of you may be struggling like that, but not most of us! That image enables you to say, "I don't struggle with laziness!" Yet we all have this tendency in our hearts, and we often do not recognize it because we measure ourselves against people whom we know are lazy.[43]

---

[43] Many of the insights here on the multifaceted nature of sloth in Proverbs come from Russell Moore's teaching on sloth in "Walking the Line."

Some of you may be struggling with wanting your needs met without having to work for them. Or you do not want to spend wisely; you just want to spend. Proverbs 20:4 says, "The slacker does not plow during planting season; at harvest time he looks, and there is nothing." As a result of this lifestyle, you depend on handouts—or bailouts! We have a slothful yet entitled society that wants others to work for what they get. We even see this with people who drive from church to church in town to see if they can get money. And they know how to work the system. The problem is that is not most of us, and so we do not think we struggle with laziness.

Some people have a problem not prioritizing what needs to be done over what we want to do! That's laziness too. This type of slothfulness is choosing to do what you want to do over what you need to do. Others have a life that is a mess because they are not taking control. They have a cluttered workspace and a car full of old fast food wrappers. Others just love to sleep too much. That is a temptation for all of us because the God-ordained rhythm of work and rest can be abused. So get out of bed and get to work.

However, for most people, their laziness is not a lack of activity; it's just the wrong kind of activity! Some people do not complete the tasks that are assigned to them or they do not finish them on time. Are you the kind of person who gets excited about new projects, but you do not complete them or you are having to constantly ask for extensions? Proverbs 12:27 talks about a lazy man who "doesn't roast his game." What an amazing picture! This person worked enough to get the meal—he did the hunt—but he will not work to finish it by cooking and preserving what he killed! Laziness can be the inability to finish tasks.

Many people struggle with laziness by being sidetracked by all kinds of diversions. Like the guy in the movie *Office Space* who says, "In an average week, I'd say I only do about twenty minutes of real, actual work." Why? You don't work as much as you could because you are checking Facebook all day, passing around YouTube clips, or calling in sick when *Call of Duty* is released. An article a few years back said that *Angry Birds* was costing businesses $1.5 billion in lost wages (Yarow, "Angry Birds"). When I posted that article, a Facebook friend commented on my post by saying, "At least 15 people I work with are playing Angry Birds continuously while they talk to customers 7 hours a day." Diversion is sloth, and Proverbs says of this kind of laziness, "The one who works his land will have plenty of food, but whoever chases fantasies lacks sense" (12:11; cf. 28:19).

Some people just constantly procrastinate at work. They start assignments the day before they are due. They repeatedly put things off to another day. Procrastination is sloth. Some people are all talk and little action. They go to meetings and make big plans, but they do not follow through in the end. It is the husband who constantly says to his wife, "I'll fix that," but never gets around to it. Proverbs 14:23 says of this kind of laziness, "There is profit in all hard work, but endless talk leads only to poverty." Do not say you will do something if you won't!

Some people do not take the initiative to provide for their family. Maybe they try to avoid child support payments, or maybe they claim some illegitimate disability to get out of work. That is not just wrong; it's ungodly. The Bible does not condemn those who are laid off or have a true disability, but some people just make excuses to avoid work or to delay having to do it! Proverbs 26:13 hilariously mocks this kind of sloth: "The slacker says, 'There's a lion in the road—a lion in the public square!'" This guy makes a "thin excuse" to avoid work, but it seems legitimate to him (Longman, *Proverbs*, 468).

I (Jon) understand this. I used to get up at 4 a.m. to run with my youth pastor, but I would love the mornings it rained because it gave me an excuse not to run. It was the best of all worlds because I did not feel guilty about bailing, since "I can't do it today anyway." But I could have gone to the gym instead! It is the same with excuses for work. People who ask for benevolence help often tell me, "I'll do any job that's available. I just want to work." Then I say, "OK. I know the manager at the grocery store over on Main. I can get you a job tomorrow stocking shelves." Then they will say, "Oh, I can't do that because I have a back problem." They say that they will do anything, but unless it is a desk job making sixty thousand dollars a year with full benefits, they shoot down every job idea I give them. That is an excuse to not work! The best scenario (in our own minds) is to be able to convince ourselves that we are hard workers without having actually to expend the energy to be a hard worker. That is why Proverbs 26:16 says, "In his own eyes, a slacker is wiser than seven who can answer sensibly." That is one of the keys about being lazy—you often do not know or think that you are! You think you are a hard worker when actually you are not.

Laziness is a destructive path not just because it will embarrass you, although it will, and not just because it'll make it difficult for you to give your family what they need, although it will, and not just because it'll make you a drain on the people around you, although it will (10:26); it is destructive because ultimately it will send you to hell. The wages of laziness is death. The desire for ease, comfort, and avoiding work kills you. Proverbs 21:25 states, "A slacker's craving will kill him because his hands refuse to work." Again, it may not turn out that way immediately because some lazy people inherit wealth, but it will turn out that way ultimately.

Proverbs 15:19 says, "A slacker's way is like a thorny hedge, but the path of the upright is a highway." Again, it is not just that you will have difficulty making your way in this life as a lazy person, although you will; but according to Proverbs there are two paths that lead to two different destinations. One leads to life and the other to death, and laziness is the path to hell. Proverbs 18:9 says literally that a lazy person is a brother to the "master of destruction," so you show yourself to be Satan's brother if you are lazy. Therefore, judgment will fall. Sloth is not just ridiculous; it is destructive!

## Our Laziness Points Us to Jesus

Laziness can be a sign of not being born again—lacking the new heart—and needing to be transformed. This is why Paul says to deal with this in the church: if you don't work, you don't eat (2 Thess 3:10). And Paul says in 1 Timothy 5:8, "But if anyone does not provide for his own family, especially for his own household, he has denied the faith and is worse than an unbeliever." If you do not have a work ethic, there is no evidence that your faith is real; you are not believing the gospel. You may get up early, sit in your favorite chair, and read Scripture for an hour, but if you constantly procrastinate on your work assignments or cannot complete tasks that are assigned to you, then you have a problem with Jesus no matter how long your quiet time is! (Moore, "Finding Jesus").

Solomon again points us to Jesus—the Wisdom of God (1 Cor 1:30). This pattern observed by the sage is centered on Christ, who upholds the world right now by his word. Your work ethic shows if you are walking toward or away from Jesus. That is, one way to know whether you are walking with Jesus is to look at your work ethic (1 Tim 5:8). The Wisdom of God on earth had a job as a carpenter. He learned and worked a trade! He also did the work his Father sent him to do. In John 4:34 Jesus says, "My food is to do the will of him who sent me and to finish his *work*." And in John 17:4 Jesus says, "I have glorified you on the earth by completing the *work* you gave me to do" (emphasis added). God worked to create the world and provide for humanity. He worked six days and finished his task, and then he rested. Jesus also worked six days of Holy

Week, said "It is finished" on day six when he completed the work of new creation, and then rested in the garden tomb on the seventh day. As N. T. Wright poetically writes, "On the seventh day God rested in the darkness of the tomb; Having finished on the sixth day all his work of joy and doom" ("Easter Oratorio"). He did this to provide for us what we cannot provide for ourselves.

The proper response to laziness in our lives is to turn away from it and turn to Jesus, who perfectly imaged the Father by working. He died for all of us who fall short in our work ethic and offers us forgiveness and escape from hell. Then he transforms us by his Spirit into his image—the image of one who labors! God worked to create, produce, and provide food and a home for his children (Gen 1–2). Part of being made in his image means that we do the same. We have failed, and the image is now distorted; but it is still there. Wisdom restores the image! Wisdom in Proverbs works to build creation (Prov 8) and a house (Prov 9). The New Testament reveals that Jesus worked to create the world, he upholds the universe right now (Col 1; Heb 1), and he worked to make all things new. He prepares a home for his family (John 14), and he feeds them (John 6). Being saved means being conformed into the image of Christ, and that means work and production.

All of this includes work in terms of vocation but also non-vocation. We are called to produce and not just to consume in all kinds of areas of our lives. Proverbs talks about women who order the chaos and build homes (14:1; 31:10-31). So tasks such as decorating, cleaning, consigning, and changing diapers are not menial but rather are the way of wisdom—the way of Christ! This also means that in the body of Christ we are called to serve: keep the nursery, teach a Bible study class, and stack some chairs. This means that Christians should be the best employees. Managers and bosses around town should call local pastors and ask for more of their people because Christians show up on time, stay on task, and put in a good day's work.

Work ethic is important for all kinds of reasons, and one reason is what God is preparing you for. Proverbs 12:24 says, "The diligent hand will rule, but laziness will lead to forced labor." This does not just mean that you will be promoted if you work hard, though it is more likely you will. Humanity was called to rule the creation in the beginning, but we handed it over to the serpent. Solomon tells his son—a son who will rule Israel—a good work ethic is necessary to rule. This principle is fulfilled in the Greater Solomon who rules not only Israel but the whole world. He regains what was lost in Eden, and one day his kingdom will cover the entire cosmos. Jesus says that those who are faithful in the small things will be put in charge of many things (Matt 25). He says his followers will rule the universe with him, but in order to do that we are called to be faithful in the seemingly mundane things. As Russell Moore says, "We are in an internship for the eschaton right now" ("Finding Jesus").[44] As you change diapers, take out the trash, carry out the project assigned by your boss, deliver the package, and paint the wall, you are being prepared to be a king or queen of the universe.

## Conclusion

We were called in the beginning to have dominion over the creeping things. Now in our fallen condition—in our lack of dominion over our lives—God calls us to look to the smallest of creeping things to learn from it: "Go to the ant, you slacker!" (6:6). This is an indictment that proves we need Jesus. We need to be made like him through the Gospel—made into the image of the one who said, "It is finished!"

## Reflect and Discuss

1. Why do we see baptism as a spiritual concern but work ethic and provision as a secular one?
2. The ground curse of Genesis 3 means that work and provision are now difficult. How do some respond to this difficulty?
3. What is your typical picture of laziness?
4. What are some ways that we are lazy other than what we typically think of?
5. How can someone practically avoid diversions in their workday?
6. Why do we often procrastinate with deadlines? How can we fight against that?
7. Why do you think Paul says a failure to provide for your house is a possible sign of unbelief?
8. What are some things that Jesus worked to finish?
9. How does the end of the age cause your work right now to have great meaning?
10. What are some seemingly menial tasks around the house or in your church that you can engage in to train for eternity?

---

[44] The conclusion to the section was also aided by Moore's insights here.

# Wrath

## PROVERBS 20:22; 24:17-18; 25:21-22

**Main Idea:** You are freed from wrath when you trust in God's wrath.

---

**I. Avoid Being a Wrathful Person Because It Will Earn the Wrath of God (24:17-18).**
**II. Trust in the Wrath of God (20:22; 25:21-22).**

---

"Hello, my name is Inigo Montoya. You killed my father. Prepare to die!" That is one of the great quotes in film history. It comes from the movie *The Princess Bride.* We loved watching that movie as kids, especially when Inigo Montoya gets his revenge on the man who killed his father. As he exacts his vengeance, he finally gets to say the line that he has been repeating to himself his entire life!

We all love "get even" stories because injustice makes us so angry. That is why revenge stories and songs are so popular. I cannot help but smile when the Count of Monte Cristo coldly pays back everyone who did him wrong. People are fascinated by shows like Maury Povich's when he brings out high school nerds who are now good-looking and jacked with muscles to show off to those who used to pick on them. People love listening to songs like Carrie Underwood's "Before He Cheats," or "Two Black Cadillacs," or Toby Keith's "How Do You Like Me Now?" Keith sings about someone who made fun of him in high school but now wakes up to an alarm in the morning hearing Keith's song on the radio. How can we not help but feel some glee in these bits of pop culture?

The reason we resonate with these movies, shows, and songs is because we all know what it is like to be wronged or for someone we love to have been wronged. Many people know what it is like to be bullied and made fun of. There are names that you can still hear today that you have not been called for twenty years, and just hearing that name still turns your stomach. Many people have experienced broken promises or the abandonment of a parent, been abused by someone they trusted, cheated on, or gossiped about. You may have been abandoned, raped, abused, or stabbed in the back by a friend, and you still experience deep pain.

Since we all know what it is like to be wronged or for someone we love to be wronged, we all love the revenge story. There is a sense in which we *should* love these stories: we are born with an innate sense of justice because we have been made in the image of a God who is just. That is why we get really angry when people get away with doing what is wrong or get off on a technicality, especially if it is someone we love who was hurt. We want the offender to get what is coming to him. We want justice to be done!

Since we are made in the image of a God who is just, and since wanting justice to be done is not wrong, why does God condemn wrath and bitterness? The problem we have is not the desire for justice to be done. The problem we have is the desire to be the ones who execute the justice, when that job belongs to God alone. Our sense of justice is right, but trying to be the one who executes it is wrong because it is an attempt to take God's place. When you refuse to lay down a grudge, you reveal that you do not trust that God is able to deal with an injustice to your satisfaction. We see this truth throughout the book of Proverbs. People are wrathful because they do not trust the wrath of God to make things right.

## Avoid Being a Wrathful Person Because It Will Earn the Wrath of God

### PROVERBS 24:17-18

Proverbs 10:12 says, "Hatred stirs up conflicts, but love covers all offenses." Therefore, according to Proverbs, being a wrathful, vengeful, bitter, angry, quick-tempered, unforgiving person is the path of foolishness. In contrast, wisdom means being a patient person who is slow to anger and quick to forgive (14:29). Holding on to grudges and seeking to get even are condemned throughout the book. Forgiveness and mercy are encouraged.

The problem is that we think since we never took a Louisville Slugger to someone's car that we are not wrathful people. Yet there are all kinds of ways to be a wrathful person. For some, they just have a kind of cold silence. They might say, "If you don't know what you did, then I'm not going to tell you." For others, they just let things fester with their spouse because they think that if they don't act mad, he will think that what he did is no big deal. Some try to lash out with bad behavior, like looking to someone other than their spouse for affection in order to teach their spouse a lesson. Some might just imagine in their mind, If that person who hurt me were sick or dead, my life would be happier.

Proverbs mentions all kinds of ways people try to get even that do not necessarily include violence. Some respond to an insult from someone else by crafting a great comeback. Some lash out by gossiping about others. For example, in one of Taylor Swift's songs where she is done wrong by a boyfriend, she tells him that she will tell everyone else that he is gay. Proverbs calls us to another path. Proverbs 17:9 says, "Whoever conceals an offense promotes love, but whoever gossips about it separates friends." People try to get even by constantly bringing up past wrongs done to them and refusing to let them go. Some just blow up in a fury and lose their temper with their wife, husband, or children by saying things they should not say and do not really mean. It damages their relationships and ability to share intimacy. Instead, Proverbs 17:27 urges, "The one who has knowledge restrains his words, and one who keeps a cool head is a person of understanding." So instead of gossiping or losing our temper or making lists of wrongs done to us, we are called to be cool-headed and let go of offenses done to us!

For some of us, we can ease any guilt we might feel over our bitterness with the fact that "I never acted on it." But even if you never act on it, bitterness—which starts in the heart, in our thought life—is still sin. Further, what starts in the heart may not stay in the heart. Proverbs 20:22 states, "Don't say, 'I will avenge this evil!' Wait on the LORD, and he will rescue you." The verse references talking to yourself—planning that starts in the heart. The intent to get even starts in the heart, and is accountable to God, even if you never act on it. Jesus says the same thing in Matthew 5!

Some of us don't do anything except get happy when things go bad for those who hurt us. When they lose their job, struggle in their relationships, or have a bit of "bad luck," it makes our day a little brighter. Proverbs 24:17-18 warns about that reality: "Don't gloat when your enemy falls, and don't let your heart rejoice when he stumbles, or the LORD will see, be displeased, and turn his wrath away from him." It's not just that people will not like you if you are a vengeful person, although that is true, but you also will go to hell for gloating. You will receive the wrath of God. Why? Proverbs 24 says that your lack of forgiveness is as much a sin—condemnable before God—as what they did to you. That is a hard truth, but it is the truth, especially for believers who have been forgiven so much.

Duane Garrett writes, "It seems perverse to refrain from gloating so that Yahweh might further injure your enemy" (*Proverbs*, 199). That may seem like a twisted bit of advice from the sage: you refrain, you forgive, and then that person will get what's coming to him! Some might think that doesn't sound like a Christian motive. As John Piper points out, we need to be careful thinking that because Jesus had that motive. That is a Christian motive for being free from wrath ("Future Grace, Part 4").[45]

> *For you were called to this, because Christ also suffered for you, leaving you an example, so that you should follow in his steps. He did not commit sin, and no deceit was found in his mouth; when he was insulted, he did not insult in return; when he suffered, he did not threaten but entrusted himself to the one who judges justly.* (1 Pet 2:21-23)

These verses answer the big practical question that hurt people have: How can I forgive? How can I let it go? How can I act like nothing really happened to me while they get away scot-free? The answer to that question is follow the example of Jesus and hand justice over to God! You trust God to handle it!

Jesus, the Wisdom of God, calls us to this: love your enemies, pray for those who persecute you, turn the other cheek, and do not revile! He is not some absentee Master who says, "Do what I say, not what I do!" He understands. It is not like a husband giving his wife advice on enduring the pain of childbirth. Jesus knows what he is talking about because he has been wronged in a greater way than you or I ever could be! He carried his cross, got punched in the face, and was whipped, stripped naked, and mocked by taunts: "If you are really God's Son, come down off that cross!" And when he went through that, Jesus looked into the faces of his murderers and mockers and said, "Father, forgive them, because they do not know what they are doing" (Luke 23:34). We might be tempted to think Jesus was wimpy in that moment and is calling us to be wimpy like he is, but that would be wrong. Jesus is no wimp. He trusted the justice of God! It takes more toughness not to retaliate and to wait for judgment day! Proverbs 24 says that if we fail to trust in God's wrath for the day of judgment, we will experience that wrath ourselves on judgment day! So, again, what is the antidote to wrath?

---

[45] My (Jon's) thinking on wrath and forgiveness has been greatly shaped by Piper's sermon.

## Trust in the Wrath of God

### PROVERBS 20:22; 25:21-22

People believe that forgiveness is the right course of action in every case with one exception—mine! Our hearts are warmed by forgiveness stories, but we all think that our situation is just a little bit different. We think, *You could not possibly expect me to forgive him or her after what he or she did to me. How can I forgive a father who killed my mother, a dad who took advantage of me, or a spouse who walked out on me?*

How? How do you forgive those who have really wronged you? It is really hard because our biggest fear is that if we let this go, it will be like what they did to me was no big deal. The answer is to follow in the path of Jesus and trust in the wrath of God that they will get what is rightfully and justly coming to them.

Proverbs 20:22 states, "Don't say, 'I will avenge this evil!' Wait on the Lord, and he will rescue you." The Bible calls us away from vigilante or self-produced justice. People resonate with vigilantes like Zorro, Batman, Dexter, or the Count of Monte Christo because we want justice to be done. But these stories are stories of unbelief. Real forgiveness is a belief issue. The fear of the Lord is the beginning of wisdom, and it is still the beginning of wisdom when it comes to bitterness and forgiveness. You trust God to redress what has happened to you. You free yourself of bitterness by trusting that God will avenge you. In Romans 12:19 the Lord says, "Vengeance is mine. I will repay" (author's translation). There is no timetable given, but there is certainty that it will happen. No matter how long it takes, you trust that God will set things right in the end.

Proverbs goes a step further. It does not just forbid revenge. Resisting the urge to take revenge is obviously a good step and something we are called to accomplish, but often that can be done through an act of will-power or through just lacking the energy or the opportunity to get back at somebody. No, Proverbs goes a step further when it says do good to those who have wronged you. Proverbs 25:21-22 says—and Paul quotes this in Romans 12—"If your enemy is hungry, give him food to eat, and if he is thirsty, give him water to drink; for you will heap burning coals on his head, and the Lord will reward you."

Why should you do good to those who have hurt you? You do so because it heaps burning coals on their heads. What does that mean? Two options are possible. First, this statement may be a metaphor for repentance similar to an Egyptian repentance ritual where a thief carried a basket of fiery coals on his head as a sign of shame. Thus, your mercy toward them may shame them and lead to their repentance and reconciliation with God and you. Or second, this statement means that your good deeds will bring even greater judgment on those who wronged you. Given the way Paul quotes this in Romans 12, the second option is better. Psalm 11:6 aids this interpretation as well because burning coals refers to God's judgment: "Let him rain burning coals and sulfur on the wicked; let a scorching wind be the portion in their cup."[46] Therefore, your good deeds lead to greater judgment because in many ways your forgiveness and mercy have displayed the cross to them, and instead of repenting they have hardened their hearts. So we forgive and do good to those who hurt us because it will either lead to their repentance or to their judgment. Either way, God will make things right.

The problem for many of us is that we think forgiveness and love of enemies are for really good Christians—like varsity-level Christians. Or we think our case is different. How can you expect me to forgive the people who made my life a living hell? But the Bible says if you do not forgive, you probably are not a Christian. Jesus says in Matthew 6:14-15, "For if you forgive others their offenses, your heavenly Father will forgive you as well. But if you don't forgive others, your Father will not forgive your offenses." And if you do not have God's forgiveness, that means hell!

These verses are not saying that you have to be a good person to go to heaven or to get God's forgiveness. They are saying that unforgiveness shows that you do not believe the gospel. Bitter people go to hell not because they are not working hard enough for God, but because they do not trust God to work hard enough for them.

The bottom line is that if we are wrathful people it is because we do not believe the gospel. There are two possibilities for the people who have wronged us (Piper, "Future Grace, Part 4"). First, if it is a Christian who hurt us, Jesus drowned in his own blood to pay for the sin he or she committed against us. God has not swept what that person did to us under the rug of the universe. He has dealt with it. He took what that person did so seriously that he killed his Son for it. If you hold a grudge, essentially you are saying that the cross of Jesus Christ is enough to forgive the sins that you have committed against God, but it is not

[46] See Waltke's discussion of these two options in *Proverbs 15–31*, 330–32.

enough to forgive the sins committed against you. That is a failure to truly believe the gospel.

Ephesians 4:32 says that we are to forgive because we have been forgiven, and our offenses against God are far greater than anyone's offense against us. So forgive. Be patient in traffic. Do not blow up in anger against your children. Jesus has been infinitely patient and merciful to you. Do good to your enemy, and it may lead to their repentance and faith in Jesus Christ, who paid for every sin that person committed against you.

Second, if it is a non-Christian who hurt you, he or she will pay for those sins forever in hell. If the person who hurt you remains unrepentant, he will suffer for eternity. You do not have to add to that sentence one second of your fury. God does not need your help to carry out that punishment.

Therefore, let go of your grudges, forgive those who hurt you, pray for those who have wronged you, do good to your enemy, and do not insist on always having the last word. The way you live that kind of life is by constantly preaching the gospel to yourself in those moments when your anger begins to simmer and seethe. It may be that your mercy leads to the salvation of the lost because they see the gospel in your kindness in a way they could never see it before. If the world began to see Christians who forgive one another and do not retaliate when made fun of by the world, then just maybe they will start to see the wisdom of God in the foolishness of the cross. When they see crazy people who forgive drunk drivers who killed their children or a wife who forgives terrorists who gunned down her missionary husband, then maybe they will start to see Jesus. Until then, they see people who are just like them. After all, Jesus says even lost people do good to those who are good to them (Matt 5:43-47).

## Conclusion

How do we do good to those who hurt us? Peter echoes the words of Proverbs when he tells us to follow Jesus who trusted in the justice of God (1 Pet 2:18-25). Peter saw this firsthand (John 18). When the mob came for Jesus, Peter took up his sword and cut off a man's ear. Jesus told Peter to put the sword away because he did not need Peter's help. Jesus could call the armies of heaven and they would respond to his voice, but Jesus was able to be non-wrathful because he knew God's wrath needed to come down and be poured out on him at Golgotha.

And Jesus knew that one day he would split the eastern sky and return to exact vengeance on all the enemies of God. Every injustice will be set right—bank on it! On that day he will not need your help or my help. As Russell Moore says, "He will say, 'No need for swords, boys. I can take it from here'" ("Why Jesus").

## Reflect and Discuss

1. What are some famous revenge stories that you love?
2. Why do we love revenge stories?
3. What is right about our desire for revenge and what is wrong about it?
4. What are some ways that we are wrathful that are not necessarily violent?
5. According to Proverbs 24:17-18, how does God feel when we rejoice over our enemies' failure?
6. How did Jesus endure the injustice of the cross? What does his model mean for us?
7. What are the two possibilities for those who have wronged us?
8. How does the cross of Jesus help you forgive others?
9. How does hell help you forgive others?
10. What are some practical things you need to do as a result of this study?

# WORKS CITED


"16 House Rules by Susannah Wesley (John Wesley's Mom)." Accessed October 18, 2016, http://www.raisinggodlychildren.org/2011/03/16-house-rules-by-susannah-wesley-john-wesleys-mom.html.

"A Daughter Needs a Dad," author unknown. Posted by Dave Roberts, June 2, 2015. Accessed December 30, 2015, http://thefrazzledparent.com/a-daughter-needs-a-dad.

Akin, Jonathan. "A Theology of Future Hope in the Book of Proverbs." PhD diss., The Southern Baptist Theological Seminary, 2012.

Akin, Daniel. "My Body Belongs to God." Accessed February 18, 2016, http://www.danielakin.com/my-body-belongs-to-god-spring-convocation-2005.

———. "The Vanity of Happy Meal Christianity." Accessed December 29, 2015, http://www.danielakin.com/the-vanity-of-happy-meal-christianity.

Alden, Robert L. *Proverbs: A Commentary on an Ancient Book of Timeless Advice.* Ada, MI: Baker, 1988.

Baklinski, Thaddeus M. "Study: Young Children Who Are Spanked Are Happier and More Successful as Teenagers." *LifeSiteNews*, January 5, 2010. Accessed October 27, 2016, https://www.lifesitenews.com/news/study-young-children-who-are-spanked-are-happier-and-more-successful-as-tee.

"Baptist Leader Claims God 'Does Not Hear the Prayer of a Jew.'" *Jewish Telegraphic Agency*, September 19, 1980. Accessed January 6, 2015, http://www.jta.org/1980/09/19/archive/baptist-leader-claims-god-does-not-hear-the-prayer-of-a-jew.

Black, Rosemary. "Spanking Makes Kids Perform Better in School, Helps Them Become More Successful: Study." *New York Daily News*, January 4, 2010. Accessed October 13, 2015, http://www.nydaily

news.com/life-style/spanking-kids-perform-better-school-helps-successful-study-article-1.457285

Brown, Francis, S. R. Driver, and Charles Briggs. *The Brown-Driver-Briggs Hebrew and English Lexicon.* Fifth printing. Peabody, MA: Hendrickson, 2000.

Challies, Tim. "Desecration and Titillation." Accessed December 28, 2015, http://www.challies.com/articles/desecration-and-titillation.

———. *Sexual Detox: A Guide for the Married Guy.* Accessed August 7, 2014, http://www.challies.com.

Chandler, Matt. "The Mission of God." Accessed August 19, 2014, http://www.thevillagechurch.net/sermon/the-mission-of-god.

"Childhood Obesity Facts." Accessed December 29, 2015, http://www.cdc.gov/healthyschools/obesity/facts.htm.

Clifford, Richard J. *Proverbs.* Louisville, KY: Westminster John Knox, 1999.

"Ellen DeGeneres Bows Out of *American Idol.*" *People,* July 29, 2010. Accessed January 20, 2016, http://www.people.com/people/article/0,,20420698,00.html.

Dever, Mark. *The Message of the Old Testament: Promises Made.* Wheaton, IL: Crossway, 2006.

Fox, Michael. *Proverbs 1–9.* The Anchor Bible 18a. New Haven, CT: Yale University Press, 2000.

———. *Proverbs 10–31.* The Anchor Bible 18b. New Haven, CT: Yale University Press, 2009.

Garrett, Duane A. *Proverbs, Ecclesiastes, Song of Songs.* New American Commentary 14. Nashville, TN: B&H, 1993.

Getty, Keith, and Stuart Townend, "In Christ Alone," copyright 2001, Kingsway Thankyou Music.

Goldsworthy, Graeme. *The Tree of Life: Reading Proverbs Today.* Sydney: AIO, 1993.

Gottlieb, Lori. "How to Land Your Kid in Therapy." *The Atlantic,* July/August 2011. Accessed October 13, 2015, http://www.theatlantic.com/magazine/archive/2011/07/how-to-land-your-kid-in-therapy/308555.

Hamilton, James M., Jr. *God's Glory in Salvation through Judgment: A Biblical Theology.* Wheaton, IL: Crossway, 2010.

"How Can I Conquer Gluttony?" Interview with John Piper, January 2, 2008. Accessed December 29, 2015, http://www.desiringgod.org/interviews/how-can-i-conquer-gluttony.

Indiviglio, Daniel. "How Americans' Love Affair with Debt Has Grown." *TheAtlantic,* September 26, 2010. Accessed December 29, 2015, http://www.theatlantic.com/business/archive/2010/09/how-americans-love-affair-with-debt-has-grown/63552.

Johnson, Dennis. *Him We Proclaim: Preaching Christ from All the Scriptures.* Phillipsburg, NJ: P&R, 2007.

Kavoussi, Bonnie. "Half of Americans Are Spending More Than They Earn, but Don't Realize It: Survey." *Huffington Post,* May 17, 2012. Accessed October 27, 2016, http://www.huffingtonpost.com/2012/05/17/americans-spending-more-than-they-earn_n_1523920.html.

Keller, Tim. *Counterfeit Gods.* New York: Dutton, 2009.

———. "True Wisdom." Accessed July 9, 2014, http://www.gospelinlife.com/true-wisdom-5411.html.

Kidner, Derek. *The Proverbs: An Introduction and Commentary.* Tyndale Old Testament Commentary. Downers Grove, IL: InterVarsity, 1985.

———. *The Wisdom of Proverbs, Job, and Ecclesiastes: An Introduction to Wisdom Literature.* Downers Grove, IL: InterVarsity, 1985.

Krasnow, Iris. "Excerpt from 'Surrendering to Motherhood.'" Accessed January 26, 2016, http://iriskrasnow.com/_pages/more_surrendering_motherhood.htm.

Kwon, Lillian. "Stop Separating Gays from 'Normal' People, Says Evangelical." *Christian Daily,* February 26, 2015. Accessed December 28, 2015, www.christiandaily.com/article/stop-separating-gays-from-normal-people-says-evangelical/49906.htm.

Leithart, Peter J. *Blessed Are the Hungry: Meditations on the Lord's Supper.* Moscow, ID: Canon, 2000.

Lewis, C. S. *The Great Divorce.* Glasgow: William Collins Sons & Co., Ltd., 1986.

Longman, Tremper, III. *How to Read Proverbs.* Downers Grove, IL: InterVarsity, 2002.

———. *Proverbs.* Baker Commentary on the Old Testament Wisdom and Psalms. Grand Rapids, MI: Baker, 2006.

Nestle, Erwin. *Novum Testamentum Graece.* Edited by Barbara and Kurt Aland. Stuttgart: Deutsche Bibelgesellschaft, 1993.

Moore, Russell. "Proverbs 5:1-23—The Horror of Adultery and the Gospel of Christ." Accessed August 7, 2014, http://www.russellmoore.com/2011/02/09/the-horror-of-adultery-and-the-gospel-of-christ-prov-51-23.

———. "Proverbs 6:6-11—Finding Jesus in an Anthill: Following Christ through Wisdom with Money." Accessed July 8, 2014, http://www.russellmoore.com/2009/01/25/finding-jesus-in-an-anthill-following-christ-through-wisdom-with-money-prov-66-11.

———. "Walking the Line: Glimpses of the Christ Life in the Book of Proverbs." A series of sermons on Proverbs. Accessed October 27, 2016, http://www.russellmoore.com/resources/proverbs.

———. "Why Jesus Is More-and-Less Violent than Allah, Planned Parenthood, and Me: Mercy, Ministry, and the Kingdom of Christ." Accessed December 28, 2015, http://www.russellmoore.com/2006/10/11/why-jesus-is-more-and-less-violent-than-allah-planned-parenthood-and-me-mercy-ministry-and-the-kingdom-of-christ.

Murphy, Roland E., and Elizabeth Huwiler. *Proverbs, Ecclesiastes, Song of Songs*. New International Bible Commentary. Peabody, MA: Hendrickson, 1999.

Murphy, Todd J. *Pocket Dictionary for the Study of Biblical Hebrew*. Downers Grove, IL: InterVarsity, 2003.

Newsweek Staff. "Survey: Mother Matters." Accessed October 18, 2016, http://www.newsweek.com/surveys-mother-matters-118835.

Ortlund, Raymond C., Jr. *Proverbs: Wisdom That Works*. Preaching the Word. Wheaton, IL: Crossway, 2012.

Piper, John. "Future Grace for Finishing the Task, Part 4." Accessed December 28, 2015, http://www.desiringgod.org/messages/future-grace-for-finishing-the-task-part-4.

———. "Future Grace for Finishing the Task, Part 5." Accessed December 29, 2015, http://www.desiringgod.org/messages/future-grace-for-finishing-the-task-part-5.

Poirier, Alfred J. "The Cross and Criticism." *Journal of Biblical Counseling* 17, no. 3 (Spring 1999): 16–20.

Roosevelt, Theodore. Address to the New York State Agricultural Association, Syracuse, NY, September 7, 1903. Accessed September 20, 2016, http://www.presidency.ucsb.edu/ws/?pid=24504.

Ross, Allen P. "Proverbs." Pages 21–252 in *Proverbs–Isaiah*, ed. Tremper Longman III and David E. Garland. Revised edition, vol. 6. *Expositor's Bible Commentary*. Grand Rapids, MI: Zondervan, 2005.

Skehan, Patrick W. *Studies in Israelite Poetry and Wisdom*. Catholic Biblical Quarterly Monograph Series 1. Washington, DC: Catholic Biblical Association of America, 1971.

Spurgeon, Charles. *Illustrations and Meditations; Or, Flowers from a Puritan's Garden*, New York: Funk & Wagnalls, 1883.

———. "Meeting of the Neighboring Churches," preached at the Metropolitan Tabernacle, London, March 27, 1861.

Stein, Robert. "Wine-Drinking in New Testament Times." *Christianity Today*, June 20, 1975.

"Surveys: Mother Matters." *Newsweek*, last modified May 1, 2005. Accessed January 13, 2016, http://www.newsweek.com/surveys-mother-matters-118835.

Ten Elshof, Gregg A. *I Told Me So*. Grand Rapids, MI: Eerdmans, 2009.

Toussaint, Stan. "Building a Happy Home." *Kindred Spirit*, date unknown.

Van Leeuwen, Raymond C. "Wealth and Poverty: System and Contradiction in Proverbs." *Hebrew Studies* 33 (1992): 25–36.

Veith, Gene Edward. "The Youth Anti-culture," *World* 14, no. 18 (May 8, 1999): 26. Accessed October 27, 2016, https://world.wng.org/1999/05/the_youth_anti_culture.

Wallis, Claudia. "The Case for Staying Home." *Time*, March 22, 2004. Accessed January 14, 2016, http://content.time.com/time/magazine/article/0,9171,993641,00.html.

Waltke, Bruce K. *The Book of Proverbs, Chapters 1–15*. New International Commentary on the Old Testament. Grand Rapids, MI: Eerdmans, 2004.

———. *The Book of Proverbs, Chapters 15-31*. New International Commentary on the Old Testament. Grand Rapids, MI: Eerdmans, 2005.

Warner, Judith. "The Myth of the Perfect Mother: Why It Drives Real Women Crazy." *Newsweek*, February 21, 2005.

Weber, Linda. *Mom, You're Incredible!* Nashville, TN: B&H, 2002.

Wiersbe, Warren W. *Be Skillful: God's Guidebook to Wise Living*. Colorado Springs, CO: Cook, 1995.

Wright, N. T. "Easter Oratorio." Accessed December 28, 2015, http://ntwrightpage.com/Easter_Oratorio_Libretto.pdf.

Yarow, Jay. "Angry Birds Costing Businesses $1.5 Billion in Lost Wages." *Business Insider*, September 14, 2011. Accessed December 28, 2015, http://www.businessinsider.com/angry-birds-losses-2011-9.

# SCRIPTURE INDEX